HOW TO SWAP LS & LT ENGINES INTO Chevy & GMC Trucks 1960–1998

Jefferson Bryant

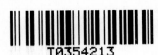

SA DESIGN

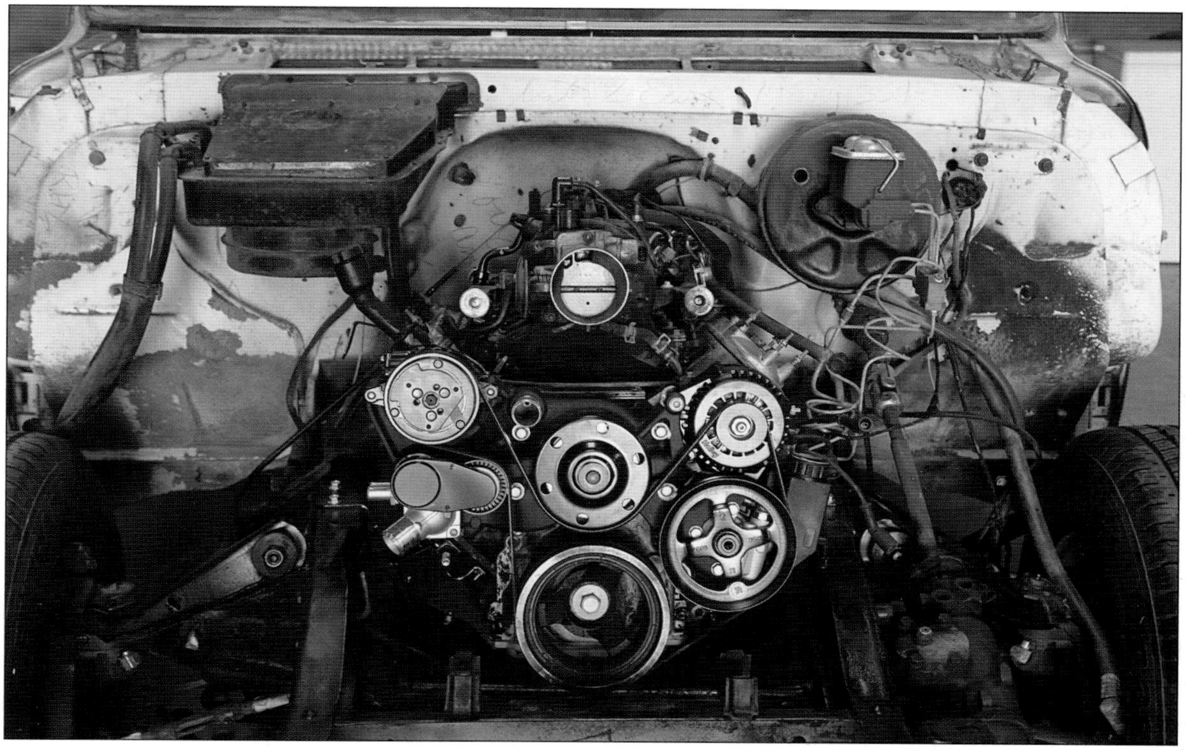

CarTech®

CarTech®

CarTech®, Inc.
6118 Main Street
North Branch, MN 55056
Phone: 651-277-1200 or 800-551-4754
Fax: 651-277-1203
www.cartechbooks.com

Edit by Bob Wilson
Layout by Connie DeFlorin

ISBN 978-1-61325-608-4
Item No. SA509

Library of Congress Cataloging-in-Publication Data Available

Written, edited, and designed in the U.S.A.
Printed in China
10 9 8 7 6 5 4 3 2 1

All photos are courtesy of Jefferson Bryant unless otherwise noted.

DISTRIBUTION BY:

Europe
PGUK
63 Hatton Garden
London EC1N 8LE, England
Phone: 020 7061 1980 • Fax: 020 7242 3725
www.pguk.co.uk

Australia
Renniks Publications Ltd.
3/37-39 Green Street
Banksmeadow, NSW 2109, Australia
Phone: 2 9695 7055 • Fax: 2 9695 7355
www.renniks.com

Canada
Login Canada
300 Saulteaux Crescent
Winnipeg, MB, R3J 3T2 Canada
Phone: 800 665 1148 • Fax: 800 665 0103
www.lb.ca

CONTENTS

DEDICATION

This book is dedicated to my wife, Ammie, and my children, Jason, Josie, and Ben. Without your patience and help, this book would not have been possible. I would also like to say thank you to all of my readers; I hope that this book and my previous books will help you build the vehicle of your dreams.

ACKNOWLEDGMENTS

This book contains information from years of hard work and effort in the world of LS/LT engine swaps. I have relied on many people to help put this information together in one place to help you perform your own LS/LT swap into GM C/K trucks and SUVs as efficiently as possible. The following people were instrumental in accomplishing this goal: Ben Bryant, Justin Johnson, Pat McElreath, Chris Franklin, and Bodie Hunt of Red Dirt Rodz; Matt Graves of American Powertrain; Jeff Lee of Martin & Co; and Blane Burnett and Evan Perkins of Holley Performance.

I would also like to thank the following companies for assisting with this project: Aeromotive Inc., American Powertrain, Chevrolet, Dakota Digital, Dirty Dingo Motorsports, Dynotech Engineering, G Force Performance, Holley Performance, HP Tuners, ICT Billet, Magnaflow, Speedway Motors, standaloneharness.com, Summit Racing, and Swap Time USA.

GEN III, GEN IV, AND GEN V ENGINES

When General Motors released the first C10 truck in 1960, it created a phenomenon that continues today. The GM C/K series is the single most popular truck line in the automotive aftermarket, and the enthusiasm for 1960–1998 GM trucks is at an all-time high. Whether you are restomodding a 1963 C10, building a 1984 Squarebody for the drag strip, or slamming a 1990 Old Body Style (OBS, which was from 1988–1998), the options are practically endless. Dropping an LS-series (Gen III or Gen IV) or LT-series (Gen V) engine into a C/K is one of the best ways to bring that sweet ride into the 21st century and increase the horsepower as well.

Each era of GM C/K series trucks has its unique issues and concerns for engine swaps. However, the great thing is that there is so much room under the hood that most factory oil pans and accessory drives can be used on an LS/LT swap, which makes this a more economical venture than most other swap projects. That doesn't mean that there are not serious issues, especially when getting into 4-wheel-drive (4WD) swaps, where things can get expensive fast.

Regardless of your plans for the

The Gen III engine platform was the replacement for LT1/LT4 engines and found its first home between the frame rails of the 1997 Corvette. Then, it was used in the 1998 Camaro and Firebird models as well as the truck and SUV lines. (Photo Courtesy General Motors)

Each Gen III and Gen IV powerplant is put together by an assembly technician. All of the Gen III and Gen IV motors are distributorless, and all but one is fuel injected. If buying a used engine, you will need all of the wiring and electronics for almost every engine swap unless an aftermarket controller will be used. (Photo Courtesy General Motors)

truck, the details needed to help complete an LS/LT swap can be found in this book. We cover everything from sourcing an engine to sourcing the engine mounts and accessories, transmission, electronics, and wiring. LS/LT swaps are the fastest-growing segment of automotive performance. The aftermarket is full of options to help complete a swap, and sorting through all of those parts can be overwhelming. Before buying any parts, an engine is needed.

LS-Series Engines

Development for the Gen III engine began in 1993 after the release of the short-lived LT1/LT4, which was the Gen II small-block Chevy (SBC) and was produced from 1992 to 1997. General Motors saw the writing on the wall with more strict emissions and corporate average fuel economy (CAFE) standards, knowing that the 38-year-old SBC's engine design was not up to the task. Starting with a blank slate, the automaker designed an all-new Gen III V-8 engine, which shared only a few basic dimensions with the original SBC. This new high-performance engine, the Gen III LS1, introduced modern engine technology while retaining the traditional pushrod valvetrain. The engine first appeared as the flagship engine in the 1997 Corvette, which immediately drove enthusiast interest into the stratosphere and ushered in a new era of high-performance small-block engines.

Although commonly referred to as "LS" engines, the official nomenclature is "Gen III" and "Gen IV." These remarkable engines produced class-leading performance and fuel efficiency. While the performance was incredible, there was a genuine fear of these new engines in the enthusiast market, as the EFI systems were far more complicated than the previous designs.

A few early adopters made headway in the swap realm, but it took several years for the LS-series engine to catch on as a reliable swap option. Once it did, practically everyone sought out Gen III and Gen IV engines for practically every vehicle ever built. The factory small-block engines produced 320 hp at the low end of the scale and reached more than 500 hp at the top end of the spectrum, kicking off what has become a horsepower war.

Gen III: The Evolution of V-8 Performance

All aluminum or cast-iron blocks built from 1997 through 2004 are basically the same with some minor differences. However, there is an important internal difference: the outside diameter (OD) of the camshaft bore was changed in 2004. While the cam itself remained the same, only the bearing OD changed, and, as such, it required a different set of cam bearings.

General Motors used the Gen III platform for the full range of GM trucks as well. With two years of experience under its belt, General Motors replaced the aging Gen I 305 and 350 small-block truck engine platform with Gen III motors.

The new truck and SUV powertrain was offered in three displacements: 4.8L, 5.3L, and 6.0L. These V-8 engines were installed in every GM truck and SUV from 1999 to 2007. The 4.8L and 5.3L engines share aluminum cylinder heads. The Vortec truck engines have proven to be a popular swap due to sheer volume. A Vortec Gen III can be picked up for next to nothing.

The scalloped holes on the top right side of the main webs on the block (shown here) are the crankcase breathing holes. This promotes proper ventilation for the air and oil vapor in the Gen III and IV motors. (Photo Courtesy General Motors)

LS1

Originally released in the 1997 Corvette, the LS1 is the engine that started it all. This 345-hp, 350 ft-lbs, 5.7L engine was a huge success for General Motors, so it began offering the 5.7L engine in the F-Body platform in the 1998 Camaro/Firebird. By 2004, the LS1 found itself in the Pontiac GTO.

The LS1 features an aluminum block and heads, but there were several different 5.7L block castings from 1997–1998 and 1999–2004. These castings are very similar, but they have subtle differences. The early blocks have two oil galleys in the back of the block with a shallow crossover passage in the rear cover, which supplies the passenger-side oil galley. These early units also have a 24.5-mm hole drilled through the main webs to promote "bay-to-bay breathing" because of excessive crankcase pressure that is caused by oil vapor being trapped between the main caps. The casting number for the 1997 to 1999 model years is 12550592.

The later blocks (1999 to 2004) are all basically the same, but they contain minor differences. The 1999 block has a reinforced passenger-side front corner, and General Motors added a deep oil slot to improve oil flow to the passenger-side oil galley. The casting numbers for these blocks are 12559378 and 12560626.

The 1256118 block is the official LS6 block for the 2001 Corvette, but a few of these blocks made it into LS1 production in 2001 and 2002. In fact, it was used for all Corvette applications from 2003 to 2004. The key difference in this block is the addition of two cast slots in each of the center mains. This cast-in feature cured the crankcase evacuation problem that existed in the earlier models that had drilled holes.

As a side note, the GM handbook states that you should limit cylinder boring to 0.004 inch for the early blocks. It also says that later castings can only be overbored 0.010 inch because the cast-iron sleeves are thin and serrated. Don't even waste time on these motors if you want to bore it out, as it is cost prohibitive.

LS6

The 5.7L LS6 motor was fitted to 2001 to 2004 Corvette Z06s. The motor, with 385-hp and 380 ft-lbs of torque, provides a significant increase in horsepower and was a serious step up in performance. In 2002, the LS6 was increased to 405 hp and 400 ft-lbs (a 5-percent increase), where it remained until its end of production in 2004. The Gen III iron block part number is 12551358.

Gen III Vortec Engines

The 1998-and-older Vortec engines (based on the Gen I small-block Chevy platform) were replaced in 1999 with the all-new Gen III Vortec engines. Most of these engines have an iron block with aluminum heads, and they are plentiful in salvage yards. These engines are often overlooked because they do not carry LS engine codes, but they are certainly worth the effort if you want an inexpensive Gen III engine. The larger-displacement 6.0L engines were coded LQ4 and LQ9 and came with "drive by wire" in heavily optioned trucks and SUVs.

LR4

The 4.8L Vortec 4800 engines were rated from 255 hp to 285 hp and 280 ft-lbs to 295 ft-lbs, depending on the year and model of vehicle. This particular engine model was available in C/K-series trucks with the base V-8.

LQ4

Installed in the Chevy Express and GMC Savana vans, the base-version Vortec 6000 is rated at 290 hp and 350 ft-lbs of torque. Therefore, these are the least powerful of the 6.0L motors. The top-rated version (325-hp and 365 ft-lbs of torque) was available in the top-trim-level trucks and SUVs.

LQ9

For truck engines, this is the motor to have. The Vortec 6000 HO motor was released in the 2002 Cadillac Escalade and EXT, but it later became available in most trucks and other SUVs. A 10.1:1 compression ratio raised the output of these engines to 345 hp and 380 ft-lbs of torque. Although these are cast-iron blocks, they are the most powerful truck engines.

LR59

This block was used for 4.8L and 5.3L engines for 2002–2007 GM C/K trucks, 2002–2006 Chevrolet Tahoes/GMC Yukons, and 2002–2006 Chevrolet Suburbans/GMC Yukon XLs. The 4.8L engine produced up to 295 hp and 305 ft-lbs of torque, while the 5.3L engine had up to 320 hp and 340 ft-lbs torque.

The 5.3L engines used both cast-iron and aluminum blocks. The cast-iron blocks were built from 1999 to 2007, while the aluminum block was available from 2003 to 2007.

The 4.8L engine used a cast-iron block (numbered 12551358), which was installed in all 1999–2004 trucks and SUVs. These engines were coded "LR4" and "LR59" and are commonly known as the Vortec 4800. The 2003–2004 models are throttle-by-wire controlled, while earlier models may be equipped with drive-by-wire throttle if the truck had rear-wheel traction assist.

LM4

This 5.3L Vortec 5300 began production in 2003 and was the first Vortec unit to use an aluminum block, thus becoming an all-aluminum engine. It was first used in extended-wheelbase 2004 Chevy Trailblazers, 2004 GMC Envoys, and 2004 Chevy SSRs. The LM4 block is 100 pounds lighter than the cast-iron LM7 block and uses the "pan-axle," which allows the front differential to bolt directly to the oil pan in 4WD vehicles. This engine's throttle is drive-by-wire controlled, except in the Chevy Express and GMC Savana vans. These engines produce 285 to 300 hp and 325 to 335 ft-lbs of torque.

LM7

The LM7 5.3L Vortec 5300 model is the cast-iron-block version of the LM4 aluminum block. The engine appeared in 2002–2005 Cadillac Escalade two-wheel-drive (2WD) vehicles, 2002–2006 Chevrolet Avalanches, 2003–2007 Chevrolet Expresses/GMC Savanas, 1999–2007 GM C/K trucks, 1999–2007 GMC Sierra 1500s, 1999–2006 Chevrolet Suburban/GMC Yukon XLs, 1999–2006 Chevrolet Tahoes/GMC Yukons. Available from 1999 to 2007, this powerful Gen III motor is rated from 285 to 295 hp and has 330 ft-lbs of torque.

L33

Commonly found in 2005–2007 GM C/K trucks, the 5.3L L33 engine features an aluminum block, new cylinder heads (LS6 based), and a high-lift cam, pushing output to 310 hp and 300 ft-lbs of torque.

LS4

The introduction of the Gen IV engine came in 2005 with the LS4 and larger LS2. These engines are based on Gen III dimensions but feature updated designs. They were designed to use displacement-on-demand technology.

LS2

The 6.0L LS2 production engine replaced the LS1 as the standard powertrain in 2005–2006 GTOs and 2005 C6 Corvettes. The LS2, initially rated at 390 hp and 405 ft-lbs of torque, received a bump to 400 hp in 2006, which is found in 2005–2006 Chevy SSRs.

Gen IV: Improving the Legend

Based on the Gen III architecture, the Gen IV engine was released in 2005. These new engines use displacement-on-demand technology, which General Motors called "active fuel management." In this system, the engine alternates firing of the pistons between all eight to as few as four pistons, saving fuel and reducing emissions. Although the technology has been offered on the Gen IV platform, this engine series was designed to accept variable valve timing (VVT) and to accept three valves per cylinder.

However, the Gen III production engines didn't disappear in 2005. The LS1 was still in production for the Holden VE and W models and the LS6-powered Cadillac CTS-V, and Chevrolet Performance continued to offer both engines. In fact, Gen III engine production continued for new vehicles until 2005, when two all-new engine platforms were released: the Gen IV LS2 and LS4.

In 2006, the 505-hp LS7 became the most powerful naturally aspirated (NA) production small-block Chevy engine ever built. The Vortec truck engine line changed over to the Gen IV platform in 2005, adding six new Gen IV blocks. By 2008, the 6.0L L76 and the 6.2L LS3 joined the Gen IV line.

As the horsepower wars increased, General Motors developed the LSA and the LS9, which were both based on the LS3 block. The LSA is a supercharged 6.2L that uses a 1.9L roots-type Eaton supercharger to build 556 brake hp (flywheel) and 551 ft-lbs of torque.

The LSA is available in the 2009-and-newer Cadillac CTS-V models as well as the 2012-and-newer ZL1 Camaro. The LS9 also measures out to 6.2 liters of displacement but uses a 2.3L Eaton roots blower to generate the 638 brake hp and 604 ft-lbs of torque, making it the most powerful GM V-8 ever produced (until the LT4 and then LT5). Just like the LS7, the LS9 features a 10.75-quart dry-sump oiling system. The LS9 is used in the 2009–2013 Corvette ZR1.

LS4

The 5.3L LS4 is used in 2006-and-newer Pontiac Grand Prix GXPs, 2008 Chevy Impalas and 2008 Chevy Monte Carlos. This is the smallest-displacement car engine in the Gen III/Gen IV lineup. It also marks the first time a small-block Chevy V-8 was offered in a front-wheel-drive car since the small-block was introduced in 1955.

Specifically designed for front-drive vehicles, the LS4 produces 303 hp and 323 ft-lbs, and it has displacement-on-demand technology. It shares the same deep skirt design and six-bolt cross-bolted main caps as all other Gen IV engines.

The LS7 was the first dry-sump LS engine. It was introduced in the 2006 Z06 Corvette and produced 505 hp. (Photo Courtesy General Motors)

Cadillac and Chevrolet needed an engine to turn the CTS-V and ZL1 Camaro into street demons, so General Motors came up with the LSA. The slightly smaller Eaton supercharger reduces the overall output to 556 hp compared to the LS9. The LSA is also available as a crate engine. (Photo Courtesy General Motors)

It is also designed for the traditional "east-west" configuration for front-wheel drive. To do this, General Motors shortened the overall length of the crank by 3 mm at the rear and 10 mm at the front for a total of 13 mm. The accessories are arranged to maximize space, and it uses the longest single belt drive in a GM engine. The LS4 also has another unique feature: the oil filter is inside the oil pan, but access is still pretty simple.

LS7

Introduced for 2006 Corvette Z06s, the 505-hp LS7 was the most powerful NA production small-block Chevy engine ever built. To achieve the 7.0L displacement goal, both bore and stroke increased to 104.8 mm and 101.6 mm respectively.

The cast-iron piston sleeves are pressed-in rather than cast-in. The pistons feature tapered wrist pins, and the rings are anodized to reduce blowby and friction. The titanium connecting rods weigh 27 percent less than the LS2 rods, which reduces the pressure on the rod and main bearings. All of these components help the LS7 achieve its 7,100-rpm redline. All-new cylinder heads were developed, featuring fully CNC-machined ports and a 1.8:1 rocker-arm ratio. The intake valves are titanium, while the exhaust uses sodium-filled valves to wick heat away from the valve face.

LS3

This 6.2L engine replaced the 6.0L LS2, raised power output from 400 to 430 hp, and increased torque from 400 ft-lbs to 424 ft-lbs. The additional 30 hp comes from the increased cylinder-head flow, larger injectors (from the LS7), larger bore (shared with the 6.2L Vortec engine), enhanced valvetrain, and new pistons. In addition, bolting on an active exhaust system adds 6 hp.

LS9

While the LS7 is the most powerful NA Chevy small-block, this supercharged 6.2L Gen IV is the most

The LS9 is the bad boy from the Gen IV line, making 638 hp with an intercooled supercharger. The 6.2L engine is available as a crate engine from GM Performance. These engines were found in the ZR1 Corvette and the ZL1 Camaro. (Photo Courtesy General Motors)

powerful production LS-series engine that General Motors has ever produced. It is also the most technologically advanced. This mill cranks out super-car performance at 620 hp and 595 ft-lbs of torque.

Gen IV Vortech Engines

The Gen IV engines followed suit with the Vortec engines in 2005, although the Gen III motors continued production through 2007. The Gen IV engines feature a mix of iron- and aluminum-block engines. While not as many of these trucks have made it to the salvage yards, some wrecked late-model trucks are available. These represent some of the most-powerful Vortec engines, but they are also the most complicated.

L76

The all-aluminum 6.0L L76 engine is one of the most advanced Gen IV engines. This powerplant uses GM's active-fuel-management technology (formerly known as displacement on demand) as well as VVT. Using active fuel management, the L76 operates on four cylinders under light and moderate loads, increasing up to 6 percent fuel economy while retaining excellent peak horsepower at 361 hp and 385 ft-lbs of torque.

The L76 uses a structural cast-aluminum oil pan specifically built for the Pontiac G8. It also features a returnless fuel-injection system that uses Multec injectors and a tank-mounted fuel-pressure regulator, which eliminates the excess fuel sent through the lines. The L76 also uses the newest version of electronic throttle control (ETC), which eliminates the mechanical link between the accelerator pedal and the throttle body. With the deletion of the throttle actuator control (TAC) module, the E38 electronic control module (ECM) directly controls the throttle motor.

The all-aluminum 2007-and-newer 6.0L L76 Vortec Max 6.0L VVT engine was available in Chevrolet Avalanches, Suburbans, and Silverados, as well as GMC Yukon XLs and Sierras. It features VVT, high-flow cylinder heads, and all the advanced technology of the E38 ECM. SAE-certified power ratings are 366 hp and 380 ft-lbs of torque.

L92

The L92 Gen IV all-aluminum engine was installed in the 2008-and-newer Hummer H2s and SUT (sport utility truck) platforms as well as 2007 Cadillac Escalades, Escalade ESVs, and Escalade EXT trucks and SUVs. SAE-certified power ratings are 403 hp and 417 ft-lbs of torque.

LC9

The all-aluminum 5.3L LC9 engine was used in 2007-and-newer Chevy Avalanches, Suburbans, Silverados, GMC Yukon XLs, and GMC Sierras. Standard features include active fuel management, returnless fuel injection, E85 compatibility, and advanced engine control. SAE-certified power ratings are 302 hp and 330 ft-lbs of torque.

LMF

This 5.3L Gen IV engine with a cast-iron block was installed in 2008-and-newer Chevy Expresses and GMC Savana vans. It features E85 compatibility and all the other Gen IV series advancements. SAE-certified power ratings are 301 hp and 325 ft-lbs of torque.

LFA

This is the 6.0L all-aluminum Gen IV engine that was designed specifically for specialized vehicles and exhaust systems. It is offered on 2008-and-newer Chevy Tahoe Hybrids, 2008-and-newer GMC Yukon Hybrids, 2009-and-newer Cadillac Escalade Hybrids, 2009-and-newer Chevy Silverado Hybrids, and 2009-and-newer GMC Sierra Hybrids. SAE-certified power ratings are 332 hp and 367 ft-lbs of torque.

LH6

The 5.3L was the first Gen IV engine introduced into the GM Vortec truck line. The engine was used in 2005–2007 Chevy Trailblazers, including EXTs, 2005 GMC Envoy XLs, 2005 GMC Envoy XUVs, 2005–2007 Buick Rainiers, 2005-and-newer Saab 9-7Xs, 2007 Chevy Silverado 1500s, and 2007 GMC Sierra 1500s. It's an all-aluminum engine developed jointly with the LS2 car and truck V-8s. Power output is rated at 300 hp and 330 ft-lbs of torque.

LH8

The all-aluminum LH8 5.3L engine was designed for 2008-and-newer Hummer H3s, 2009 Chevrolet Colorados, and 2009 GMC Canyons. It has a new quad catalytic converter system, which was required for the H3 application. It includes a compact exhaust system design. SAE-certified power ratings are 300 hp and 320 ft-lbs of torque.

LMG

The 5.3L cast-iron-block LMG Gen IV engine was installed in 2007-and-newer Chevy Avalanches, Suburbans, Silverados, Tahoes, GMC Yukons, Yukon XLs, and Sierra models. Active fuel management, returnless fuel injection, E85 compatibility, and advanced engine control are standard. SAE-certified power ratings are 320 hp and 340 ft-lbs of torque and 315 hp and 338 ft-lbs of torque.

LY2

New for 2007, the 4.8L LY2 features a cast-iron block and aluminum heads that power Chevy Tahoes and Silverados as well as GMC Yukon and Sierra platforms. The LY2 uses the E38 ECM for advanced system control. Drive by wire and displacement on demand are standard. Power output is rated at 295 hp and 305 ft-lbs of torque.

LY5

The LY5 is another 2007-and-newer cast-iron-block 5.3L Gen IV engine manufactured for Chevrolet Avalanches, Suburbans, Tahoes, and Silverados as well as GMC Yukons, Yukon XLs, and Sierra models. SAE-certified power ratings are 320 hp and 340 ft-lbs of torque.

LY6

The LY6 engines are built for 2008-and-newer Chevrolet Suburban HDs and Silverado HDs as well as GMC Yukon XL HDs and Sierra HD models. The cast-iron-block Vortec 6.0L VVT engine mates with the 4L80 and 6L90 6-speed transmissions. SAE-certified power ratings are 353 hp and 383 ft-lbs of torque.

Gen V LT-Series Engines

Pushing the envelope even more, General Motors released the Gen V platform in 2013. It replaced the LS-series engine in all platforms (the exception being 2500 and 3500 GM trucks) from 2014 and onward. The

General Motors introduced the Gen V LT1 in 2014, which was installed in all Corvettes and produced 460 hp and featured direct injection. This technology injects the fuel at very high pressure directly into the combustion chamber, which gives the ECM absolute control over the entire combustion process.

The LT4 engine is a supercharged version of the LT1. Basic changes included lower-compression heads (down from 11.5:1 to 10:1) and a big supercharger. The LT4 produces 650 hp on the stock tune but capable of so much more.

Because everyone needs more horsepower, the LT5 was released. This beast adds 100 hp more than the LT4 for a total of 750 hp and 715 ft-lbs of torque. The last C7 Corvette, the ZR1, had this engine in 2019.

Gen V shares the look of the III/IV series, but in reality, it is all new.

The biggest advancement in the LT series is the use of direct injection, where the fuel is sprayed directly into the combustion chamber at high pressure (2,175 psi for the LT1). This aids in fuel economy and overall performance through better fuel atomization. Direct injection also makes cylinder deactivation more efficient, further increasing fuel economy. The 2014 LT1 Corvette can get up to 29 miles per gallon (mpg). Other advancements include piston oiling jets, active fuel management, and continuous VVT.

With active fuel management and displacement on demand, the Gen V engines can sound and feel as if they are missing at idle. In fact, these engines can idle as low as 400 rpm. This is because the ECM is dropping cylinders to reduce fuel consumption. Don't be concerned if your engine feels like it has a miss at idle, it is just the ECM dropping cylinders.

Chevrolet Performance has released several crate versions of the Gen V. There is a naturally aspirated 6.2L 460-hp LT1, which is the same engine installed in the base-model C7 Corvette, and the supercharged 6.2L 650-hp LT4, which comes in the Z06 version of the C7 Corvette. The LT1 engine for Camaros is rated at 455 hp.

6.2L LT1

Making 460 hp without a supercharger is not easy, and to do so while hitting 29 mpg is even harder, but the LT1 does exactly that. The 4.06-inch bore combined with the 3.62 stroke create an 11.5:1 compression ratio, which makes efficient use of the fuel that is pumped through the direct-injection nozzles. A forged crank, hypereutectic pistons, and forged powdered metal rods yield light weight and durability. The heads are conventional aluminum castings and feature lightweight sodium-filled valves.

6.2L LT4

To pump up the output of the LT1, General Motors dropped a supercharger onto the 6.2L block to make 650 hp. To make that work long term, it made changes to the rotating assembly. The crank is the same, but the rods were slightly redesigned to increase strength in key areas. The pistons in the LT4 are forged and the combustion chamber was opened up, decreasing the compression ratio to a boost-friendly 10.0:1. The heads are rotocast, making them stronger and better at handling higher heat ranges. The valves are solid titanium, and the oiling system is a dry-sump design.

6.2L LT5

For 2019 Corvettes, the LT5 expanded upon the previous successes of the Gen V design. The LT5 generates 755 hp and 715 ft-lbs of torque with the assistance of an Eaton TVS supercharger and intercooler. This massive power increase comes from the direct-injection system that is augmented by port injection (like the LS platform).

6.2L LT2

Designed specifically to work with a mid-engine platform for the all-new mid-engine C8 Corvette, the LT2 builds 490 hp and 465 ft-lbs of torque. This engine uses a dry-sump oiling system.

Starting in 2014, all GMC/Chevrolet trucks and full-size SUVs with V-8 gasoline engines came with Gen V engines. There are currently six truck versions: 4.3L (the LT-based V-6), 5.3L V-8, and 6.2L V-8. The V-6 is an LT-series engine that essentially has two cylinders cut off. The V-8s are the most common for trucks and SUVs.

4.3L LV3

A V-8 isn't always needed, and that is where the LV3 fits in. This powerful V-6 engine is based on the Gen V platform, but it has two fewer cylinders. Up to 297 hp and 330 ft-lbs of torque make this engine capable of handling modest loads in the bed of a full-size truck and still get excellent fuel economy. This engine is known as the EcoTec3.

5.3L L83

This engine features a 3.78-inch bore with 3.62-inch stroke. These engines make 355 hp and 383 ft-lbs of torque with gas, while E85 produces 376 hp and 416 ft-lbs of torque.

5.3L L82

For lower-trimmed 2019-and-newer trucks, the L82 is a 5.3L engine with active fuel management instead of the new dynamic-fuel-management system, which uses 17 different firing orders that can change which cylinders fire and when.

5.3L L84

For 2019-and-newer GM trucks with mid- and upper-level trim packages, the L84 provides the new DFM system. Instead of four cylinders of deactivation, the L84 can deactivate all eight cylinders in 17 different configurations.

6.2L L86/L87

The L86 is a modified LT1, making 420 hp and 460 ft-lbs of torque. The LT1 and L86 are very similar, down to the compression ratio of

11.5:1. In 2019, the L87 replaced the L86. This new version has dynamic fuel management, which can change the program every 125 milliseconds, allowing these trucks to get fuel economy in the low 20s.

6.6L L8T

For the heavy-duty trucks, General Motors needed a better option, and that is in the form of the L8T. It is similar to the L86 but features an iron block and a longer stroke (98 mm), pushing displacement to 6.6 liters.

These are not monster horsepower engines. At 401 hp, it is 19 less than the L86/L87, but it makes slightly more torque at 464 ft-lbs. The main difference is the L86/L87 prefers 93-octane fuel, whereas the L8T uses 87 octane gas. The engine also has a stronger iron block and does not have stop/start run operation nor does it have any cylinder deactivation controls.

All 2019-and-newer GM Gen V engines come with ECMs that are hardware locked by the factory, making them more expensive to swap. An aftermarket ECM can be used or a factory ECM can be unlocked, which can cost upward of $2,000. Keep that in mind when looking for an engine at a salvage yard.

Sourcing an Engine

There are many places to find an engine for your project. Chevrolet Performance has quite a few variations on the crate engine—from the basic block to build your own engine to complete kits that provide almost everything that is needed to swap an LS/LT into a C10. There is also the salvage route, where you can purchase a used engine from a salvage yard or you can buy one directly from someone online or at a swap meet.

The key to buying used LS/LT engines is to make sure to get as many components as possible from the original vehicle. This includes the engine, the transmission (when applicable), the ECM, the accessory drive, and the engine harness.

The factory wiring harness probably won't be used, but it can be used if you choose to do so. If you can get the harness, then the sensors and terminals will remain intact. Another component that is needed from a donor vehicle is the gas pedal and throttle body for any drive-by-wire engine. These are matched to the ECM and engine, so you have to make sure that you get the right one.

LT-series engines are not as tricky when it comes to the throttle pedal, which is now referred to as an accelerator-pedal sensor. The standard swap part is actually from an LS-powered Cadillac CTS-V. Get the fuel-control module and transmission-control module for any LT-series engine because these are required for controlling the pulse width modulation (PWM) fuel-pump system and transmission if you are planning on running the original

There are several ways to obtain an engine for your swap: 1) buy a crate engine like this 2015 LT1, 2) buy an engine from a wrecked vehicle, or 3) buy all of the pieces and build your own. With a crate engine, buyers typically get a warranty.

The fuel-injection system is under the intake on Gen V engines. The injectors are pressed into the heads by the rails and connected to the mechanical fuel pump that sits about where a distributor would be on a small-block Chevy. The pump is driven off the fuel lobe on the camshaft.

Preparing a vehicle for an engine swap requires removing the original drivetrain and, in many cases, cleaning it up. This is the perfect time to address any paint or body issues under the hood. This 1966 GMC Suburban came to the shop with no drivetrain or front sheet metal, which provided ample room to work.

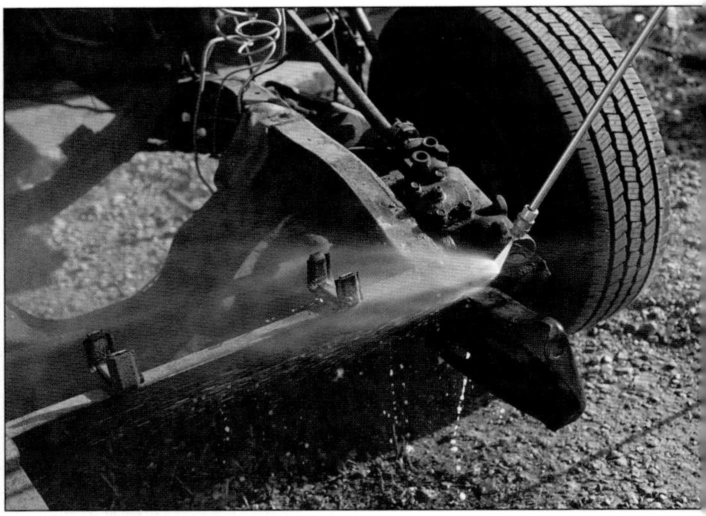

The intended look for this Suburban was to retain the original patina. However, this project requires a clean workspace, so we fogged the entire engine bay with degreaser and pressure-washed the chassis to get down to the original finish. This allows us to not have to deal with greasy hands all the time.

The same goes for the engine. This is a 2001 Gen III LM7 takeout engine that is absolutely caked with crud. Note the large mechanical fan, as only some trucks came with mechanical fans on Gen III and Gen IV engines

transmission for the LT engine.

To simplify this, simply opt for one of the Chevrolet Performance Connect and Cruise crate engines. These come with the engine, ECM wiring harness, accessory drive, throttle pedal, and in some cases, a new transmission and controller as well. These crate engine packages truly simplify the process of choosing and swapping an LS/LT series engine into your vehicle. They are pricey, but they come with GM quality and a warranty.

Sourcing an Engine

1 *Make sure that the engine is clean. We had to soak this engine with degreaser (make sure that it is safe for aluminum) a few times to remove the grime.*

Sourcing an Engine *continued*

2 *After the engine is dry, separate the transmission from the engine. A plastic trim cover sits between the starter and the bellhousing with one bolt holding it in place. Remove the starter and the bolt to the trim cover.*

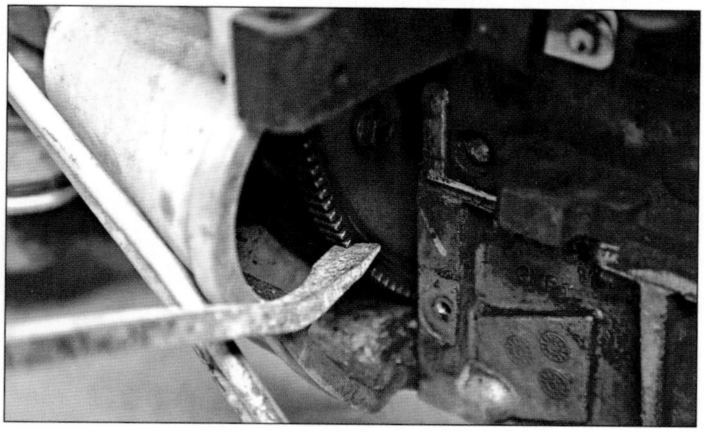

3 *Next, remove the flexplate. This flexplate was locked in place. There is a special tool for this, but a prybar works too.*

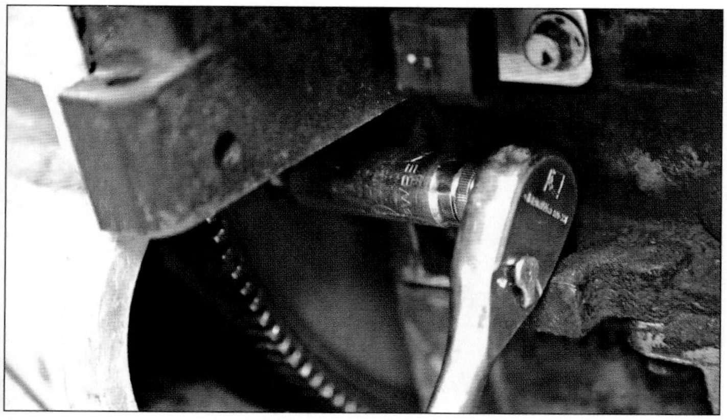

4 *Three bolts hold the torque convertor to the flexplate. Remove each one, spinning the motor by hand to bring the next bolt into the starter opening.*

5 *With the transmission off, the bellhousing bolt pattern is visible. Note that there is a dead space at the top passenger's side of the pattern. Any GM SBC bellhousing will bolt to these blocks (it just won't use all the holes). The Gen V has a similar layout.*

6 *For the 1991 C1500 that is featured in this book, we sourced a complete 2018 Chevrolet Silverado 5.3L drivetrain with a 6L80 transmission and an NQH transfer case. Make sure to get all of the pieces that go with the takeout engine, as it will make the swap easier.*

Vortec 5.3L Truck Engine Removal

While some swappers purchase crate engines or salvage takeout engines, cash can be saved by finding a wrecked vehicle and yanking out the motor yourself. The most abundant source for LS-series engines is GMC and Chevy trucks. The key is to locate one with less than 200,000 miles on the odometer. When properly maintained, an LS engine can go 300,000 miles before needing to be rebuilt, so at 150,000, there is usually a lot of life left in an LS engine.

We picked up a 2003 Chevy 1500 truck with rear-end damage. The engine and transmission ran. Heck, the truck still drove and could have been repaired, but it had a salvage title. For $500, you can't beat it.

We rolled the truck into the shop and began stripping it down. We started by removing the fenders. This step isn't necessary, but it makes accessing all the bolts much easier, and the truck is slated for the scrap yard anyway. Within 10 minutes, the fenders were off.

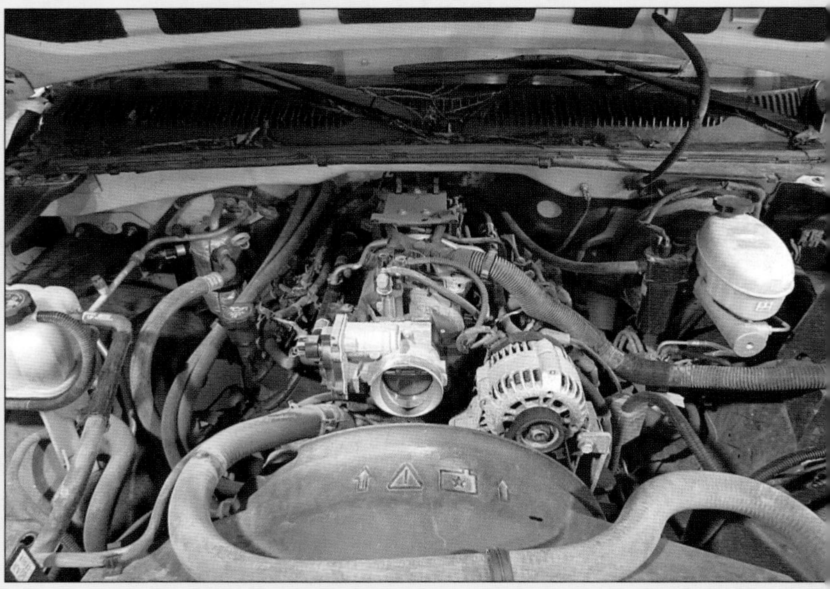

If pulling your own engine, there are a few items you need to be prepared to do. This 2001 Chevrolet 1500 has an LM7 5.3L engine, which is by far the most common Gen III engine.

1 ***First, remove the fenders, grille, and hood to access the engine without having to work around those parts. Next, disconnected the airbox and remove the shrouds.***

2 ***Disconnect the wiring to remove the engine. This includes the computer, which is located in the driver-side inner fender well.***

3 ***Remove or cut the hoses. However, we left the air-conditioning system intact, as those parts are ·ood salvage parts, and opening them to the atmosphere ·amages the components themselves.***

4 ***Now, only the radiator stands in the way. Remove the radiator last to minimize the mess.***

5 ***The throttle actuator control (TAC) module is a key component of the drive-by-wire system. Don't ›rget to remove it as well as the wiring harness that ›oes with it.***

6 ***The pedal mounts to the firewall. Remove its 10-mm bolts, and it is now ready to swap into your vintage C/K truck.***

Next, we removed the core support. This opens up the front ⁻ the engine, making removal from the chassis easier. There ·e many hoses and wires attached to the engine. Carefully ·move each wire connector from the engine, cut any zip ties or ·raps holding the harness to the engine or chassis (don't cut any ·ires!), and remove the harness. The hoses can be removed or ·mply be cut, as new hoses will be needed for your swap install.

At this point, the engine should be unfettered. Unbolt ·e transmission from its mount, support it with a jack, and ·move the transmission crossmember. Unbolt the engine ›om the motor mounts on the frame and attach an engine hoist. Lift the engine and slide it out of the chassis.

Since this vehicle is drive by wire, we have to remove the pedal and TAC module. The TAC module is located on the firewall next to the power brake booster. Don't forget these two items. They will be needed if you are planning on using the stock computer. If not, take them anyway because someone will want them.

A little degreaser and elbow grease will have your new LS engine ready for prime time in just a few minutes. Don't forget to save the secondary sensors, such as the mass airflow (MAF) sensor from the air inlet tube. ■

ENGINE AND TRANSMISSION MOUNTS

Swapping an LS or LT engine into a C10 requires sorting out the physical mounting of the engine and transmission first. Everything else will be based on where the engine sits in the chassis. Luckily, most C10-series trucks already have small-block engine mounts in the chassis, but not all of them do. The LS and LT motor mounts are similar but not interchangeable, and there are engine-placement considerations that must be factored in that are different between the two engine generations.

The LS block uses a four-bolt mount that bolts to the side of the engine block. The most common solution for this change is simply converting the LS engine to the common early-style three-bolt engine mounts. The original 1955 small-block featured the three-bolt mount configuration, and the same motor-mount pattern continued in production through the second-generation small-block of the LT1 and LT4 engines (not to be confused with the 2014-and-newer LT1 Gen V series).

There are numerous companies making adapter plates to convert the LS mount to accept an SBC three-bolt mount. With so many adapters (there are literally hundreds of different brands available), deciding which one to use is the tough part. Both LS and LT engine blocks are shorter than the SBC. The SBC bellhousing plane is about 1 inch behind the crankshaft, whereas the bellhousing plane is in line with the crank on LS/LT engines.

The stock LS engine motor mounts are located more toward the bellhousing than on the Gen I and Gen II blocks. Therefore, if a motor mount is bolted to the frame using these holes, in most vehicles the engine sits too far forward. This increases the nose weight of the vehicle, causing instability.

Universal adapters with offset mount locations, such as 1.25 inches forward and 0.5 inch upward, better facilitate engine placement for chassis and body clearance. Dirty Dingo

This 1966 GMC Suburban originally came with a 302-ci V-6, which is a rare engine but not what the owner wanted. After sourcing a 2001 5.3L LM7 engine and 4L60 transmission, we began the swap. All of the front sheet metal was removed to provide access. The early trucks (1960–1972) require a little more chassis prep than the later-model C/K trucks.

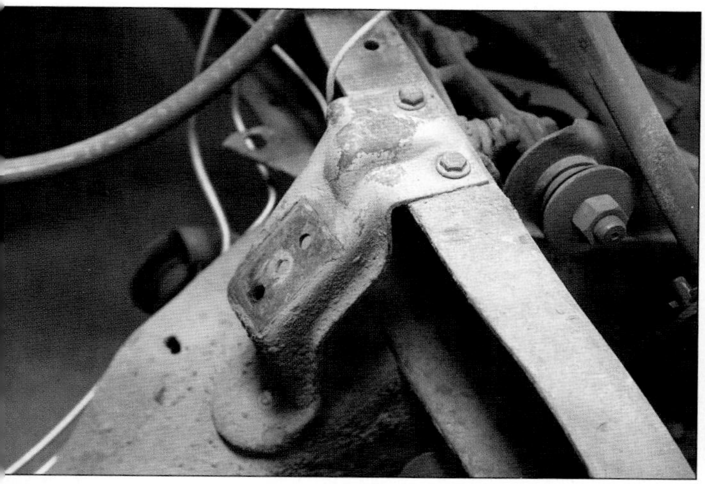

hese frame stands are only useable for the 302 V-6. They re very rare and should be kept for reuse or resale. Unlike he factory V-8 mounts, they cannot be used for any LS/LT wap. Straight-6 frame stands cannot be used for LS/LT waps, either.

The 1963–1967 frames feature a wide top rail that is 2⅜ inches wide, but 1968-and-newer frames were 1¾ inches wide to accommodate big-block engines. Frames were often swapped on these older trucks, so measure to verify before ordering new frame stands.

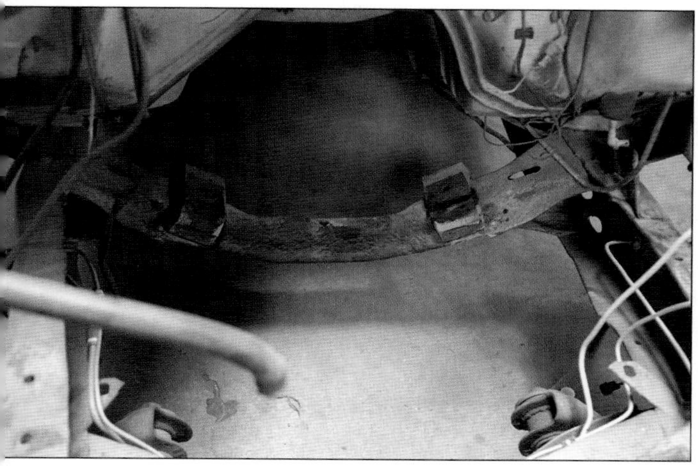

The transmission crossmember on the early trucks is in the way, so this always has to be removed. The engine can't be swapped with this in the way. The crossmember is riveted in place. Don't try to save it; just cut it out.

ffers adjustable adapter plates so nat you can get the positioning just ght for your application.

Simply bolt the adapter plate to ne engine block to get the mounting rovisions for the old-style three-bolt ngine mount. For most C10 trucks nat originally came with an SBC ngine, this allows the LS-series ngine to drop right into the chas-s with no re-engineering. However, mply fitting the engine into the hassis is only part of the consider-tion, as there are clearances that must be checked, specifically the oil pan and low-mount accessories.

Much like the LS platform, the LT-series engines use a four-bolt engine mount that is just forward of the block centerline. The rear two bolts split the center cylinders and the SBC has mounting bosses on the block that sit roughly between the two front cylinders. This pushes the LT forward of where the typical SBC sits.

Dimensionally, the LT is about the same size as the SBC, although the back of the block is shorter, as there is no ledge for the bellhousing. Additionally, the mechanical fuel pump is at the back of the block, requiring a little extra clearance. Most swappers simply adapt the LT block mounts to the commonly available SBC mounts and then go from there. With so many options for placement, it can get a bit sticky trying to figure out exactly what is needed.

The Gen V LT-series factory engine mounts are wildly different from SBC-style mounts or LS factory mounts. The LT-series mounts use a large polymer bushing to dampen the engine vibrations, which bolt to the frame instead of a clamshell that is secured with a single through-bolt. In some instances, the factory mounts can be used, but they are very large and require substantial fabrication to the get the alignment right. Using SBC mount adapters provides more options, and they are generally easier to fabricate frame stands for.

Typical installations need the engine in the factory SBC location,

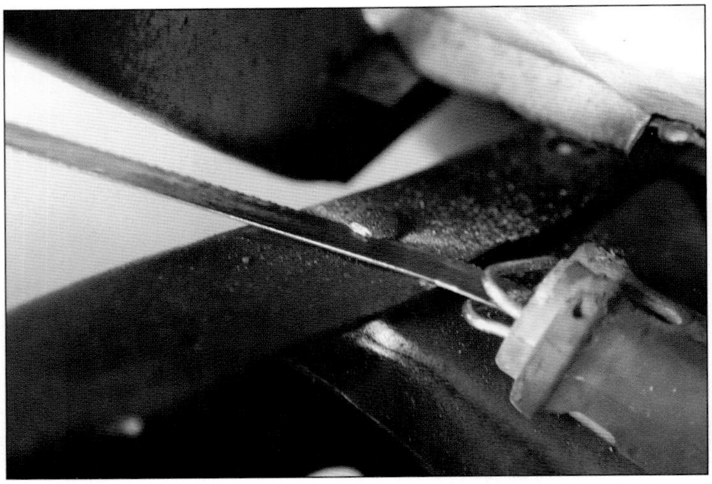

Various methods can be used to remove the rivets. The top rivets are easy to access, and a reciprocating saw makes quick work of removing them.

The bottom rivets are much trickier. If you are using a lift, a reciprocating saw is a good choice. If you are brave, lie on the floor but put safety first and use a hot wrench or plasma cutter. This will get the job done fast, and you won't end up with metal shavings in your eyes.

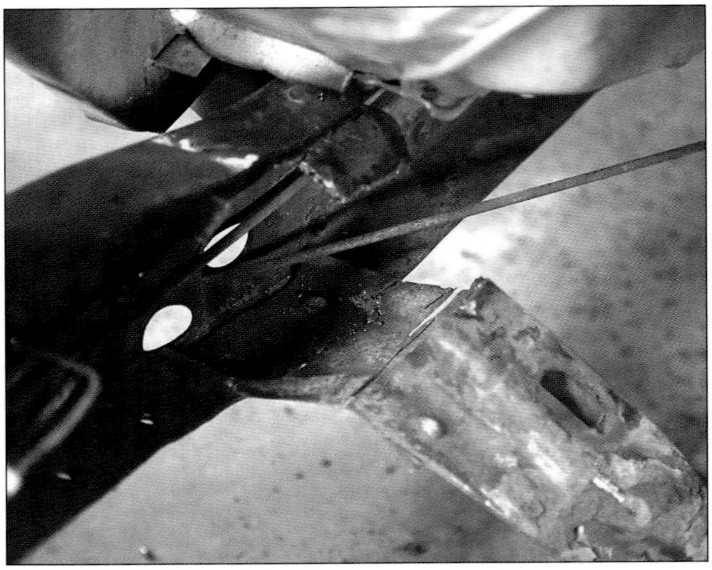

Sometimes these rivets are stubborn to remove. We had to remove the crossmember in sections.

If you don't want to ruin your back, LS mockup motors ar available, such as this one from Speedway Motors. They allow you to do all the mockup fabrication and setup to check fitment without having to use the complete engine.

which references the bellhousing mounting plane. This is 1[1]/8 inch rearward from the factory LT mounting point, so these are known as 1[1]/8-inch rearward adapters. This position works well in most GM trucks and SUVs, but not in all applications. Using the stock bellhousing location works well for engine-only swaps, where the original drivetrain is being used. This is the most common placement used in 4WD applications because it simplifies the transfer-case location and operation.

If the entire drivetrain is being replaced, there are several other considerations to be made. The type of transmission makes a big difference, as the only comparable physical transmission to any stock unit used in any C10/1500 truck is the 700R4 and the 4L60E. These transmissions use the same mount. If swapping newer-model transmission into th truck, a more forward position is usu ally warranted.

Adapting an LS/LT to factory GM SBC frame stands is a balancing act The firewall clearance as well as th front of the engine have to be deal with. The oil pan and accessories ca get in the way, especially if using fac tory components. In most cases, th

ʾactory truck-only vacuum pump will clear most truck frames, but it will do so only in the most forward positions.

Additionally, the factory air conditioner (AC) compressor location is on the passenger's side, down low, right to the block. Many aftermarket adapter mounts simply will not clear the factory compressor, and the compressor does not clear the frame or crossmember in most vehicles, so you have to sort that out. We have a solution, though. It is mentioned in Chapter 4.

1963–1966 C10

Three types of frame stands are available for these trucks, depending on which engine was originally installed in the truck. In most cases, the stock frame mounts will work for an LS or an LT swap with a basic adapter, but not all of them will. You need to know what engine was originally in the truck to determine if the frame stands will work.

230/250/SBC

If your truck had one of these engines originally installed, then the frame stands will work as is with adapter plates to the engine. Straight-six frame stands can be used in the rearward position or moved to the forward position. This is all relative to the adapter plates that have been chosen, which provides a lot of placement options for additional clearance.

292 Straight-Six

The larger straight-six engine used a unique offset (one sits farther forward than the other) frame stand that works with the 292 only. These stands will not work for LS or LT swaps and must be replaced.

GMC 302 V-6

GMC trucks and Suburbans with the 302 V-6 use unique frame stands that are not compatible with LS/LT swap adapters and require replacement.

1967–1972 C10

Two types of frames were used for these trucks: wide and narrow. The 1967 frames were a carryover from the previous bodystyle and featured wide frame rails (not the overall width of the frame, just the rails themselves). In 1968, General Motors switched to a narrower frame rail to accommodate big-block engines, providing better clearance for the exhaust. Because of this, the frame stands are different on these trucks.

When LS/LT swapping and using a replacement frame stand kit, such as the Holley Hooker Blackheart swap system, verify the width of the frame rails, as it is common to find that your truck has been frame-swapped. This applies to all 1960–1972 GM trucks.

Installing the Engine

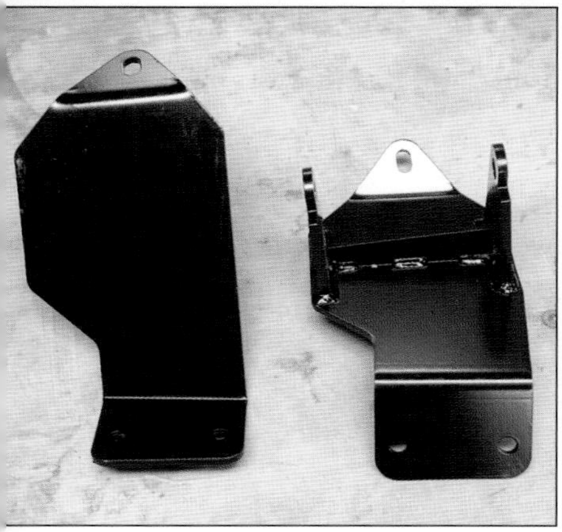

1 *We selected a Hooker Blackheart LS swap kit for this 1966 Suburban, and these are the new frame stands. They are left and right, and they use late-model clamshell-mount bushings for a clean install.*

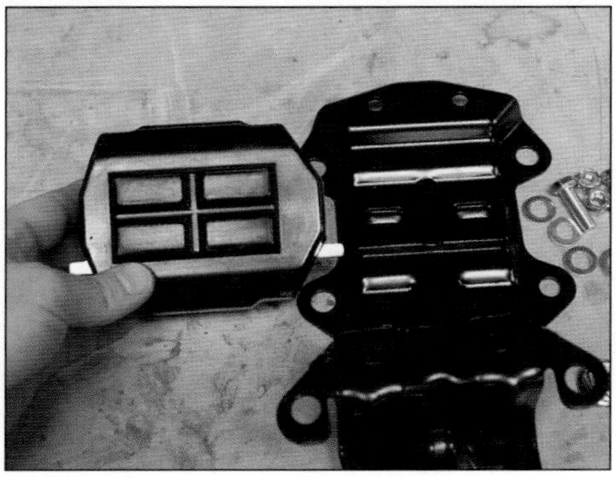

2 *The clamshells are a bolt-together design that has locating features that lock it into place, but the isolator can still be installed upside down. These mounts look very similar to the factory GM clamshell, but they are not the same dimensions, so they can't just be interchanged.*

3 *With the base on the table, a raised section and a flat section can be seen. The raised section is the bottom of the mount, toward the ground.*

Installing the Engine *continued*

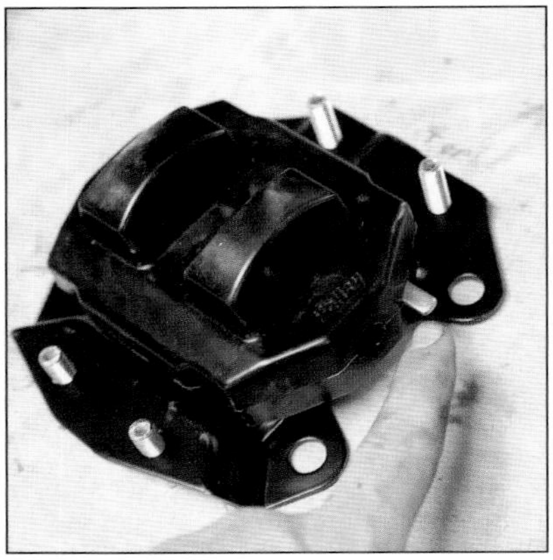

4 *The isolator installs onto the base using four smaller knobs down to the base and the steel fingers on the sides toward the top two bolts. This is key for the mounts to locate correctly to the frame stands.*

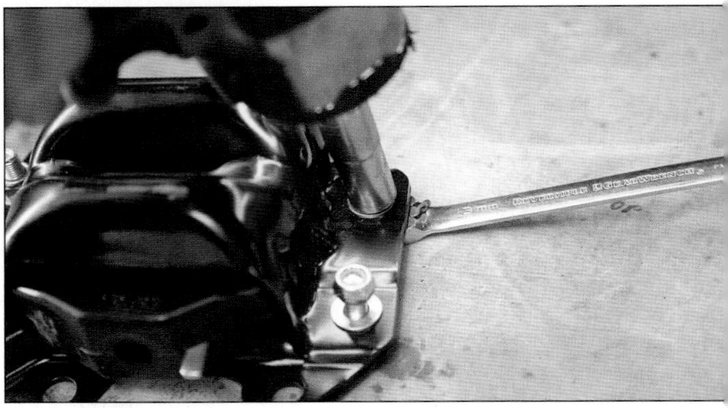

5 *Bolt down the top half of the clamshell with a 13-mm bolt and nut.*

6 *The complete assembly bolts to the engine block in the stock location as shown. The steel tabs should be above the motor-mount through-bolt.*

7 *On the chassis, secure the new Hooker frame stands using factory holes and the new included hardware. The lower bolt can be a bit tricky to access with a wrench, as it has to go through a small slot in the crossmember.*

8 *Finally, drop the engine onto the new frame stands. Unlike the early-style SBC mounts, these clamshells self-locate. A pry bar may need to be used to get the isolators to line up perfectly with the frame stand holes side to side, but these mounts are super easy to work with.*

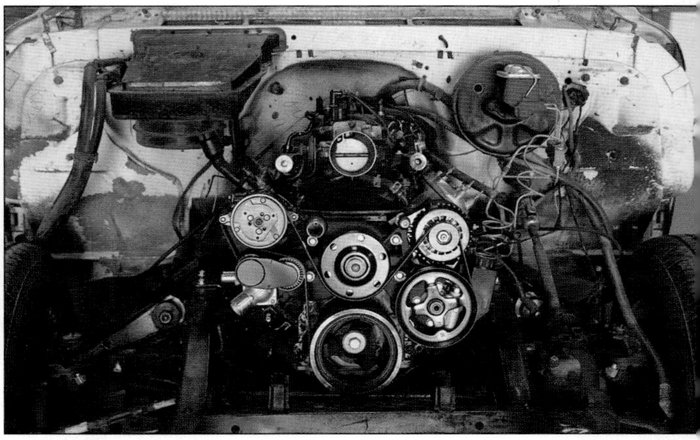

9 *The LM7 engine looks right at home in the chassis of the 1966 Suburban. With these Hooker Blackheart mounts, everything clears quite well with no issues.*

1963–1972 K10

The main issue for 4WD swaps is the clearance from :he front axle housing to the oil pan. The frame stands ınd engine plate adapters for 2WD trucks work to phys-cally install the engine in 4WD frames, but there may)e crossmember clearance issues, depending on how low he engine sits in the frame. This is dependent on the ıdapters. There are a few solutions to this.

.ifted Suspension

Most 4WD swaps with LS/LT engines require the uspension to be lifted at least 2 inches. This is to pro-vide clearance for the front axle housing. The pumpkin center section) of the housing will hit most LS/LT swaps, regardless of what oil pan is used at stock height. The engine can be raised in the chassis, which requires a custom frame stand or adapter plate.

Frame Mods

If the engine is mounted in the stock frame stands, there is a good chance the corners of the front crossmember will hit the oil pan or accessories. This is remedied by cutting out the offending sections and welding in some angle iron or plates that are cut to size and shape. This is done on a case-by-case basis, as the clearance depends on the mount style, position, and oil pan. In most cases using stock frame stands, the crossmember requires modification to clear the oil pan, low-mount AC, and low-mount power steering.

Replacing the Crossmember

1 ***If starting with a 1967–1972 4x4 model, swapping an LS/LT requires a bit more work. The front :rossmember simply will not work with an LS/LT ıngine. You could try to notch it, but there is a much ;impler solution: the Dirty Dingo replacement cross-nember system. After removing the original crossmem-)er, clamp the engine-mount assembly into position.***

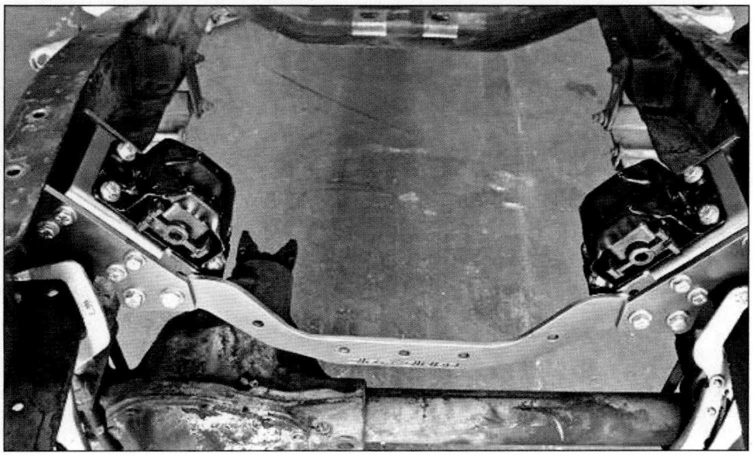

2 ***Then, loosely bolt the crossover brackets in place to ensure that the motor mounts are square to the chassis.***

3 ***Drill each of the straight-6 frame-mount bolt holes while the assembly is clamped into place. As each one is drilled, place a bolt into the new hole to ensure that everything stays aligned.***

Replacing the Crossmember *continued*

4 ***Once all of the holes are drilled, bolt down the brackets with the supplied hardware and machined backing plates. These plates provide additional strength to the chassis by spreading the clamping force across the entire assembly.***

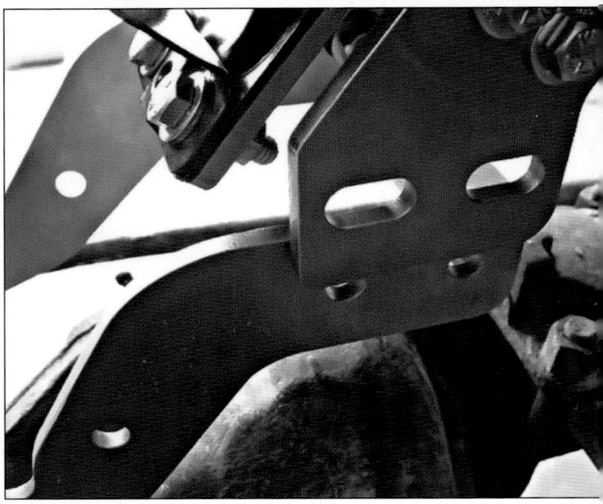

5 ***Next, bolt the crossmember braces to the motor-mount assembly.***

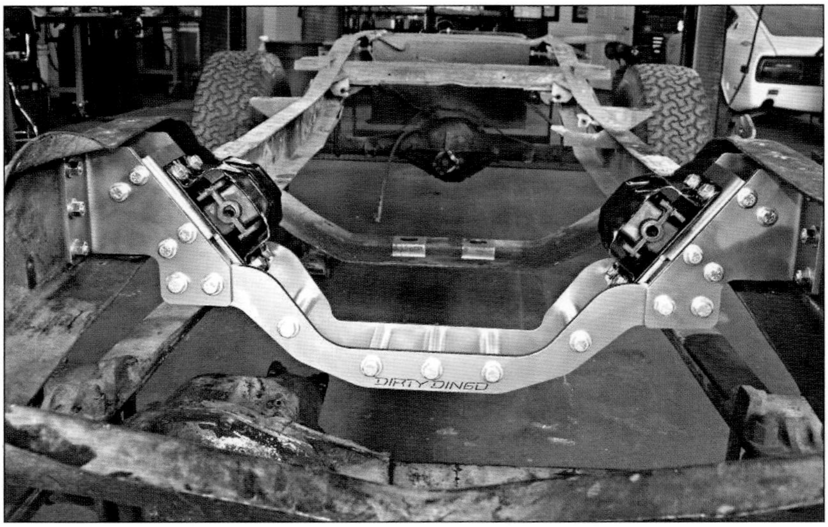

6 ***For the last step, install the crossmember stiffening bushings between the front and rear crossmember arms. This ensures there is no twisting or flexing while also saving weight.***

New Crossmember

There are a few options for replacing front crossmembers: build one or buy one. For a relatively low cost, Dirty Dingo offers a kit for these trucks to accommodate LS/LT swaps without a suspension lift. Built from 1/4-inch steel, the crossmember is CNC cut for precision fitment and fully welded. Installation does not require welding, as it is a complete bolt-in part. Once it is installed and the engine is mounted, the center section can be removed to service the engine, which is really handy.

The Dirty Dingo crossmember works with a GM hot rod pan (H3 Hummer), a Holley oil pan, or a Vortec truck oil pan in the stock bellhousing position. For applications that require the engine to sit farther forward, the 1998–2002 F-Body oil pan is required. The 2010–2015 Camaro manifolds work great with this crossmember as well. Low-mount AC components require a frame notch and for the engine to be set as far forward as possible.

1973–1987 C10

The most plentiful truck on the planet, the 1973–1987 C10, is one of the most popular candidates for an LS/LT swap. There are numerous options for adapter mounts for these trucks and SUVs, and they are relatively simple to do. The factory V-8 frame stands work with most motor-mount adapters. However, the V-6 frame stands do not work.

Hooker Blackheart System

The Holley Hooker Blackheart LS/LT swap kits for these trucks greatly simplifies the entire process with a complete kit or á la carte components. These pieces are designed to work together, so when this system is used, the exhaust, transmission mount, oil pan, and accessory drive all work together. You can just use the pieces from the kit that you need as well. The adapters fit the factory SBC clamshell mounts, and Hooker offers an updated version that uses a polyurethane bushing. A transmission crossmember is optional for various transmission swaps as well.

Dirty Dingo

For both LS and LT swaps, Dirty Dingo offers an adjustable adapter that allows a total of 3 inches of movement for your specific application: 1/2 inch rearward and 2½ inches forward. Once installed and torqued, they do not allow the engine to move. These use the original SBC clamshell-style frame mounts and help position the engine for various transmissions.

LS engines clear truck pans and low-mount truck AC with limited engine placement adjustment. They will not clear Corvette or Camaro/GTO low-mount AC brackets. Low-mount alternators will clear with limited placement adjustment.

LT engines require an aftermarket oil pan or frame notch. Low-mount AC does not work with these adapters, but it will clear the vacuum pump with limited engine placement adjustment.

BRP Muscle Rods

This LS-swap kit does not use the factory clamshell mounts. Instead, it uses a proprietary frame mount with a cylindrical bushing. The stock truck pan does clear, but the LH8 pan is recommended, as the truck pan hangs way too low for proper ground clearance. This kit clears the factory truck accessory drive and most aftermarket drives. The BRP kit comes with a transmission-specific crossmember, so order the correct kit for your transmission.

The BRP kit for LT swaps requires the BRP LT oil pan and comes with a custom transmission crossmember.

1973–1987 K10

Several adapter mounts are available for the 1973–1987 K10, including Dirty Dingo LS and LT mounts as well as BRP mounts.

Dirty Dingo LS Mounts

Adjustable by 3 inches total, these mounts clear the truck low-mount AC drive, but the engine cannot slide rearward, setting the engine 2.5 inches forward of the original bellhousing plane. The Corvette and Camaro/GTO low-mount AC does not clear. Low-mount alternators do fit, but they limit the adjustment for engine placement. These mounts work with the stock truck oil pan.

Dirty Dingo LT Mounts

Laser cut from 1/4-inch-thick plate steel, these mounts are adjustable just like the 2WD versions. These mounts clear low-mount alternators with limited adjustment. The stock LS truck pan requires a small notch on the driver's side of the crossmember, but aftermarket pans should clear without modification.

BRP Muscle Rods

This kit is designed around the GM LH8 Hummer oil pan or a Moroso high-clearance steel pan. The mounts do not use the factory clamshells. Instead, they feature a round bushing on a plate that bolts to the frame. Clearance is maintained in regard to the stock components under the hood, including the AC box, crossmember (with the LH8 or Moroso oil pan), and brake booster. When used with the BRP transmission crossmember, ensure the proper driveline angle. Kits are transmission specific, so make sure to know what you are using before you order one of these kits.

1988–1998 C1500

Hooker, Dirty Dingo, and BRP offer adapter mounts for the 1988–1998 C1500.

Hooker Mounts

Hooker has a few options for LS/LT swaps in these trucks. If you think an LT upgrade is possible in the future, the Hooker premium version is the ticket. With these brackets, an LS can upgrade to an LT by just changing the clamshell on the frame stands. Premium adapters require using the matching Hooker clamshell isolators.

If the goal is an LS only, then the standard mounts will cost significantly less to purchase, and the stock clamshells will work. Choices are dual position, rear position, or front position. For 2WD trucks, the rear position optimizes the engine placement for retaining the rest of the original drivetrain, as it locates to the original bellhousing plane. The front-bias position moves the engine forward for better accessory clearance and better fitment for T56 Magnum transmission clearance.

Installing the Drivetrain

1 *This 1991 Chevrolet 1500 4x4 is getting a complete 2018 Silverado 4WD drivetrain, including the Gen V L83 5.3L engine, 6L80 transmission, and NQH transfer case. A Hooker Blackheart 4x4 swap kit was chosen to make the swap simple. First, remove the factory motor mounts.*

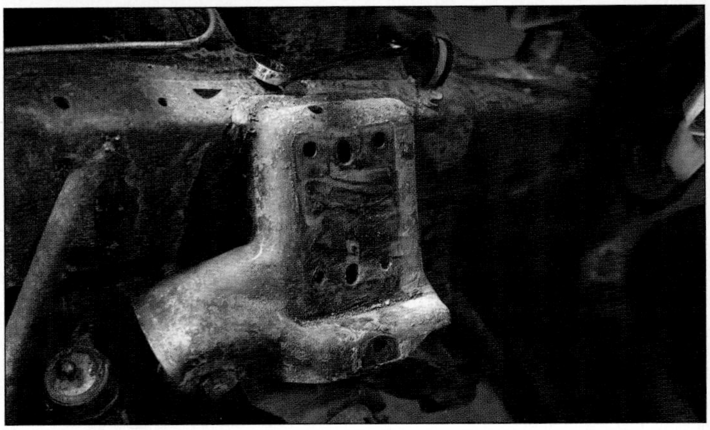

2 *There is no crossmember in the 4x4 trucks, as the engine is part of the chassis. This truck sat in a field for about 15 years before being pulled out for a rebuild, so it is fairly crusty. We will sort that out a little later.*

3 *The new frame stands are nearly identical, but they are left-side and right-side specific. The top of each one has a small "V" notch to note its orientation.*

4 *Using the supplied hardware, bolt each frame stand to the chassis. These are rear-biased mounts to position the transmission and transfer case in the stock position, allowing the original driveshafts to be reused. If you have a T56 manual, use front-biased mounts.*

5 *Because this is a 4x4 project, checking the fitment with the transmission and transfer case is a bit cumbersome and tricky, so we used a spare LT short-block as a mockup. The reason we did this is because these mounts were designed to use the Holley-swap oil pan, but we wanted to see if it would work with the stock pan.*

6 *Without the transmission in place, it is difficult to set the engine at the exact angle. The interference location of concern is the edge of the oil pan to the front axle housing. It does touch ever so slightly.*

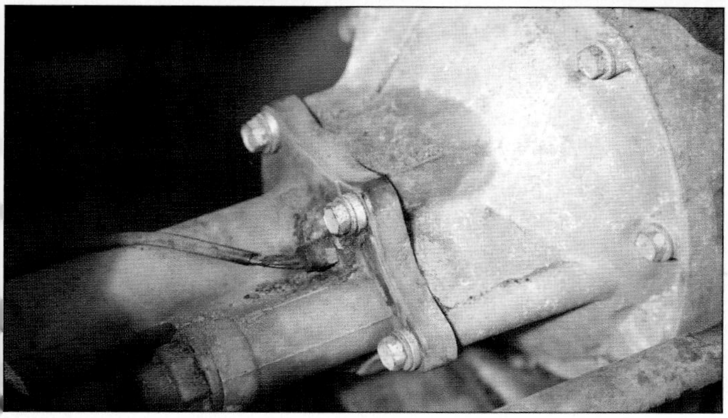

7 The top-center-bolt flange is the offending culprit. We could have swapped oil pans, but there is another solution that worked quite well: shaving down the boss.

8 Using a grinder with an 80-grit flap wheel, shave down the boss to the edge of the raised pedestal. We removed about an 1/8 inch, which was not enough to cause any loss of strength but was just enough to provide the clearance that we needed to the oil pan.

9 Then, reinstall the engine to the stand and check the clearance. There was more than enough room to move forward with the stock pan. Once the transmission was installed, there was approximately 1/4 inch of clearance, so it would have cleared without the modification, but the added clearance gives some extra peace of mind for engine flex.

10 With that issue sorted, set the entire drivetrain into place as a unit. Removing the original drivetrain required yanking the transfer case, but we were able to do it in one piece during reinstallation.

11 The original transmission crossmember was removed, but the torsion bar mount cannot be removed. Using a floor jack, raise the transfer case enough to clear the torsion-bar crossmember so that you can slide the rest of the drivetrain rearward and set it in place. With the Hooker Blackheart system, the original transmission crossmember bolted right up to the 6-speed transmission.

Dirty Dingo LS Mounts

The Dirty Dingo mounts provide up to 3 inches of adjustment for the engine placement with similar caveats to the other sliding mounts. These clear low-mount truck AC units in the 2.5-inch forward position. They do not work with Camaro/GTO or Corvette low-mount AC drives. Low-mount alternators do clear but with limited adjustment. Truck oil pans clear the crossmember.

LT swaps with the Dirty Dingo adjustable mounts do not clear low-mount AC drives. The vacuum pump will clear with reduced engine placement adjustment. The truck oil pan requires notching the engine crossmember for clearance or using an aftermarket oil pan.

BRP Muscle Rods

Similar to the Squarebody kits, the BRP kit is transmission-specific and clears the stock truck pan, but the LH8 pan is recommended for ground clearance. The frame stands are replaced with a cylindrical bushing. This kit clears the factory accessory drives as well as the aftermarket drives. The engine is located in line with the original bellhousing plane.

1988–1998 K1500

For the 4x4 version of these trucks, there are a few options for adapter mounts. Hooker and Dirty Dingo both make adapters for these 4x4 trucks.

Hooker LS Mounts

Hooker has two distinct versions of its adapters for these trucks: standard and premium. The standard mounts are designed for LS swaps, whereas the premium units allow for future conversion to an LT (or back to an LS from an LT) by simply changing the frame stand clamshell. The premiums require using the Hooker clamshell mount. Both styles come in rear-, forward-, or dual-mounting positions.

The forward position is for LS swaps with 6L80/6L90 transmissions and transfer cases into the stock position in relation to the driveline.

The dual-mount adapters have both positions, should plans change in the middle of the build. These mounts work with all the other Hooker LS swap components: headers/manifolds, the oil pan, accessories, etc. The stock truck oil pan or Holley 302-2 or 302-3 pan clears the front crossmember without modification.

Hooker LT Mounts

Three versions of these motor-mount adapters are available for the 4x4 trucks: rear bias, front bias, and dual mount. The rear-bias position puts the LT engine inline for the stock transmission and transfer case to stay in the stock location, keeping the drivelines undisturbed. This also retains the stock transmission crossmember position.

The forward position is for LT swaps with the 6L80/6L90 transmissions and transfer case into the stock position in relation to the driveline.

The dual-mount adapters have both positions (should plans change in the middle of the build). These mounts work with all the other Hooker LT-swap components:

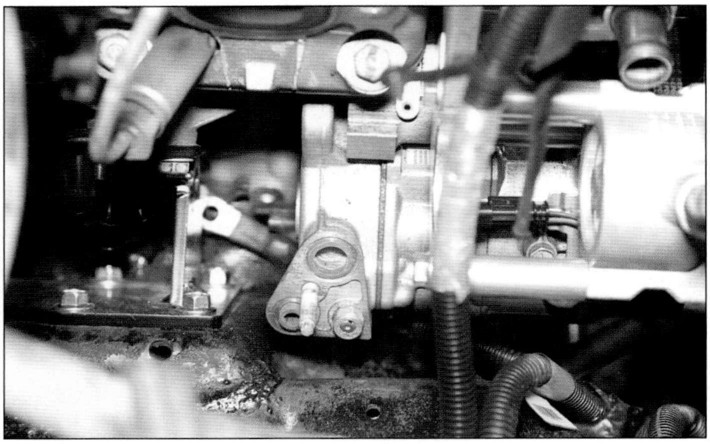

One of the key issues with LT swaps is the factory AC compressor. In this 1991 model, the AC unit fits and clears, but fittings will be an issue.

For 1973–1988 Squarebody trucks (1998 for SUVs), the chassis readily accepts the LS/LT engines, and even the stock manifolds fit.

The stock vacuum pump that was used on 2014–2018 models even clears the frame. However, it is unnecessary and has been eliminated by General Motors on 2019-and-newer models. These pumps have a high failure rate.

headers/manifolds, the oil pan, accessories, etc.

Dirty Dingo LS Mounts

These adjustable mounts provide up to 3 inches of engine placement adjustment using the factory clamshell mounts. Low-mount alternators clear with limited engine placement adjustment. Truck oil pans require a small notch on the driver's side of the crossmember.

Dirty Dingo LT Mounts

Like the other versions of Dirty Dingo mounts, these allow 3 inches of adjustment for engine placement and use the factory clamshell mounts. With the LT engine, the low-mount AC will not clear and the vacuum pump will clear with limited engine-placement adjustment. The stock truck oil pan will not clear the crossmember, so an aftermarket pan or crossmember notch is required.

BRP Muscle Rods

This kit uses the BRP cylindrical bushings and requires the BRP extended-sump LT-swap oil pan.

Universal Adapter Plates

Most swappers elect to use adapter plates because they are simple and allow the use of readily available (and inexpensive) SBC mounts. Many options are available for adapters—from single-position adapters (which are the most common and simple) to multi-position and even sliding mounts. We have used all three types, and they have their benefits and drawbacks.

The biggest issue with single-position adapters is that they are just that: one position. If you run into a clearance issue, purchase a new set that works with your project. The 1963–1972 trucks use the early-style isolator that bolts to the engine, whereas the 1973–1987 trucks use the clamshell isolator that bolts to the frame itself. These clamshells have a recessed triangle at the bottom of the clamshell, away from the engine. The 1988–2002 SBC clamshells are similar but have a protruding triangle that sticks out toward the engine.

The two styles of clamshell are not interchangeable. The adapter plate must match the style of frame mount that the truck uses, or the frame will need to be converted to correspond. Be sure to check your frame mounts before ordering, as frame swaps were common, especially on 4WD trucks.

Early-Style Adapters

Early-style adapters are available from Trans-Dapt, ICT Billet, and Dirty Dingo.

Trans-Dapt

These basic adapters are built from laser-cut steel, they are painted black, and they work. They come in three types: 1⅛ inch rearward, 5/8 inch rearward, and 5/8 inch forward as well as with or without rubber or polyurethane engine mounts. They fit well, clear all of the components, and do precisely what they are supposed to—all for less than $80 (plates and hardware only, no mounts).

The measurements reference the relative position of the engine to the factory LS/LT position (not the mounts themselves). So, 5/8 inch

A complete kit does not have to be used. There are plenty of adapter-plate options that allow the use of factory frame stands for two-wheel-drive C10 trucks. Pay attention to the type of mounts you have, though. There are two types of early SBC mounts: tall/narrow and short/wide.

Both of these mounts bolt up to the same engine pad, but they require the correct frame stands. First, measure your existing mounts or frame stands to determine which ones are needed. In 1973, General Motors switched to a clamshell-style mount.

The Dirty Dingo sliding mounts bolt to the engine block with a spacer. These use countersunk Allen-head bolts, so if you have to take them off, the mount has to be completely disassembled.

The slider uses a standard three-bolt early-SBC motor mount. The front part of the slider will hit the factory air-conditioner compressor, so if you plan on using it, the rearward movement will be limited.

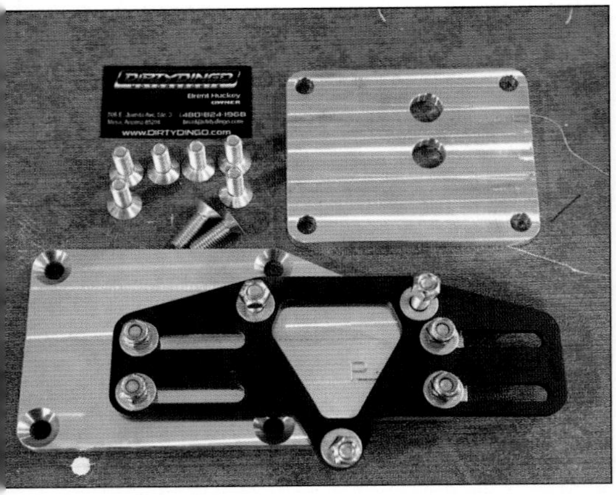

If your truck has a frame swap or has specific engine-placement needs, a set of sliding motor-mount adapters, such as these from Dirty Dingo, are an excellent choice. Before there were vehicle-specific swap kits, these adapters were often used.

Single-position and multiple-position adapter plates are available. These adapters from Trans-Dapt are single position, so you need to know where the engine will sit before ordering them.

rearward means the engine itself sits 5/8 inch from the LS/LT-series mount, which is half the difference between the SBC and LT positions.

ICT Billet

ICT Billet also has multi-position mounts for LS/LT swaps. This means you get three unique position options with a single adapter. All positions move the engine 0.72 inch up in the chassis, which may not work for those using the truck intake, which is very tall. However, this provides clearance for the crankshaft-to-front-crossmember clearance, which is a problem in some vehicles.

The three positions are set at the stock SBC position (1⅛ inches back), 1⅝ inches forward, and 2¼ inches forward. This measurement refers to the actual engine position.

ICT Billet states that its adapters will allow the use of the factory AC compressor and vacuum pump in the 1 ⅝-inch position with the plates trimmed to remove the factory SBC-position mounting holes. Although, this may cause a clearance issue between the oil pan and the steering linkage or the front crossmember.

Dirty Dingo Sliding Mounts

These mounts allow the engine to be positioned in the stock SBC location and up to 2 inches forward and anywhere in between. This allows making minor adjustments for your specific application where static mounts won't. These mounts are quite long and a little complicated to secure. They do not clear the vacuum pump or AC compressor using the factory accessory drive.

1973-and-Newer Clamshell Universal Adapters

The 1973–1987 adapters from ICT Billet (part number 551928) are made from steel and folded into shape. These mounts are affordable and directly fit the 1973–1987 clamshells. This set is designed to place the bellhousing plane in the stock position (rearward bias). These should work with truck oil pans and truck accessory drives.

Transmissions

As mentioned several times in the motor-mount section, the transmission being used can absolutely wreak havoc on installation plans. The key is whether the original (or similar to original) transmission is being used or if the entire drivetrain is being replaced. The type of transmission makes a big difference because older transmissions were physically smaller than modern equivalents.

The 700R4 and the 4L60E are the only comparable physical transmissions to any stock unit used in any C10/1500 trucks that were also originally installed with LS engines. These transmissions use the same case. In fact, they are essentially the same transmission.

The 700R4 is controlled via a TV cable, which can be adapted to a drive-by-cable LS/LT, whereas the 4L60E is the same transmission only electronically controlled. The internals are upgraded on the 4L60E, and they are even better in the 4L65E.

When selecting engine mounts, the transmission placement is critical. If it does not matter where the transmission mounts, then focus on engine clearance. However, with the complications of 4WD systems, the location of the rest of the driveline may be more critical. For example, if you are keeping the stock transmission and transfer case in a 1980 K10, then position the engine in the rear-bias position to mate with the transmission. This keeps the transfer case along with the front and rear drivelines intact and aligned.

Installing the Transmission Mount

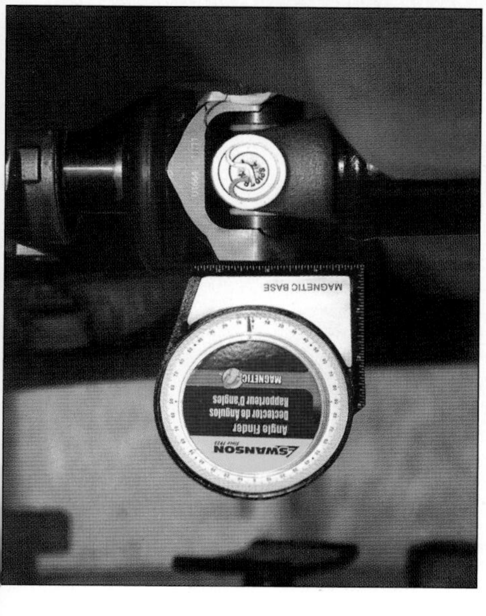

1 ***When setting up the transmission mount, check the pinion angles using a magnetic angle finder. Use the flat transmission mount flange or the edge of the slip yoke (if it is square and not angled). The ideal angle is 2 degrees down on the transmission and 2 degrees up on the pinion yoke, but 1 to 5 degrees is acceptable. The key is that the angles should match each other as close as possible in the opposite direction. This ensures that the U-joints are "working" and not running flat, which leads to excessive wear.***

2 ***Depending on the engine position, an adjustable mount, such as this one from G-Force Performance Products, may be needed. It provides 1 inch of rearward adjustment and 2 inches of forward adjustment to get the mount aligned with the crossmember. It also features a polyurethane bushing.***

Installing the Transmission Mount *continued*

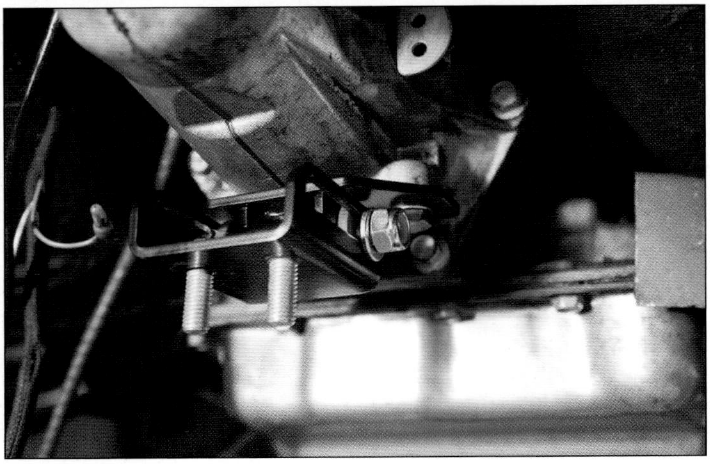

3 *The two-piece design makes it easy to remove and install the transmission crossmember for service as well.*

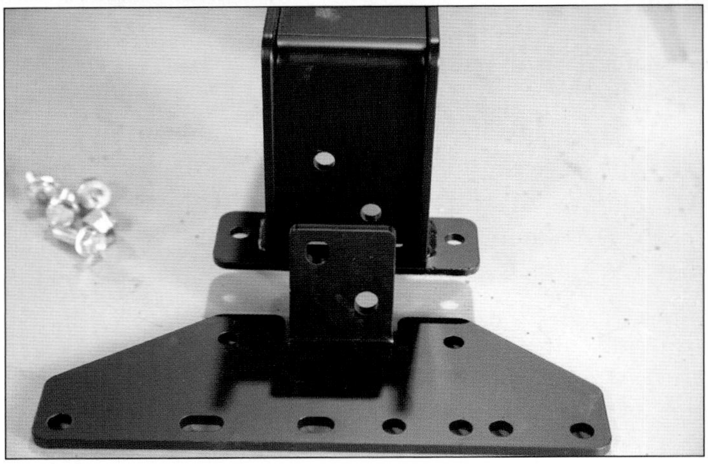

4 *For the 1966 Suburban project, we opted for the Hooker Blackheart transmission crossmember as part of the full kit. This unit is modular and has several bolt locations.*

5 *The unit is bench-assembled loosely to ensure that the parts are put together correctly and in the correct orientation.*

6 *This is a subtle difference, but the front of the crossmember angles upward, running down toward the rear of the car. Note that the front is above the notch in the front plate, while the rear is flush.*

7 *For our application using a 4L80, a 1-inch spacer is provided for the transmission mount itself. This yields the correct driveline angle. Only a T56 transmission does not use a spacer; all others require various spacing.*

8 *A standard transmission mount works with this kit. Rubber or polyurethane can be used. We used polyurethane, as the engine mounts are polyurethane and they should match.*

9 *On the 1966 GMC, the frame is slightly different from the Chevy models. Only one hole lined up on either side. We loosely bolted the crossmember to the chassis. All of the bolts are loose at this point.*

10 *We selected a new hole location and drilled a pilot hole. Then, we stepped up a few sizes and re-drilled.*

11 *Frames can be difficult to drill through, so we used four different sizes of drill bits to get to the final 3/8-inch bolt size.*

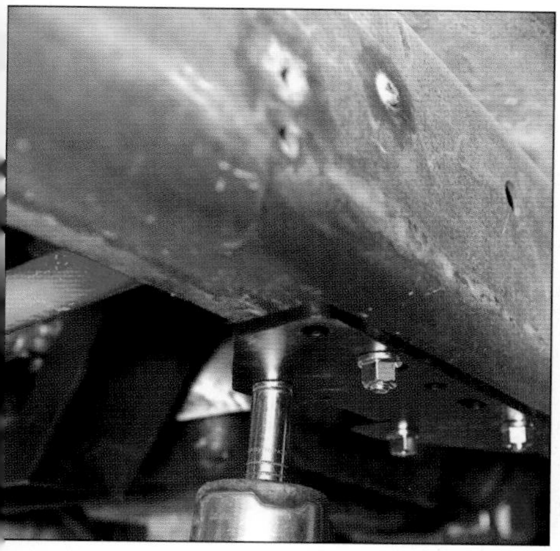

12 *Finally, all of the bolts were installed and torqued down. The crossmember sits on top of the frame brackets just in case something comes loose down the road. If you use the locking washers and tighten the bolts properly, that should not be an issue.*

13 *The last step is lowering the transmission onto the crossmember and bolting the mount to the plate.*

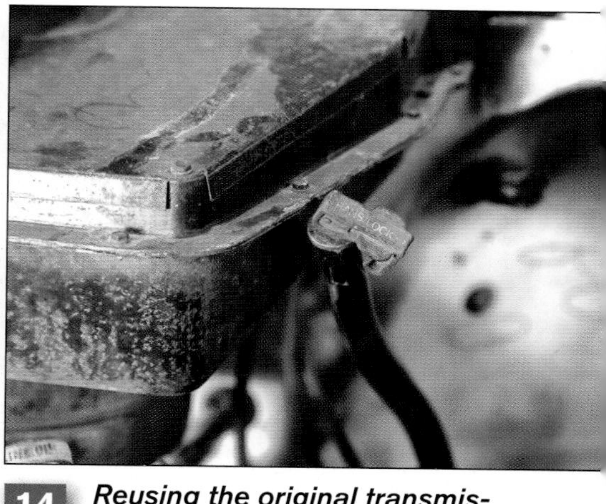

14 *Reusing the original transmission dipstick can be tricky, as they are very long and don't always cooperate. On the 1966, the stick hit the factory heater box. A slight bend made it compliant.*

The 1992 K1500 that is featured in this book received an entire 2017 L83 driveline, including the 6L80 transmission and NQH transfer case. In the forward-biased position, it is very close to the original driveline location.

Purchasing a complete kit for engine and transmission mounts is the easiest solution to a C/K truck swap. In most cases, a complete kit fits the vehicle better and can be cheaper than trial-and-error swaps and even fabricating mounts. Some kits, such as Hooker, Dirty Dingo, and BRP swap systems, have other components such as oil pans, exhaust, and accessory drives that work together with the mount kit to truly make the swap as easy as possible.

OIL PANS, PAN MODIFICATIONS, AND AFTERMARKET OPTIONS

After the engine mounts, the oil pan is the trickiest part to sort out. In fact, the pan can be more difficult, depending on the engine mounts being used. For most 2WD C10 trucks, stock oil pans fit relatively well. However, they tend to hang too low for safe driving.

Unlike a steel SBC oil pan, all stock and most aftermarket oil pans are cast aluminum, so they can be broken by road hazards if they hang too low. Additionally, some motor-mount adapters are designed to work only with certain pans, while others are more universal.

Stock Oil Pans

Using a stock oil pan can greatly simplify installation, if the right one is selected. There are many stock oil pan designs, but only a few are desirable for engine swaps. The most commonly used stock oil pans are the 1998–2002 Camaro pans, the 2002–2006 truck pans, the LH8 or Hummer pans, and the CTS-V pans. These pans have proven to be the most versatile stock oil pans that fit most C10 trucks.

Oil pan issues must be addressed when mocking up the motor mounts and modifying the front crossmember. Sump depth also needs to be considered, as several of the stock pans may clear the chassis itself, but the sump depth can become an issue when the sump hangs below the crossmember, especially on lowered vehicles.

Camaro

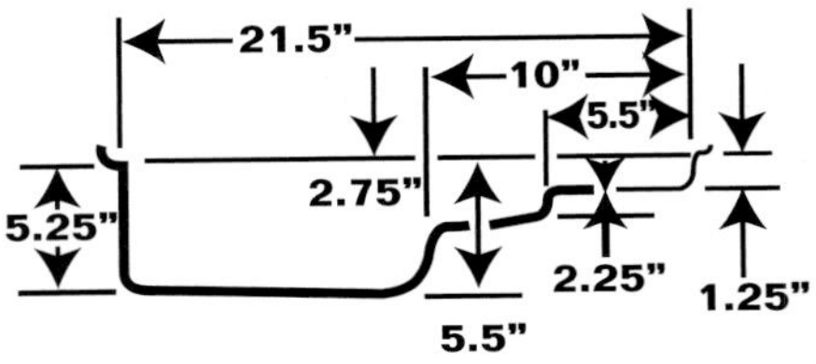

PN 12558762 Camaro/Firebird (5/5.5 qts.)

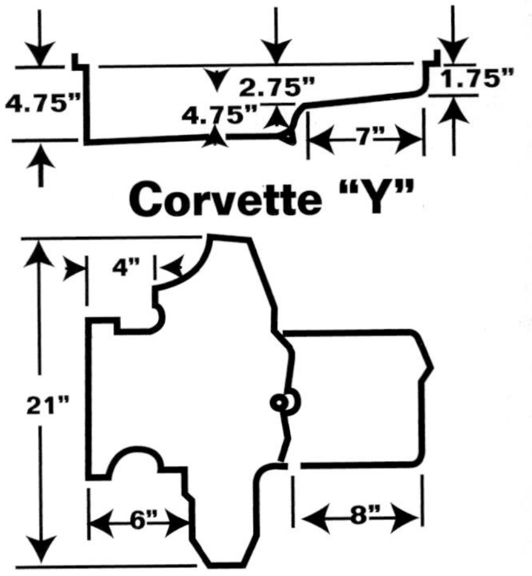

PN 12561828 Corvette (6/6.5 qts.)

Truck "C/K"

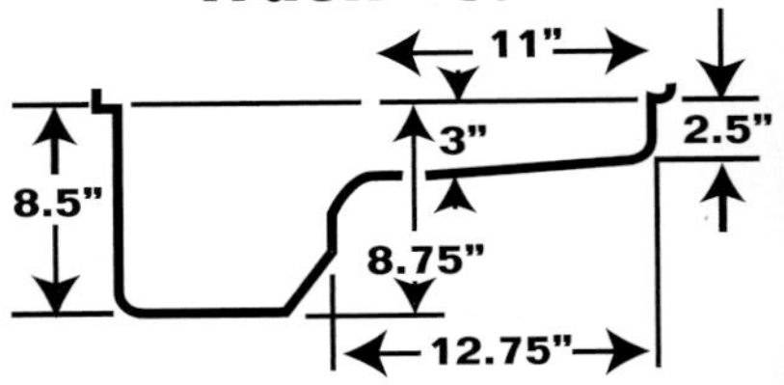

These dimensions show the various measurements for the Gen III Camaro, Corvette Y, and truck pans.

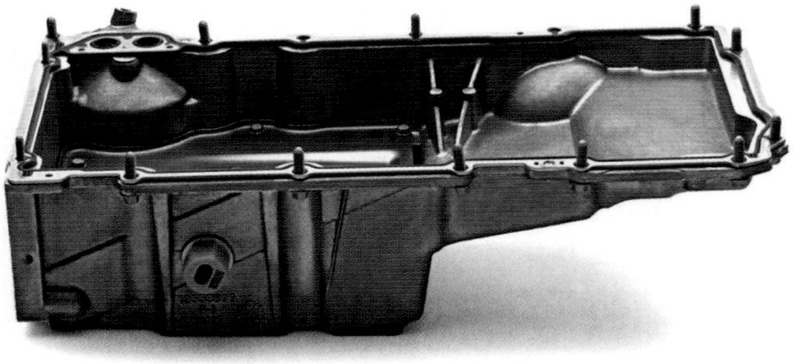

The most-used factory LS oil pan is the 1998–2002 F-Body LS1 pan, which is typically referred to as the F-Body or Camaro pan. This fits most trucks.

The early Vortec oil pans fit many vehicles, but the deep rear sump can be problematic due to potential road debris damage. Most trucks accept this pan with ease, though.

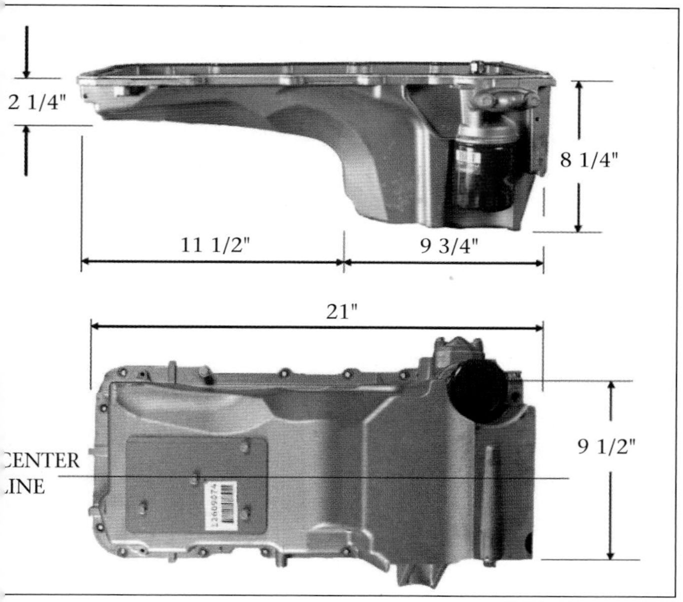

he 2007-and-newer Vortec pan also works well in the 960-and-later GM truck swaps. (Photo Courtesy Paul :hiver)

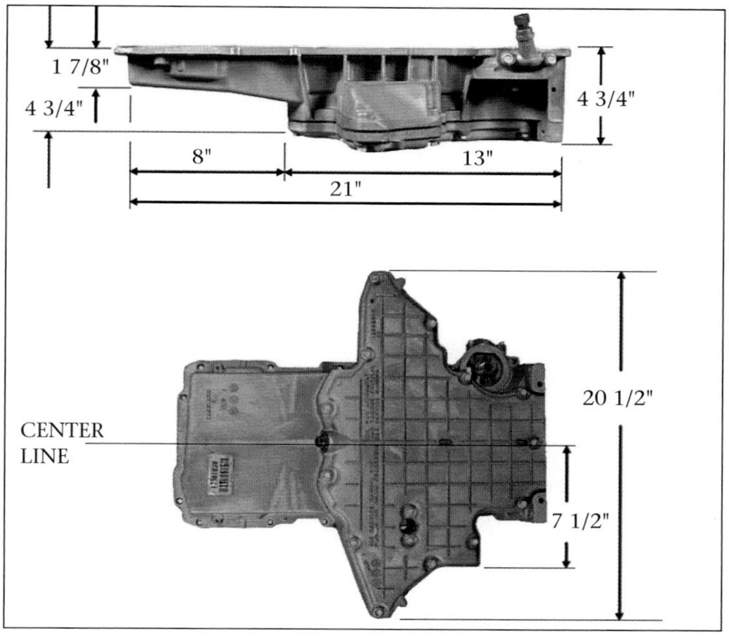

This is the Corvette "batwing" pan. It is not suitable for any truck application.

Each oil pan requires its own spe-ific windage tray, pickup tube, and ipstick. When purchasing an oil pan, nake sure to get these parts with it. here are also several blocks and oil an configurations that place the dip-tick tube in the pan rather than the lock. If you are using one of these ngines that needs a non-dipstick ıbe pan, then the machined boss on ne passenger's side of the block must e drilled out. Using a 3/8-inch drill it, drill through the block (about 1/8 ıch of material), and then the tube ill slide right in.

LS Oil Pans

An abundance of LS oil pans are vailable, including an F-Body pan, the C/K truck pan, a Corvette pan, and more.

F-Body Camaro/Firebird Oil Pan (Part Number 12558762)

The Camaro/Firebird pan was used on 1998–2002 Camaro/ Firebird Gen III engines. This pan fits all years of C10 trucks without modification. Some applications require this pan, as it allows the engine to sit farther forward than the truck pans. The F-Body oil pan's rear sump is 5 inches deep, and it is 11.5 inches long x 9.5 inches wide. The shallow front section is where most of the interference is located. The front section is flat for 4.25 inches and then slopes down at a steep angle for 4.75 inches.

2002–2006 C/K Truck/Escalade Pan (Part Number 12579273)

This oil pan is fitted to all of the 4.8L, 5.3L, and 6.0L C/K trucks and Escalades. This pan features a long, shallow front section (12.25 inches) with a crossmember-friendly short 8.75-inch-long rear sump. The rear sump is quite deep (8.25 inches), though, which typically hangs about 2.5 inches below the crossmember in most C10 trucks. This pan is not a good fit for any 4WD application, as the pan is simply too deep to clear the front drive axle.

2007-and-Newer GM Truck Oil Pan (Part Number 12609074)

The 2007-and-newer GM trucks with the 4.8L, 5.3L, 6.0L, and 6.2L

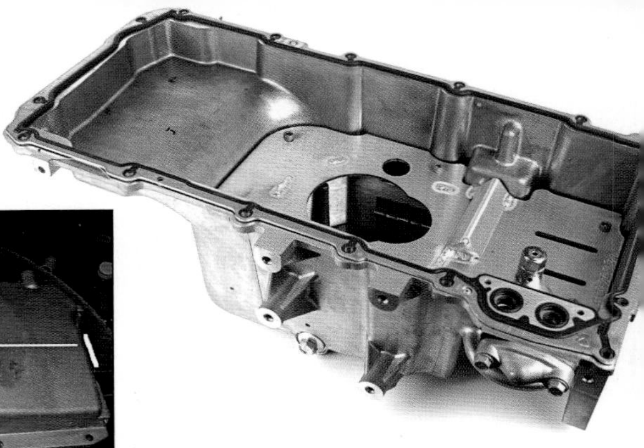

The 2010-and-newer Camaro oil pan, used under the LS3 and LSA engines, has provisions for mounting an oil cooler. Its odd shape makes it a trick pan for swappers. The internal baffling on this one is made by Improved Racing. (Photo Courtesy Improved Racing)

Gen IV engines come with this oil pan. It is basically the same as the 2002–2006 C/K truck pan, but the later pan has a shorter, shallow front section at 11.5 inches and a slightly longer rear sump at 9.75 inches. The rear-sump depth remains the same at 8.25 inches. Just like the earlier truck pans, these have a deep rear sump that hangs down past the crossmember in C10 trucks.

Some manufacturers have used the LH8 oil pan for all of their LS swap kits. For universal-style adapter plates, it may or may not hang too low under the crossmember. This works for trucks as long as the suspension is not lowered. (Photo Courtesy Paul Chiver)

C5 Corvette "Y" Oil Pan (Part Number 12561828)

With one kickout on each side, this pan is typically referred to as the "batwing" pan because the kickouts resemble wings. This race-inspired design allows for consistent pickup coverage under high lateral G-force turns. The pan is very shallow (4.74 inches top to bottom), and it has 20.5-inch-wide kickouts that preclude it from working in C10- or K10-chassis trucks.

Cadillac CTS-V Oil Pan (2004–2007, 2009-and-Newer)

Available on the Cadillac CTS-V, this oil pan is basically a cross between the F-Body and the C/K truck pans. The rear sump is 5.5 inches deep, 3 inches less than the truck and 1/2 inch deeper than the F-Body pan. The shallow front section is 11 inches long, which is shorter than the truck pan but longer than the F-Body. In turn, they can use standard adapter plates, setting the motor low in the car and clearing the engine crossmember.

The CTS-V pan does hang below the front crossmember by about 2 inches on most C10s. It depends on which motor mounts are used. Some mounts, such as the Trans-Dapt adapter plates, sit the engine

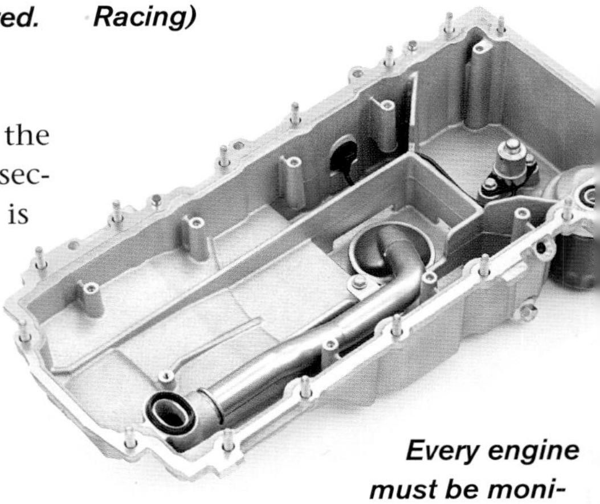

Every engine must be monitored, and the Gen III and Gen IV engines are certainly no exception. The stock oil pans feature a factory bypass plug, which may or may not be drilled and tapped for a sending unit. These two plugs represent the two main versions. Both can be drilled and tapped. There is a third version that is already tapped.

The CTS-V Cadillac oil pan works well in trucks and muscle cars, although the rear sump is deeper than the F-Body pan. This means that the pan might hang below the crossmember (depending on the motor mounts), but it is still a great option for a stock pan.

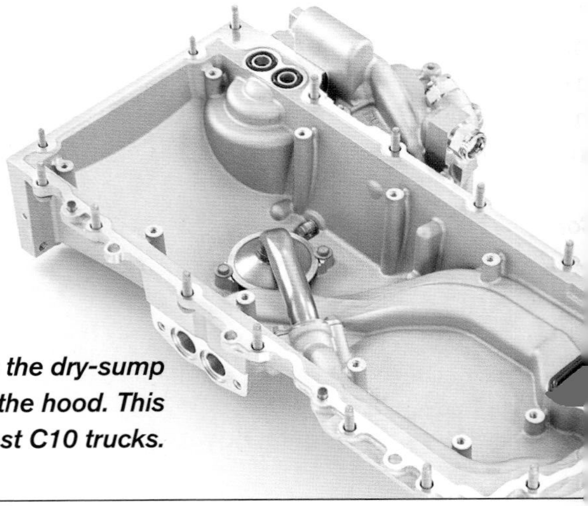

This LS7 oil pan shows the dry-sump output lines, and these must run to the dry-sump oil tank. They can be mounted in almost any convenient location under the hood. This dry-sump pan requires crossmember modification to fit in most C10 trucks.

slightly higher in the car, reducing the amount of overhang. The later-model CTS-V cars with the LSA engine use a similar oil pan with a few minor differences. The external dimensions are the same, but the LSA pan has larger oil filter threads, a different oil sending unit boss, and bosses for the oil cooler.

Hummer H3 Alpha 5.3L Oil Pan (Part Number 12614821)

The H3 oil pan, commonly referred to as the LH8 (for the Hummer H3 5.3l LS engine code), is a very popular stock oil pan for swaps. First available in late 2007, its measurements caused quite a stir in the LS-swap community because the long 13-inch shallow front section allows this pan to clear most stock GM crossmembers without modification. Again, though, this pan has a 7.5-inch-deep rear sump, making it hang about a 1/2 inch below the crossmember. The Chevrolet Performance muscle car LS swap pan is essentially an LH8 oil pan.

Corvette LS2 Oil Pan (Part Number 12581810)

The LS2 Corvette oil pan, not to be confused with the LS7 pan, falls in the "maybe" category of fitment. The 5-inch-deep rear sump would certainly clear the road, but the 13.5-inch length of the sump prevents this pan from being used in C/K10 trucks with stock front crossmembers.

Corvette LS7 Dry-Sump Oil Pan

The LS7 is a specialized pan that only fits the LS7. This is a dry-sump oiling system and requires a lot of special consideration. If you are swapping an LS7 into a C/K10, modify the front crossmember or use an aftermarket oil pan. Modifying the stock pan is not a simple task because of the internal oil routing design.

GTO LS3 Pan

The GTO pan is a front-sump design and will not fit stock C/K crossmembers.

LS3/LSA 2010-and-Newer Camaro

The fifth-generation Camaro uses a different oil pan from the fourth-generation F-Body. The newest Camaro pan has a long rear sump that won't clear the front crossmember on the C/K10, leaving it out as an option for swappers.

LS9 Corvette ZR1

Like the LS7, the LS9 in the ZR1 Corvette is a dry-sump design. It can be retrofitted to other blocks, but you could have saved money on an aftermarket dry-sump pan that will likely better fit your application.

Gen V Oil Pans

Four factory pans are available: truck, LT1 wet sump (car), CTS-V/LT4 wet sump, and LT1/LT4 dry sump. They are all cast aluminum with integral pickup tubes and oval oil ports to the block. This means that it can't simply be cut and welded to the oil pan. The factory oil pans all have a fairly large sump, which is far forward on the pan itself. Most 2WD trucks will accept the factory car wet-sump oil pans without additional modification, but the truck pan does not.

Truck Pan

The truck pan is quite large. Not only is the shallow section of the pan very short but also there is a sheet-metal extension pan that bolts to the bottom of the main sump. It is very deep, which makes it impractical for use in lowered truck swaps. The truck pan will fit 1972-and-older trucks without modification, but 1973-and-newer trucks requires special motor mounts and crossmember modifications, depending on the motor mounts. The oil capacity is 8 quarts.

LT1 Car Wet Sump

Found on most LT1-powered cars, the standard wet-sump oil pan is shallow, measuring just 4.75 inches from the bottom of the block. The main sump is 15 inches long, and measures 4.75 inches at the back to 4.5 inches deep at the front. The shallow section is 7 inches long, and it tapers from 2.5 inches deep at the rearmost section to 1.5 inches at the front of the pan (front of the engine). This pan will fit C/K10 stock chassis if the engine is set higher in the chassis. The oil capacity is 7 quarts.

2016–2017 CTS-V/LT4 Wet Sump

This pan is very deep, making it unlikely to be suitable for most swaps. The shallow front section is 11

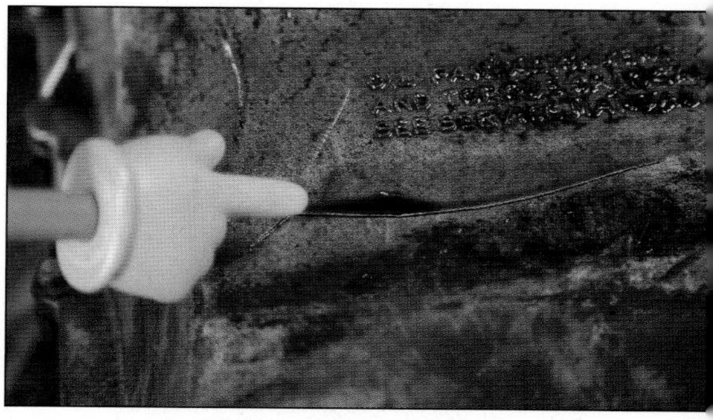

When inspecting an engine, it is important to look at all of the parts, including the cast-aluminum oil pan. On this LM7, the pan was split across the bottom. If this was discovered after finishing your swap, and it had to all be yanked out, it would be a bad day.

The oil pan on LS/LT engines is part of the block's strength. The bolts can be removed in any order, but installing them must follow the factory sequence: inside out and side to side in three torque steps—just like standard cylinder-head bolts.

Drilling the rivets is easy—just don't try to remove the gasket without verifying that the rivet has been fully removed. Otherwise, it will ruin the gasket.

LS engines use an aluminum gasket with a silicon sealing ring, and the LT pans use gray RTV only. Both require prying to release them from the block.

LS pans have a few rivets that hold the gasket in place. This needs to be drilled out if the pan or the gasket is being reused. The gasket is reusable if it is not bent.

inches long, so it will clear the stock crossmember, depending on you engine setback. The shallow section i 1.5 inches deep at the front, taperin to 2.5 inches at the shelf for the mai sump. The 7-inch-deep sump is 1 inches long. The main issue with thi pan is that it is quite deep, leaving i exposed to road debris and potentia destruction. If your vehicle is lowere at all, this pan should not be consid ered. The oil capacity is 10 quarts.

LT1/4 Dry Sump

Certain vehicles and crate engine come with an optional dry-sump sys tem. The pan for this is similar to th wet-sump car pan, but the shallov section is a little bit shorter than th wet-sump pan. This difference make this a difficult swap for most truck without modifications to the cross member. This pan has two oil drai plugs. The oil capacity is 9.8 quarts.

Pickup Tube and Windage Tray

One more note on factory o pans: the pans can be swapped fro engine to engine, but there are few points to pay attention to. The pickup tube and windage tray go with the oil pan (not the engine). These items are a matched set, so any time the oil pan is swapped, the correct tube and windage tray need to be swapped as well.

Additionally, displacement-on-demand engines have an oil-pressure bypass valve built into the oil pan. If you are not using the displacement-on-demand system, it doesn't matter. If you are using a displacement-on-demand engine and planning to use the displacement-on-demand system, an oil pan that has the bypass valve is needed.

One of the benefits of an aftermarket pan is that many of them have internal baffles designed to keep the oil surrounding the pickup tube at all times, even under severe g-forces. The baffles trap the oil so that it doesn't slosh around inside the pan, potentially uncovering the pickup tube. There are some options for modifying a factory pan with an internal baffle.

The F-Body oil pan is one of the biggest culprits for high g-force oil starvation. Improved Racing designed a bolt-in baffle for the F-Body pan (the company also offers these for the Gen 5 Camaro and GTO pans) that is a direct bolt-in with no welding required. By reducing the sloshing and aeration of the oil, the engine can maintain oil pressure without oil starvation.

Front Crossmember Modification

In regard to fitting an LS engine in a stock chassis, in most cases a stock oil pan and stock crossmember can be modified to a particular chassis. The front engine crossmember is large enough to support significant modification, provided that the removed section is boxed in to eliminate flex points. Cutting a small notch on the back side of the crossmember then filling it with 10-gauge steel (1/8-inch) reinforces and strengthens the engine crossmember while allowing the engine to sit in place. The front brake crossover line also requires relocation, and a few simple bends should do the trick.

The main issue with 4WD truck front crossmembers and LT-series engines is the width and depth of the pan in regard to the corners of the front crossmember. Using the stock LT pan in 4WD trucks with the factory crossmember may require squaring the rounded corners of the front crossmember to clear the sump of the oil pan. Additionally, the bolt-on sheet-metal sump on the truck oil pan may not clear the front axle housing in stock-height trucks, depending on the engine mounts used.

Aftermarket Gen III and Gen IV Oil Pans

With so many options and potential pitfalls, many builders choose an aftermarket oil pan that fits specific vehicles. There are many versions, and most are centered on two platforms: the first-generation F-Body 1967–1969 Chevy Camaro/ Pontiac Firebird and the 1965–1972 GM A-Body cars.

Most of the fabricated (meaning welded steel or aluminum, not cast) aftermarket oil pans require the use of a remote oil filter. This is sometimes seen as a major drawback for some builders, as you now have to find a place to locate the filter and run the lines. This is not always the case, as there are several aftermarket pans that maintain the pan-mounted filter, such as the Holley LSX-swap cast-aluminum pan.

It took the aftermarket a few years to get going on LT-swap components, but it has finally come around, and there are now several LT-swap pans available. Currently, there are four oil pans available for the Gen V LT-series engine: the Holley Retro-Fit (standard and drag racing versions), Moroso fabricated pan, and two pans from BRP Hot Rods that have a high clearance and extended sump. All of these pans are designed to add clearance for LT swaps, and they should work for most applications. The details set them apart, as does the price. All of these pans are designed for wet-sump oiling systems.

Holley Retro-Fit Street (302-20) and Drag (302-22)

Holley has been at the forefront of the LS swap game for quite some time, and things are no different when it comes to the LT-series engines. As with its LS pans, the LT Retro-Fit pan is cast aluminum, has a built-in oil filter port that matches the factory placement, and has all the other fittings seen on a factory pan. The pan reduces the rear sump length by 5 inches, providing plenty of clearance for full-frame vehicles. It is only 1 inch deeper than the factory sump, so there is good ground clearance for lowered vehicles. This pan fits just about any application where an SBC or an LS would clear. The shallow front section is just 1/4 inch deeper at the front than the factory wet-sump car LT pan.

The 302-22 model is the exact same oil pan, only with an added set of baffles that bolt into the pan. These baffles are used for controlling oil slosh in extreme G situations, and they are specifically designed for drag race applications. This keeps oil in the sump surrounding the pickup where it needs to be.

At just under $500, it is the cheapest solution to the factory pan that there is. Unless you really want to modify the frame, you can't get a pan for less. It comes with the Holley quality that is expected, and it looks good. It is cast aluminum, which can be polished, painted, powder coated, or left raw. This is a simple solution for a difficult problem.

The only potential issue with this pan is that it is cast aluminum. If it is hit hard enough, it could crack, leaving a driver without oil. Is this likely? No, not even a little, but it *could* happen. The factory pan is cast aluminum as well, so this really isn't much of a drawback. Because it is cast aluminum, adding additional fittings to the pan is more difficult.

Installing the Oil Pan

1 *With the pan off, the factory windage tray and pickup tube are visible. This engine is getting a new Holley swap pan, so the tube will be replaced.*

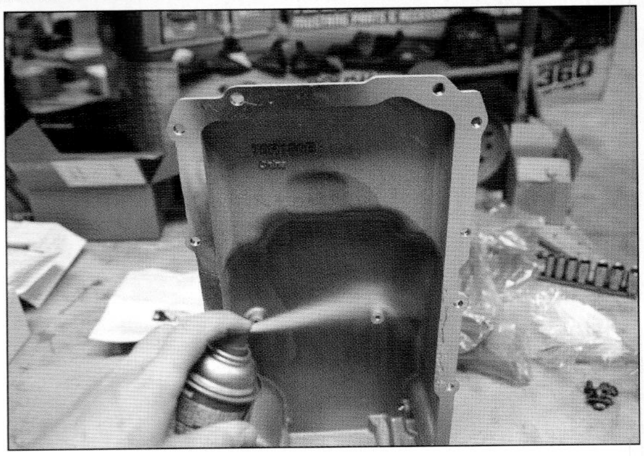

2 *Before installing the pan, clean it with some brake cleaner to remove any contaminants from the casting process.*

3 *Always use a new O-ring on the oil pickup tube and make sure that it is lubed with oil. If it is put on dry, the O-ring could stick and it won't have a good seal, which results in no oil suction.*

4 *The pickup tube is attached with two Allen-head bolts. Be careful not to strip them.*

5 *The Holley pan requires modifying the windage tray, as the new pickup tube touches it. If it is left as is, there will be problems with the oil suction.*

Installing the Oil Pan *continued*

6 *We marked the tray as noted by Holley's instructions. Modifying means removing essentially the entire front section of the tray and adding a notch for the tube.*

7 *With the tray removed from the engine, trim away the offending section with a reciprocating saw. A band saw or even a cutting wheel can be used as well, as long as the result is a clean cut.*

8 *Then, use a die grinder to clean up the edges.*

9 *Now the tray fits as it should. Only the first two rods are exposed from the tray.*

10 *Install the new pickup tube with ample clearance.*

11 *Before installing the new pan, use a gasket-scraper tool to remove any remaining gasket material.*

Installing the Oil Pan *continued*

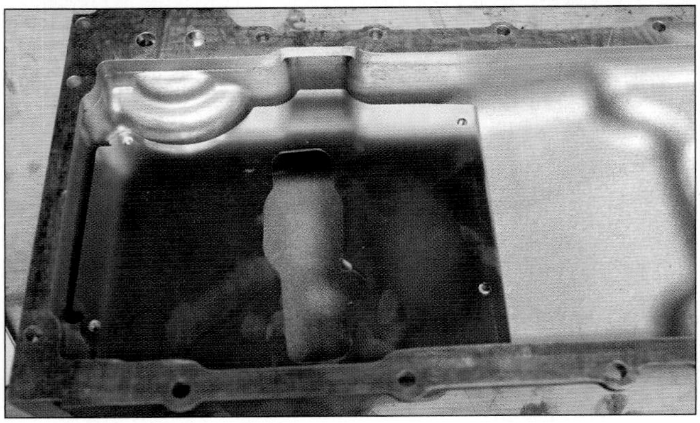

12 *Inside the Holley oil pan, a sump screen helps keep the oil from sloshing. Holley also offers a full race pan with trap doors.*

14 *Before dropping the pan on the block, place a bit of gray RTV silicone on the front and rear covers, which are bolt-on pieces. If you skip this step, you will have leaks.*

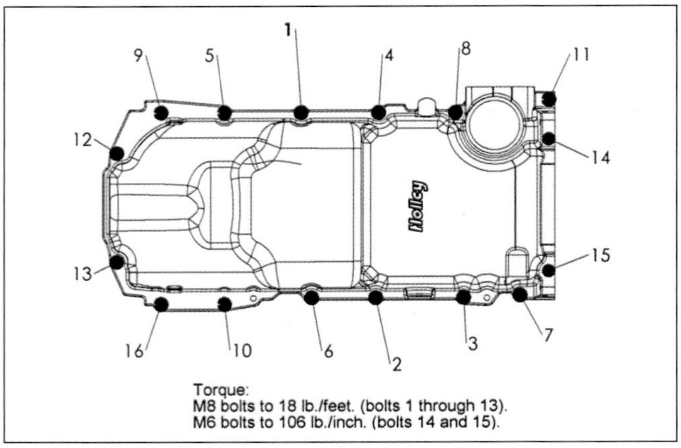

17 *This diagram shows the correct bolt-torquing sequence. It is not simple, and it must be followed exactly as shown. We use three sequences: hand tight, half torque, and full torque to ensure that the pan is square and secure.*

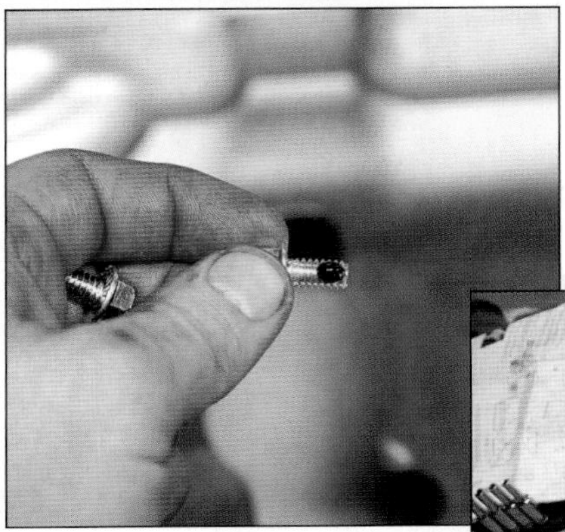

13 *The supplied bolts require medium threadlocker so that they don't rattle out.*

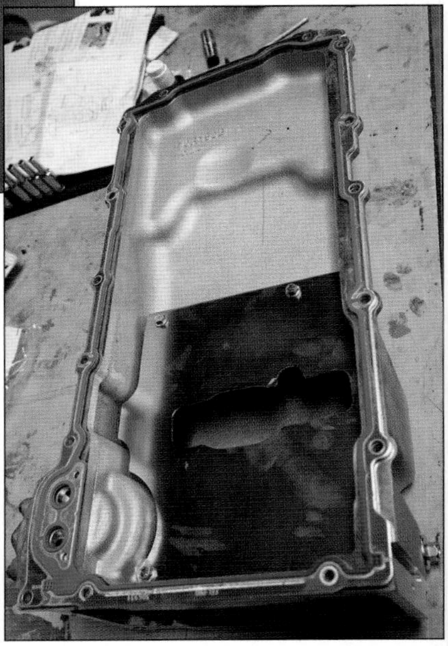

15 *The new aluminum/silicone gasket and pan are ready for installation to the block. LT blocks have alignment pins to ensure proper location of the pan; LS blocks do not.*

16 *Set the pan on the block. It is ready to be bolted down.*

18 *Finally, install the oil filter adapter. The adapter comes with the pan and is already coated with threadlocker.*

Moroso Wet Sump (20155)

This fabricated pan is made from sheet aluminum, which means that the pan is flat and square. There are not any little bumps or raised sections in the middle of the flats that can cause clearance issues. This pan features a billet aluminum O-ring rail to match up to the block and a removable pickup tube. It uses Moroso's billet oil filter adapter, so the stock location for the filter can be used. No remote filter is required like most sheet-metal pans on the market.

The front shallow section is 1⅞ inches deep, and 14½ inches long. The rear sump measures 5⅞ inches deep and 8½ inches long, so there is plenty of clearance for most crossmembers. Included with the pan is a trap-door baffle and windage tray for better oil control.

Sheet-metal construction makes it lightweight, which is an advantage. Adding other fittings to the pan, such as an oil return for turbos, is easy. Because it is not cast, road debris is less likely to crack or split the pan, as the sheet-metal aluminum will dent rather than crack.

However, it is nearly double the price of the Holley pan, which is a big drawback. It might make up for it if you are adding a return fitting for a turbo system, but that can be done on both.

BRP Hot Rods (000-6490-00 High Clearance)

Designed specifically to work with BRP's MuscleRods swap kits, this pan is a fabricated sheet-metal pan. It features the correct O-ring placement and pickup tube. It is a very good-looking oil pan, and the aluminum is easily polished. The high-clearance version is for applications that require maximum clearance, such as Tri-Five Chevys.

BRP Hot Rods (000-6451-00 Extended Sump)

If you have front-steer-style steering system, the extended-sump pan is suggested by BRP to gain the clearance without losing the 5-quart capacity.

The sheet-metal construction for less weight is an advantage. It also fits BRP swap kits.

A disadvantage is that these pans are very expensive to build, and that is reflected in the price.

Regardless of which pan you use on your swap, the pan will likely need to be removed at some point. This is a bit different from every other GM engine that came before it. There is no oil-pan gasket; instead, General Motors opted to use gray RTV silicone. Gray high-torque silicone is specifically used for high-torque applications where sensors and oil are present. It is important to use the gray silicone on the oil pan, as it is the only defense against leaks.

Another potentially catastrophic issue with the oil pan install/removal are the oiling fitting O-rings. There are three oiling fitting O-rings: one on the pickup tube to the block and two on the oil-filter ports that run to the external cooler or bypass cover. These have a habit of sticking to the engine block when removing the pan, so the pan will come off with these missing. If this is missed during the process, they can be lost, which would mean a massive internal oil leak and no oil pressure. If you are replacing the pan or putting on a new O-ring but the old O-ring is still on the block, you will have a really tough time getting it all back together.

Sump Eliminator Kit

An interesting take on the stock truck oil pans is the ICT sump eliminator kit from ICT Billet. This billet aluminum–machined piece replaces the stamped-steel sump extension on the truck oil pan. When installed, the engine gains 1.92 inches of additional ground clearance. This does require modifying the stock oil pump pickup at the bottom of the pan.

Oil System Modifications

The LT engine is not designed for use in non-factory installations. This means that it has some factory components that are not suitable for swaps, and some required sensors are not available on these engines from the factory. This includes the optional factory oil cooler, the vacuum pump, and finding a location for an oil-pressure sensor.

Some vehicles can accept the cooler and the vacuum pump, but most do not. They are simply too large to fit in most older vehicles. Removing them presents a few challenges, but these are easily rectified if it is taken care of before installing the engine.

Oil Cooler

The oil cooler is found on all 6.2L car engines with wet-sump oiling and some truck engines. The cooler is quite interesting, as it is an oil-to-water cooler. This means that the cooler is connected to the vehicle's main radiator. Coolant is pumped to the cooler (mounted on the driver's side of the oil pan), and it flows through the cooling tubes and then goes back to the radiator. The oil is pushed through the cooler by the oil pump.

This unit is very large and will not clear most frame rails, much less a recirculating ball-type steering box, so it must be removed. The remaining ports can be used for the external cooler or covered with a factory or aftermarket bypass cover. This is also the main access point for oil-pressure sensors on most LT swaps.

Vacuum Pump

LT-series truck engines, specifically the L83 5.3L and L86 6.2L, use a block-mounted oil pump to supply the braking system with enough vacuum to operate safely. This unit sits low on the block. In most cases, it will not clear the motor-mount adapters, and in some cases won't even clear the chassis itself. Car engines do not use this pump.

Removing the pump is required for most LT swaps, but that leaves two oiling ports on the block that must be plugged. They are 12 mm x 1.75 thread, but the GM plugs need to be used. Otherwise, oil pressure could be lost should a standard non-shouldered plug come out.

GM part number 1546665 is the correct plug, and it even comes with threadlocker on the threads. Two are required. You can use the press port that normally feeds the pump with fresh oil as a port for an oil pressure gauge, but most motor-mount adapters will interfere.

Adding Oil Coolers

Oil temperatures are important, especially if you are road racing or running a supercharger or turbo on your LS. Maintaining proper engine oil temperature is critical to both the life of the engine and the usable life of the oil itself. Chevrolet suggests running engine oil between 220°F and 240°F at full warmup. This is higher than the previously acceptable range of 190°F to 220°F, and it is a point of contention among experts. That doesn't change the fact that anything over 250°F begins to break down the oil and dramatically reduces its usable life. Synthetic oils have higher resistance to heat; 300°F is the industry standard for loss of lubricity.

Colder oil temperatures are also an issue and will rob an engine of power. LS engines run tighter tolerances than the old SBCs, and the cooler the oil, the thicker it is. That means there is less oil inside the bearings, increasing friction and reducing power. Heat up the oil a little more and the oil flows better, reducing the friction, freeing up a little extra power, and adding life to the engine. Another side effect of running the engine oil too cool is the lack of sufficient burn-off temperature.

Engine oil gets contaminated with fuel and water through condensation. When the oil reaches 200 degrees, the fuel and water begins to burn off. While this is necessary for a naturally aspirated engine, it is critical for a turbocharged engine, as the turbos are cooled through the engine's oil system. Water and fuel in the oil can ruin turbo bearings in a hurry. Using an engine oil with a ZDDP level of 1200 or higher gives an engine and related components better protection from heat-related lubricity breakdown.

Adding an oil cooler to an LS swap is an easy way to maintain the correct engine oil temperature, but simply adding an inline cooler is not the answer. If the oil is allowed to simply flow through the cooler, it will take longer to warm up and will run cooler overall. The key to a proper oil-cooling system is thermostatic bypass.

Making an Oil-Bypass Cover

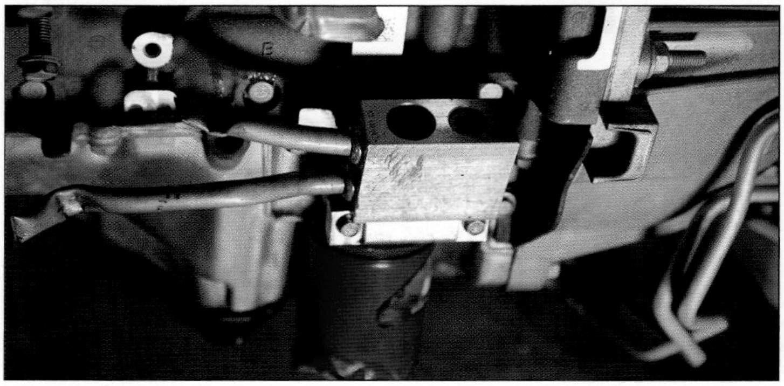

1 *Gen V truck engines may have an oil-cooler adapter, such as this, instead of a bypass cover. Most trucks with a towing package or 4WD have a remote oil cooler. It can be used, or the adapter can be replaced with a bypass cover.*

2 *This is the stock bypass cover. It does not have any oil-pressure boss options.*

Making an Oil-Bypass Cover *continued*

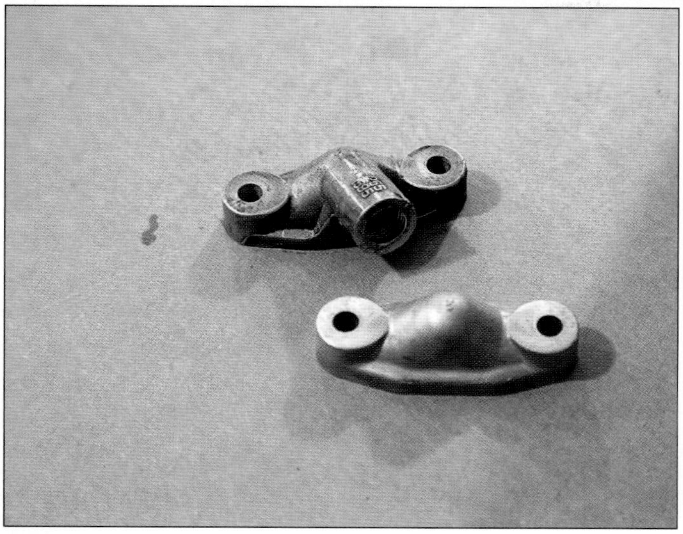

3 ***Some LS engines have a bypass cover that has a boss for a pressure sensor (top), but the center is not actually drilled. Most LS-series engines have the lower cover.***

4 ***If you have the boss, it needs to be drilled out to make it work. It doesn't have to be drilled to the maximum size, but if using it for a turbo oil return line, it needs to be opened all the way.***

5 ***We re-tapped the cover on this one, as the threads did not match our sending unit.***

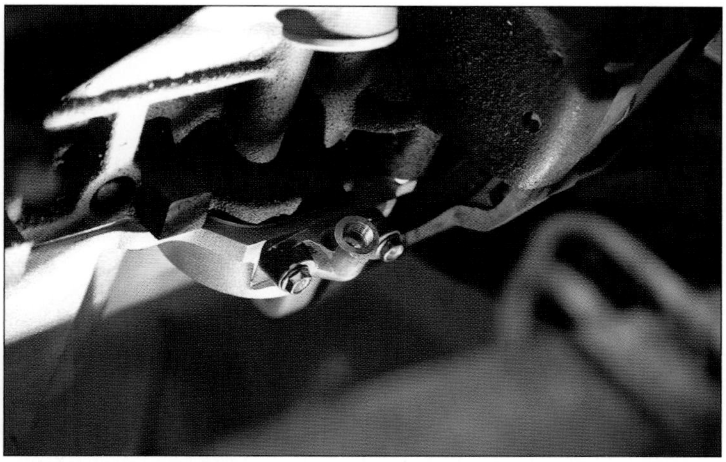

6 ***Another option is to simply buy a new bypass cover that is already drilled and tapped.***

All of the factory LS engine oil pans have an oil-bypass port built right into the side of the pan above the oil filter. These ports can be used for the oil-cooler lines as well as the oil-pressure sending unit, or an oil filter sandwich-type adapter can be used. Several companies make oil-cooler adapters for these factory ports.

A thermostatic bypass port allows the engine oil to circulate through the cooler only after it reaches a certain temperature. This allows the oil to warm up faster. If it cools too quickly in the cooler, the bypass will close, maintaining a consistent minimum temperature. These types of valves can be found in adjustable versions but are typically sold in static ranges, typically opening at 180 degrees and are fully open at 200 degrees.

Several of the newer Gen III and Gen IV LS engines even have oil coolers built into them, namely the high-performance and some of the Vortec heavy-duty applications. If you choose to run an aftermarket oil pan with a remote oil filter, the plumbing will allow the addition of an inline cooler. There are thermostatic bypasses available for this design as well.

Locating the cooler is fairly simple most of the time. The cooler is mounted in front of the radiator or AC condenser, but they don't have to go there. You can mount the cooler just about anywhere as long as it gets airflow. For example, hot rod–style coolers mount on the frame itself. Some even have 12-volt fans for forced air cooling. There are many options, but the simplest solution is a radiator front mount.

As previously mentioned, many of the aftermarket oil pans do not have the factory-style oil filter mounts—only ports for the oil feed and return lines. This means that a remote oil filter must be used. Locating the oil filter can be a challenge in many applications, but it is a necessary component.

If you plan to use an oil cooler, the filter can be located in the same location. The key here is easy access to the filter and protection from road debris. If the filter is hanging too low, it could get damaged, leading to a shattered engine. The lines for the oil filter do not have to be high pressure, but braided lines certainly look cool and reduce the chances for leaks or blowouts from cut or damaged lines.

There is an important note for the installation of a remote filter on the LS engines: the ports are not labeled, and some oil pans do not include instructions indicating which port is pressure and which port is return. The pressure port is the front (toward the belts) port, with the return being the rearmost port.

Building a Dipstick

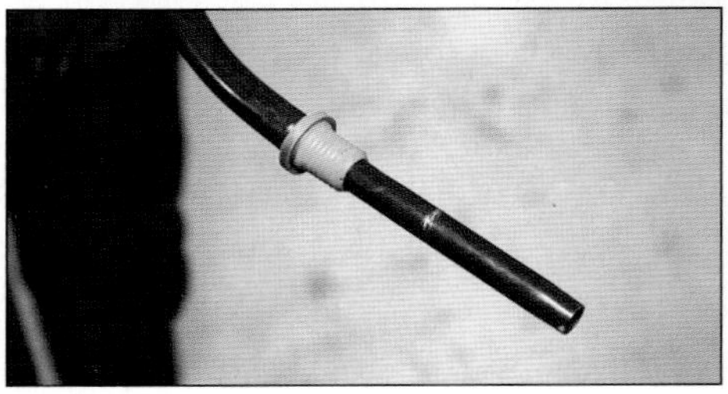

1 ***Dipsticks can cause issues, and on the 6L80 transmission in the 1991 1500 truck, it was a real issue. Instead of buying a new one, we chose to modify the original unit. One of the problems was that the tube was too long to let us install it in the transmission once the transmission was in the truck. We marked what we needed to remove. The green bushing doesn't move, so this will not affect the dipstick length.***

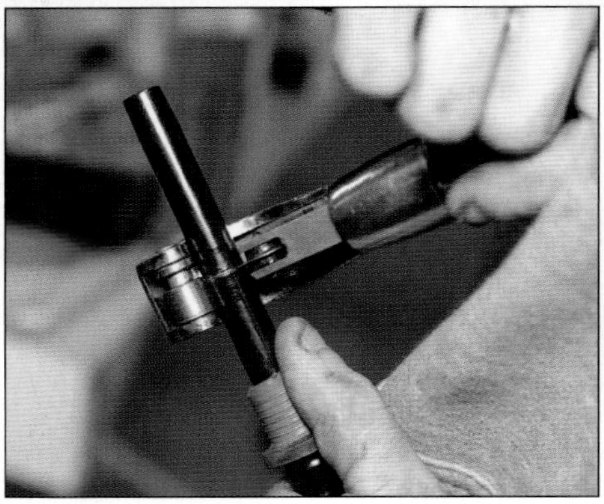

2 ***Use a tubing cutter to make a clean cut.***

3 ***Bend the tube itself to a location above the engine. This thing stuck up above the hood. We didn't want to cut the tube up here because that would require trimming the dipstick length itself. We slipped a coil-style tubing bender inside the tube to keep it from creasing.***

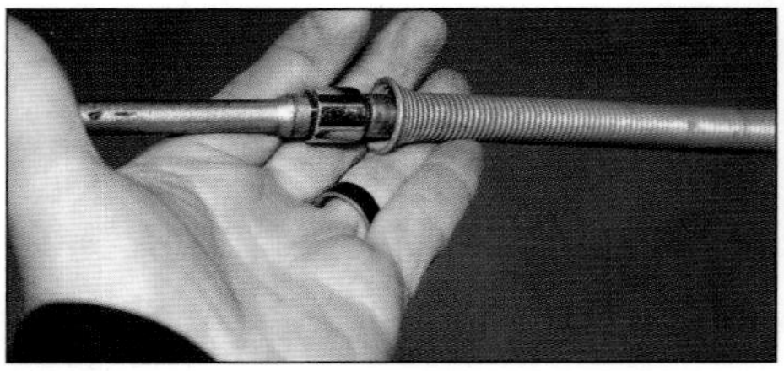

4 ***To get extra torque and control where the tube bends, slip a socket extension into the coil-spring bender to the depth that is desired.***

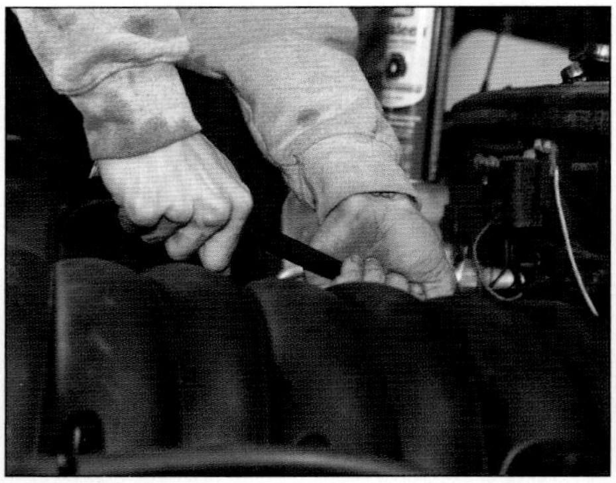

5 ***Then, carefully bend down the tube about three-quarters back from the front of the engine. Then, about halfway back, bend the tube upward to make filling the transmission easier.***

6 ***This is the finished tube. It looks good, is fully functional, and didn't cost anything.***

Accessory Drives and Cooling Systems

The stock accessory drives were designed to fit in the late-model vehicles with modern frames and spacing. Depending on which accessory drive is used, clearance may or may not be an issue. However, the AC compressor constantly presents an issue. It's typically mounted low on the passenger's side of the engine, and it tends to hit the frame rail or the upper A-arm on the suspension at this location.

Again, it all depends on the chassis and drive system being used. On the other side of the engine, the power-steering and alternator placement becomes an issue. The stock recirculating-ball steering gearbox gets in the way. Each chassis is different, and each accessory drive is different. However, there are some simple solutions for accessory drives.

Specific stock accessory drives work on specific chassis. A used engine will need compatible drive parts. If the drive system that you have won't fit your car, there are several options. The first is to find a stock drive that fits the chassis, but these can be difficult to find, especially the older 1998–2002 F-Body drives.

There are also quite a few aftermarket drive kits available. They will not only relocate the offending components but also add some flash to the install. The last solution of relocating the problem component with a home-fabricated bracket requires a little more ingenuity and fabrication.

When swapping an LS engine into a C/K10, there are a few limitations on the accessory drive, mostly for the AC compressor. Vehicles that will not run AC and/or power steering will certainly be easier to fit and modify than one requiring all of the accessories. Keep that in mind when choosing an accessory drive. An alternator alone is much easier to relocate than three components.

The accessory drives on Gen III and Gen IV engines are interchangeable throughout the product line.

LS/LT engines have crank pulleys of different lengths. The Corvette/CTS-V crank balancer is on the left, and the mid-length F-Body/GTO is on the right. Vortec pulleys are even longer.

Vortec engines have the longest pulley setup. The depth of the balancer must match the rest of the system.

However, each accessory drive is based on two components: the water pump and the harmonic damper (or harmonic balancer). LS engines are internally balanced, so it is technically a harmonic damper, but it is commonly referred to as a harmonic balancer.

The crank pulley is part of the damper. They are one piece as opposed to a separate pulley that bolts to the balancer. There are three balancer designs for LS engines. The Corvette (Y-Body and CTS-V) damper is the shortest of the three, placing the drive belt close to the motor. The F-Body (also GTO) damper is 3/4 inch longer than the Corvette engine, and the C/K (GM truck engines 4.8L, 5.3L, and 6.0L) unit is 1½ inches longer than the Corvette unit. This correlates to the water pump as well. Each intended drive system uses a specific water pump, and there are differences among the years of the water pumps.

Three water-pump offset options are available: the 1998–2002 F-Body, the Corvette, and the C/K trucks. Within these groups are subgroups. The F-Body water pump remained the same throughout its production run for 1998–2002. The Corvette (also GTO and CTS-V in 2004) used one water-pump design with some internal differences. The 2005-and-newer Corvette/GTO water pump for the LS2, LS7, and LS3 used the same offset, but it contained a different internal design.

The same story goes for the C/K truck pumps. The 1999–2005 trucks use a specific water pump, but in 2007, the design changed to displacement on demand. Not all 2007 C/K engines use this pump. The offset remains the same as the early pumps, but you would not want to swap a displacement-on-demand pump onto a non-displacement-on-demand engine. The LS1/LS3 pumps are interchangeable; the LS3 pump uses a lighter pulley with about 4 pounds of weight savings.

Stock Gen III and Gen IV Accessory Drives

Several different accessory drives are available for Gen III and Gen IV engines.

C5 Corvette

The C5 Corvette (Y-Body) accessory drive fits and clears the stock chassis and stock chassis components with most motor-mount adapters. The AC compressor sits low on the engine's passenger's side and back quite far, making engine placement a concern with the C5 accessory drive. The power-steering pump mounts in front of the driver-side cylinder head, and the alternator rides up and over the power-steering pump.

This system will work on 1967-and-newer C/K trucks, depending on the AC compressor and engine placement. It does not work as well in the 1960–1966 chassis.

F-Body Drive

This drive system places the AC compressor very low and tight to the block, with the AC centerline just below the center of the crank. The alternator is tucked up to the left of the crank pulley, and the power-steering pump is mounted directly above the alternator. This drive works well on all C/K trucks.

This engine has the 1998–2002 LS1 F-Body drive system. The accessories fit somewhat tightly to the engine, but the AC compressor and alternator can be difficult to fit to the chassis.

This shows the 1997–2004 Corvette dual-belt drive. The alternator is raised, so it clears most frames. The AC compressor does not work well for 1960–1966 trucks.

This engine has the 2005–2006 GTO accessory drive. The AC compressor is mounted fairly wide, so it is more difficult to fit between the truck frame rails. (Photo Courtesy Blane Burnett)

The 1999-and-newer Vortec drive fits all of the classic truck applications with the exception of the AC compressor in the 1967-and-newer trucks. The compressor hits the crossmember. The solution is to either relocate the AC compressor or notch the crossmember.

Vortec Truck Drive

The Vortec accessory drive positions the AC compressor just below the crank centerline, tucked in really tight to the passenger's side of the block. This makes it tough to use 1967-and-newer C/K trucks without modifying the crossmember. The power-steering pump mounts tight to the block, midway between the crank and the water pump. The alternator is out of the way at the top of the engine, above the power-steering pump, next to the throttle body. An aftermarket AC compressor bracket works best for 1967-and-newer trucks or you can notch the crossmember. This drive works well in 1960–1966 C10s.

CTS-V Drive

The CTS-V drive also positions the AC pump tight to the block (lower passenger's side) and uses the short pump design, maximizing the radiator-to-engine clearance. The power-steering pump is in the midway point between the water-pump pulley and the throttle body on the driver's side, so there is plenty of hood clearance.

The CTS-V accessory drive has been used as the starting point for some of the most popular aftermarket systems. The key exception is the AC placement, which is a consistent issue for using the stock accessory drives in C/K trucks.

Gen V Accessory Drives

Unlike the LS platform, the Gen V LT-series engines only use four versions of the accessory drive: one for Corvettes, one for Camaros, and two for trucks. The 4.3L V-6 is slightly different from the truck drive but only in belt routing and idler/tensioner placement. The bracket and pump are the same as the truck.

The car drives, as well as 2014–2018 truck systems, use an offset water pump that is a radical departure from anything that General Motors used in the past. This allows the accessories themselves to reside in a much more compact location than the LS drives.

This certainly does not mean that there are no issues with swaps. The main issues for these drives are the lack of power-steering pumps and the AC compressor location. (Nearly every new GM car and truck uses electric power assist for steering; there simply is no need for a power-steering pump.) Alleviating these problems is relatively easy through the aftermarket, but choosing your drive requires knowing exactly what you plan on doing with your vehicle.

For the 2014–2018 LT1, General Motors went a completely different direction. The water pump is offset to the passenger's side with a high-mount alternator and a low-mount AC compressor. There is no power steering, and the AC compressor is very close to the chassis in most trucks, but it does work. The most common clearance issue is the motor-mount adapters.

The truck version of the 2014–2018 accessory drive has no frame clearance issues with C/K trucks. However, the same potential clearance issue exists with the AC compressor and your choice of motor mounts.

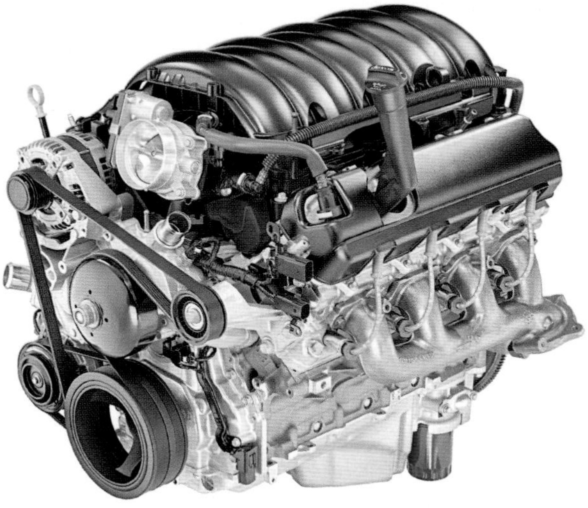

Starting in 2019, the Gen V water pump moved back to the center and the failure-prone vacuum pump was eliminated. These drives should work well in any truck. (Photo Courtesy General Motors)

In 2019, General Motors updated the 5.3L and 6.2L engines, with L84 (5.3L) and L87 (6.2L) monikers. The accessory drives on these engines feature a water-pump drive in the center of the engine, like the LS design. Additionally, there is no vacuum pump on these engines. General Motors also added the L8T 6.6L iron-block engine, which is different still. However, this engine features a power-steering pump, which is unique to the LT-series engines.

Stock Drives

The stock drives are very compact, and if it were not for the lack of a power-steering pump, they would work almost unaltered in most swap applications. The alternator is mounted high on the passenger's side of the engine, while the AC compressor is low and tight to the block.

For most truck swaps, the factory drives work quite well. Any GM truck will readily accept the factory accessory drive (car or truck version) without modification if you don't need a power-steering pump.

Corvette Drive

This version positions all of the accessories to the passenger's side of the engine. The AC compressor is mounted low and tight to the block just under the centerline of the crankshaft and slightly inboard of the centerline of the water pump pulley. There are no accessories on the driver's side of the engine. Adapting a power-steering pump to this drive would require a convoluted series of idler pulleys or an adaptation of the LT4 accessory drive.

The LT1 is naturally aspirated, but the LT4/5 engines are supercharged. This presents an opportunity for swappers. The LT4/5 crank pulley has two sets of ribs: one for the main accessories and one for the supercharger. It is possible to swap an LT4 crank pulley and fabricate a power-steering bracket. There are numerous bosses on the car water pump for the idler and tensioner pulleys that would be required.

Camaro Drive

The Camaro drive is similar to the Corvette drive in that the water pump is offset to the passenger's side, but that is where the similarities end. The crank pulley is spaced out farther from the block and the alternator is mounted low on the passenger's side, while the AC compressor is mounted low on the driver's side. The AC unit is driven off a separate belt.

2014–2018 Truck Drive

The truck drive positions the water pump pulley to the driver's side of the engine. This is mostly done to provide a path for the block-mounted vacuum pump. That is the major departure from the car version. The vacuum pump runs off a four-rib belt that is driven off the back of the crank pulley. The crank pulley is deeper than the car pulley.

Similar to the LS platform, they are not interchangeable without changing the rest of the components. The alternator is mounted up high on the passenger's side, residing just outside of the valve cover. This does not present any clearance issues for most swap applications.

The vacuum pump is used to pull crankcase pressure out of the engine and to provide adequate vacuum for the power brake system This pump is removable and, in most cases, does not need the pump. It will clear some installations, depending on the engine mount adapters. However, it will limit the placement of the engine in the chassis. It is possible to fabricate a bracket for a power-steering pump to run off the rear belt.

The AC compressor shares the same problems as the car unit: the compressor is an "always on" unit, meaning it runs all the time, regardless of whether the AC is on or not. The compressor is controlled by the body control module (BCM). Without the BCM, the unit does not operate properly.

There are swappers who have used these compressors, which are similar to LS units. The problem is that the compressor will freeze up the system because it does not cycle on and off as needed. There is a solution to this problem. See Chapter 6 for more details.

Even if you could use the compressor, the location fits in the C/K chassis but will limit the placement of the engine. The placement is low and tight to the block, so the unit clears the frame. It may be necessary to get creative on the hose fittings, depending on its exact placement.

2019-and-Newer Truck Drive

For the L84 and L87 update, General Motors moved the water pump back to the center position (which is similar to an LS engine, as they do share the same port spacing as an LS) and eliminated the vacuum pump. The AC compressor is still mounted low and tight to the block on the passenger's side. Running off its own belt, the alternator is in line with the passenger-side head, and there is an idler pulley on the driver-side head where the water pump pulley is on the earlier drive design. This is a two-belt system.

For the L8T 6.6L iron-block Gen V engine, which is used in 2500-and-larger trucks, General Motors needed a power-steering pump because these trucks use a hydroboost braking system. The hydroboost system requires hydraulic pressure from a power-steering unit.

To add power steering, General Motors added a bracket (part number 12654286) to the new accessory drive. This is the main reason for the 2019-and-newer truck accessory drive change, to accommodate the power-steering pump. To add this pump to any L84 or L87 (must be used as a complete system), you need the following parts:

- Power-steering pump bracket: 12654286
- Power-steering pump to bracket bolts: 11588725 (x3)
- Power-steering pump pulley: 12682902
- Power-steering pump antilock braking system (ABS) reservoir: 84768806
- GM Type II power-steering pump

Adapting an AC Compressor

1 This is the stock AC compressor from a Gen V LT. It is a variable-compression unit, so we have to wire it to work. The fittings are the problem. In the 1989-and-newer chassis, the stock fittings can't be used, and no one makes an adapter that fits.

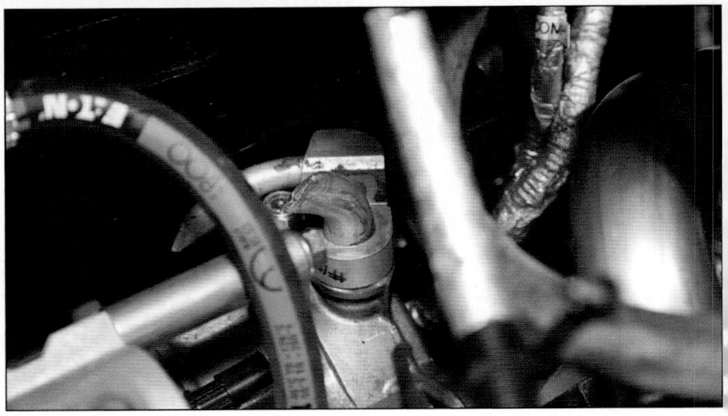

2 Pull the fitting stud and check the stock fittings. They will work if they are modified.

3 Using an aluminum -10 and -8 AC fitting, redirect the hoses to clear the frame.

4 The large -10 fitting (top) was cut off and the new fitting was welded in pointing straight out (it was a 90 here). The smaller -8 line needed more work. We drilled the fitting body from the inlet port and welded in the -8 fitting straight out. The factory port came out the side, which we cut off and welded. We had this done at a local machine shop for about $30 in labor after we provided the fittings.

5 New seals are needed for the fittings. Unlike older cars, LS/LT compressors use metal O-rings that cannot be reused. Before installing the fittings, the seals are coated with PAG 40 mineral oil. If you install them dry, you will be chasing a leak.

6 The modified fittings work perfectly in the chassis and seal well. If the stock fittings are needed for your project, call a salvage yard. New hoses cost hundreds of dollars.

7 The -8 AC line that runs to the condenser in front of the radiator was made with a 90-degree service port fitting.

8 *Using a Mastercool vise-mount AC line crimper, we crimped the lines. These can be made at any hydraulic shop if you don't have these specialty tools.*

9 *This truck is old enough to still use R12, which this compressor will not function with. It must be converted to R134A. We cleaned out the system by spraying a can of brake cleaner into the port that runs through the firewall; the cleaner shoots out the other port. The drier, condenser, and hoses are all new and R134A compliant. A new drier and condenser is required for this job.*

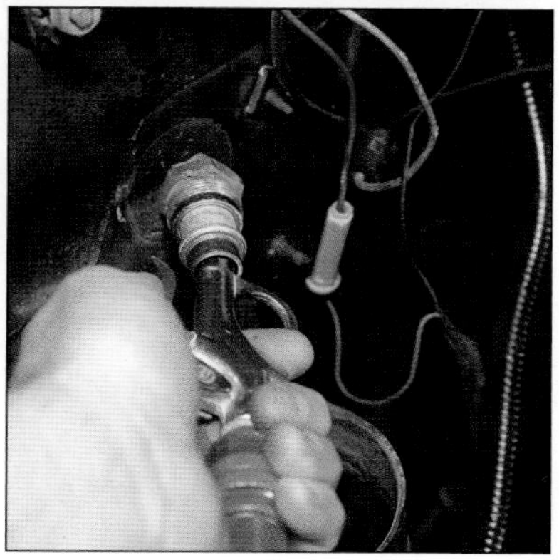

10 *Dry the evaporator coils by spraying compressed air through the port. Do this process twice just to be sure it is clean. R12 PAG oil will seize up if mixed with R134A PAG oil.*

Aftermarket Drives

While running a stock accessory drive is absolutely a cheap option, the look and fitment is definitely not there. If planning on running AC or swapping a Gen V engine and need power steering, it can be cheaper in the long run to scrap the stock drive and switch to an aftermarket system.

There are quite a few aftermarket systems available, and some, such as the Holley and Dirty Dingo systems, are designed to match with the rest of the swap kits. There are simple Gen V kits that use the stock water pump, and there are the kits that replace the stock drive altogether in favor of the LS-style water pump and components. Both have their merits.

Installing an Aftermarket Drive

1 *Most Vortec LS engines came with a mechanical fan. It can be kept or pulled off. The water pump is the same, so it doesn't hurt either way.*

2 *While the stock accessory drives work, changes are required if you want to upgrade your engine and add power steering. For the 1966 Suburban, we opted for this Holley mid-mount drive, which locates all the accessories directly off the water-pump housing. Because LS/LT engines have the same water-pump mounts, this system works for both. It just needs the correct spacing for the application.*

Installing an Aftermarket Drive *continued*

3 *The water pump is not a one-piece unit. Instead, the pump itself is a small drop-in unit. First, install the gasket using this pin to locate it.*

4 *This is the pump itself. This makes servicing the system much easier.*

5 *Another really slick feature of the mid-mount system is the twin heater-hose ports. You can choose which ones you need and block the other two.*

6 *All LS engines use steam lines that have to be ported into the radiator or the water pump. The Holley mid-mount system has a port already machined into it on the passenger's side of the engine to make it easy.*

7 *If you are using a different-style accessory drive, simply drill the top of the water pump, thread it, and put the steam line port into the adapter.*

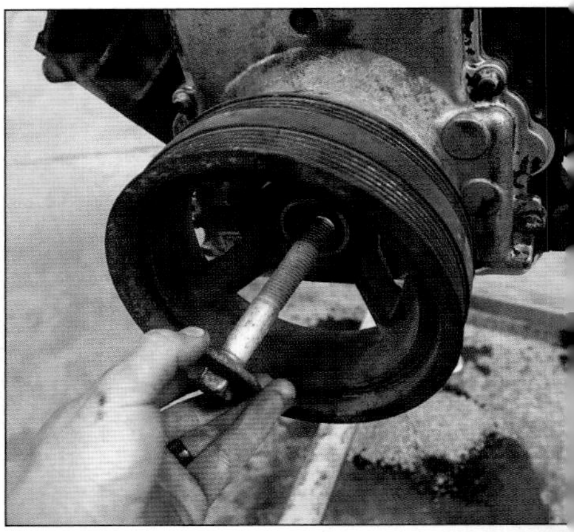

8 *Changing the accessory drive usually means changing the crank pulley. These bolts are torque-to-yield, and they cannot be reused. Always use a new crank bolt.*

9 *Use a puller to remove the crank pulley. Borrow one from a local parts store or buy one like this for around $25 to $30.*

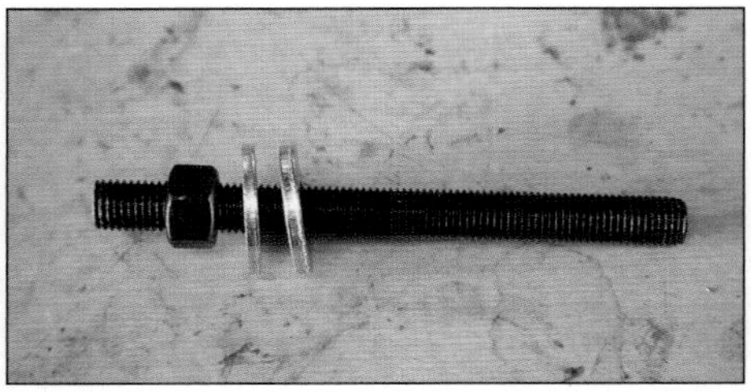

10 *Use this tool to reinstall the pulley. Most parts stores do not have a tool that will work for LS/LT engines, as they are not long enough. We bought this on Amazon for about $20. It is simple but effective. The piece of all-thread must be Grade 8, otherwise it will strip.*

11 *To install a new torque-to-yield bolt, set the bolt at 59 ft-lbs. Don't forget to put some RTV silicone on the bottom of the washer on the new bolt. This is required.*

12 *Select a random point on the pulley for the 0-degree point and mark it. Then, measure 125 degrees from the 0-degree point and make a mark.*

13 *Using a breaker bar and ensuring that the crank is locked at the flexplate, rotate the bolt to the 125-degree point. A torque-angle gauge can be used for this as well, but this works in a pinch if you don't have one.*

14 *With the new crank pulley installed, install the mid-mount pump housing into the factory water-pump location with new bolts and gaskets.*

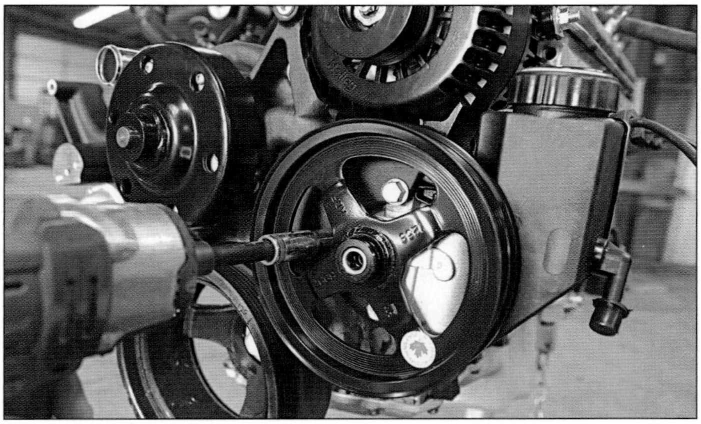

15 *Next, install all of the accessories onto the housing. The power-steering pump can be bolted on before or after the pulley is installed.*

16 *The finished installation looks great and fits without any issues in the 1966 Suburban. This setup is designed to work with all of the Hooker Blackheart LS/LT swap systems.*

LS

There are so many options on LS swap accessory drives that the key is to make sure to order a kit that matches your crank pulley. Another option is to swap out the crank pulley to match whatever kit you are ordering. There are three crank pulleys: the Corvette/CTS-V/G8/SS, the 1998–2002 Camaro/GTO, and the truck/2010–2015 Camaro.

The Corvette pulley is the most shallow, the truck pulley is the longest, and the early Camaro is in the middle. The entire drive must match the pulley. Some accessory kits swap out the water pump, and others use spacers.

ICT Billet offers the most inexpensive option, as it has kits that allow the use of the main components from the existing accessory drive and provides an AC bracket that clears the frame. A complete drive system can be ordered for 1988–1998 C/K trucks that use the 1988–1998 alternator and power-steering pump if you want to do that.

Dirty Dingo offers complete systems and add-on components as well—from a $150 alternator-only system to a complete system. Keep in mind that the Dirty Dingo and ICT systems do not come with any of the actual accessories, but if you have the originals from your engine, they will bolt right in.

The Holley accessory drives are essentially the same for LS/LT engines. The only difference is the balancer spacing. You can purchase Holley kits in individual components or as a master kit with all new components, including an AC compressor, an alternator, a power-steering pump, and a water pump. Its mid-mount is incredibly simple. All of the components bolt to the Holley-designed water pump housing for a truly unique and clean system.

Gen V

General Motors did us all a favor by keeping the water-pump mounts and spacing exactly the same as the LS. The only thing needed is a water-pump spacer. This allows an LS pump, typically an F-Body unit, to bolt onto the block. Some systems require a truck pulley and others need a Corvette pulley. It just depends on the design of the system.

Holley Standard Mount (Part Number 20-170)

The Holley accessory drives are essentially the same for LS and LT engines. The only difference is the balancer spacing.

The Holley LT accessory drive is based on its standard LS engine brackets, which are similar to the factory CTS-V LS accessory drive. This is a very versatile, well-designed, and well-built kit. It is the best-fitting accessory system for the LT engine that we have found. It works very well, and all of the components fit and integrate very well together without much guesswork.

Using the fourth-generation F-Body (1998–2002) water pump and the truck Gen V crank pulley, this system is the standard for the LT swap. The alternator is mounted on the upper driver's side with the power-steering pump just below, inboard toward the engine. The AC compressor is mounted high on the passenger's side. This system fits well in most trucks. All of the accessories are below the valve covers, so hood clearance is not an issue.

That does not mean this system does not have its drawbacks. The accessories are very wide, giving the engine a 35-inch wingspan, which is 15 inches wider than the engine itself. While this sounds like a lot (and it is), this is not out of line with most SBC accessory drives. It will not work with the LT4/5 engines.

Another drawback to the Holley system is that it missed an opportunity to add a second coolant port in the water pump adapters. The LT engines do not have any alternate water ports to pull the water temperature, so swappers have to either drill and tap the adapters (one already has a port for the factory sensor) or drill and tap the water pump itself. This is a common procedure for LS swaps, and it carries over to the LT as well.

This accessory drive is available with or without AC, and it is very versatile. The instructions for the kit are also very well thought-out, making the install a breeze.

Holley Mid-Mount (Part Number 20-200)

For those who need to limit the width of the engine, the mid-mount system is a great option. This design completely redefines the LT accessory drive, as Holley developed an all-new water pump housing that integrates all of the mounts into the pump housing. That means you bolt on the housing, assemble the components, and you are done. It is very simple, very clean, and narrow. In fact, this system is narrower than the engine itself, so this drive will fit into just about any application without issue.

The main drawback of this system is the cost. It is significantly more expensive than the standard-mount Holley system, which is not a budget piece in its own right. The benefits certainly come at a cost, but when a tight-fitting accessory drive is needed, there is simply nothing else out there that is even close. Rest assured that you are getting good quality, as these Holley systems are very well designed.

Dirty Dingo

Dirty Dingo was the first company to bring a power-steering retrofit kit to market, and it is rather ingenious. Instead of trying to work with the offset LT water pump, the Dirty Dingo system replaces the LT water pump with the older LS1 Corvette center-driven pump by using a pair of billet aluminum spacers. The LT and LS share the same bolt and gasket configuration, so it is an easy swap. The spacers also provide a mounting point for a temperature sender, as the LT block does not have any alternate cooling ports to tap into.

The center-drive pump allows the other accessories to mount on the heads and block like a typical system. Dirty Dingo uses an aluminum plate and spacer design that fits well and looks good on the LT engine. The caveat for this is that spacing of the water pump requires the use of the truck crank pulley.

For a Chevrolet Performance LT crate engine, you will have to purchase this pulley separately. The pulley is difficult to remove and install, so make sure to use the correct pulley-removal tool. A few wiring harness items must be moved as well: the cam VVT solenoid, which needs to be re-clocked, along with the removal of a portion of the steel wiring harness sleeve. The alternator moves to the driver's side of the engine, so you may have to reroute or modify the wiring harness to reach the alternator.

This drive system uses either a fourth-generation Camaro Type-II power-steering pump with Dirty Dingo's own pulley or a Type-I Saginaw pump (different brackets). To use a Type-II pump, a press-in or thread-in reservoir feed fitting for the pump is needed, which Dirty Dingo sells. The kit is also available with either no AC, Sanden 508-type AC compressor brackets, or GM R4-type AC brackets, which give you several options when it comes to adding AC.

Dirty Dingo provides multiple listings for belt lengths depending on the options, including alternator pulley and case size, AC type, and idler pulley location.

ICT Billet

A budget option for LT accessory brackets is made by ICT Billet. For about $200, you get the brackets, idler, bolts, and spacers to put power steering onto a Gen V LT engine. It is a very simple kit that does one job: add power steering. It doesn't come with any fancy designs or extravagant components, but it does provide power steering on a budget.

This system uses the truck accessory drive and crank pulley, but it does not come with it. All of the components are user-supplied, meaning the alternator, power-steering pump (1997–2004 Corvette *only*), and belt must be purchased separately.

The power-steering pump is mounted below the alternator, and it sits roughly 7 inches outside the alternator to the passenger's side, just below the centerline of the water-pump pulley. The system allows the use of the factory AC compressor and bracket, which can be altered to use a Sanden S7 compressor using the bracket described earlier in the chapter.

Installing Power Steering

1 ***If you stick with the factory accessory drive on a Gen V LT engine, you will likely want to add power steering. This power-steering add-on kit from ICT Billet also relocates the alternator slightly. We opted for this on the 1991 1500 LT swap.***

2 ***Begin by removing the AC compressor. (Weirdly, there was no tensioner on our belt—it was just the compressor and the crank.) The belt comes off easily enough, but reinstalling it is a real pain. First, remove the nut from the stud. Then, remove the stud. It is a bad design.***

Installing Power Steering *continued*

3 *Remove the upper bracket for the AC and alternator. Save these pieces for possible reuse in the future.*

4 *Remove the press-in bushing in the rear ears of the AC compressor. We used a socket, a bolt, and a vise to press it out.*

5 *Reinstall the AC compressor using the provided spacers along with the belt. Put the belt on the crank pulley and compressor and bolt it on as a unit. Be very careful not to cross-thread the bolt. There is less than a 1/2 inch of play, so the belt can't just slip on afterward (not easily, anyway). This is required due to the removal of the upper accessory-drive bracket.*

6 *The system is designed for the Corvette LS power-steering-pump pulley. The F-Body pulley shown here can be used, but it requires a different belt. The pump is preinstalled on the bracket with the center bolt (as shown).*

7 *Bolt the rear bracket to the head. The front bracket bolts to the rear bracket with the provided spacers.*

8 *To mount the alternator, use a short spacer and a bolt that threads into the head.*

9 *This is the finished system with the ICT Billet power-steering kit. This kit is for the truck drive. Car drives are available as well, which place the power-steering pump on the other side.*

Cooling Systems

Swapping LS engines into non-V-8 vehicles can raise some challenges for the cooling system. The stock copper and brass radiator for a V-8 should be capable of cooling an LS, but the steam lines need to be changed. An aftermarket aluminum radiator is an easy solution that will handle the load and provide the input for the steam line. These are readily available for all C/K platforms.

In addition to the radiators, the car Gen III and Gen IV engines were designed for electric cooling fans. Only the Vortec engines have mechanical fans. Gen V engines do not have any mechanical fan capabilities, so all Gen V swaps require an electric fan.

Radiators

The Gen III and Gen IV engines are typical V-8 engines in respect to the cooling system, so they do not require huge radiators or special metals. What they do require is a radiator that is rated for the job. With the smallest LS/LT motors easily making 300 hp, it wouldn't be a good idea to use a stock 4-cylinder or V-6 radiator.

Making horsepower means making heat as a byproduct, although the LS motors are pretty efficient when it comes to that. Considering that most of the C/Ks used V-8 engines as the base engine from the factory and there is a massive aftermarket that caters to these vehicles, V-8 radiators are easy to find. The exception is the 1960–1966 models, as these radiators are two-core copper and brass. They really should be replaced when doing an LS/LT swap.

Fabricating Radiator Hoses

1 *The owner of this 1966 Suburban provided an aluminum radiator that was close to fitting. We made some brackets to secure the radiator to the core support. As long as it is big enough, it will work. This one worked quite well.*

2 *We hit the local parts store for some random coolant hoses that matched the guide we made with some bailing wire. The hose will be sectioned to make it work.*

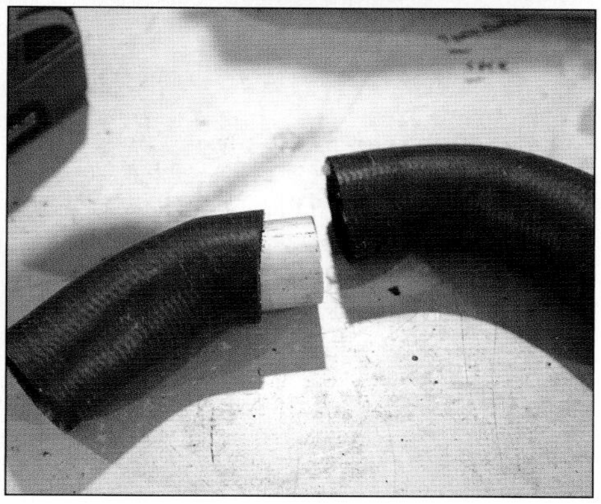

3 *To secure the hoses together, use a section of aluminum tubing that matches the diameter of the hose.*

4 *This is a really simple way to make your own radiator hoses. It works very well—just make sure to get the clamps tight.*

5 *For the upper hose, make another one by using some silicon elbows and another piece of aluminum tubing.*

In most vehicles built up through the 1970s, the OEM radiators are constructed of copper-brass. These radiators are expensive and not the most effective means for cooling an engine. Copper-brass quickly absorbs and dissipates heat at a rate that is faster than aluminum.

Aluminum radiators absorb and dissipate quickly as well, but they do so at a slower rate than copper. Aluminum radiators are stronger, so the cooling tubes are made with thinner walls. The radiator can be fitted with more cores and rows than a traditional copper radiator for increased cooling surface area, which in turn increases the cooling capacity. In addition, aluminum is cheaper than copper-brass, which certainly plays a part.

Another point to consider is electrolysis. Anytime two differentiating metals are in a coolant system, there is the potential for electrolysis. Electrolysis happens when one weaker material gets eaten away and deposited on the other. This can be disastrous for an aluminum engine because aluminum is generally the sacrificed material. When running a copper-brass radiator, there is potential to ruin an aluminum component on the engine, and the simple solution is to install an anode kit in the radiator.

Anodes are used in machinery and marine applications to protect the cooling systems and other components from damage due to electrolysis (or coolant additive failure and breakdown). Flex-a-Lite offers a zinc anode kit (part number 32060) for installation as a replacement drain petcock in radiators, which are equipped with a 1/4-inch NPT bushing welded into the tank. The anode may also be installed in any 1/4-inch NPT hole that is available in the cooling system.

Aluminum parts may disintegrate from electrolysis in the cooling system. The introduction of the zinc anode protects the cooling system from galvanic action, as it eats away at the zinc rather than the cooling system.

Coolant

There has been much discussion about which coolant is best for LS engines, particularly in engine swaps. GM's DexCool is the factory engine coolant and is recommended by General Motors. With that being said, those recommendations are for stock vehicles using all stock components.

The DexCool coolant is specifically designed for aluminum radiators, not for copper-brass radiators. DexCool's harsh and resilient organic acids attach to the solder in copper radiators, rendering them useless in such systems. The DexCool coolant also has a tendency to sludge up in the system over time due to contaminants that find their way into the system. When swapping an LS engine, most builders suggest flushing the engine with water three or four times until it comes out clear and there are no more hints of orange color.

Once the coolant system is clean, it's time to add new coolant. Most builders agree that the aftermarket (non-GM brand) orange long-life equivalent works well in systems with copper-brass radiators. Make sure that the coolant used says it is compatible with both types of coolant, such as Prestone. With that being said, the good old green antifreeze will provide more than adequate performance as long as the system has been properly flushed.

Inlet/Outlet Positioning

One major point for choosing a radiator is the inlet and outlet positioning. All LS engines have the same inlet and outlet position: on the passenger's side of the motor. In most cases, the easiest solution is to purchase a radiator with passenger-side inlets and outlets. Since there is no mechanical fan in the way, running the upper return hose to the driver's side is a pretty simple solution if you are keeping the stock radiator and it has a driver-side upper mount.

The lower feed hose is more difficult to cross over to the driver's side, depending on the distance between the engine and the radiator. It is possible to have the inlet and outlets moved, but the expense would likely be just as much as purchasing a new radiator.

LT engines use two different inlet and outlet positions: one for car pumps and one for truck pumps. The truck pump positions both inlet and outlet on the driver's side of the motor, necessitating driver-side

In most cases, the factory mechanical fan on Vortec engines will not fit the earlier trucks because there is not enough space. We opted for a 16-inch electric fan and shroud that came with the radiator. There is just enough clearance between the engine and the fan.

An electric fan can be wired to operate whenever the key is on, or a sending unit kit can be used like this one from Maradyne Fans. The sender slides into the radiator fins and provides the controller with an accurate temperature to turn the fans on and off.

We mounted the controller, which is a clean little block with built-in replaceable relay, to the core support on the 1991 1500.

It is also possible to pull water temperature from this port (the Allen plug to the left of the exhaust manifold) on the head of an LS engine.

inlet/outlet radiators for the most part. Car pumps place both inlet and outlet in the center, biased slightly to the passenger's side. The inlet points straight out, while the outlet is angled toward the passenger's side. The water neck can be rotated on the three-bolt flange if necessary.

However, these are for the factory LT water pumps, which you may not be using if you have an aftermarket accessory drive that uses an LS-based water pump. Most of the aftermarket systems use the F-Body pump, but others use the 1997–2004 Corvette pump, making things more complicated.

Aftermarket Offerings

Many aftermarket radiator offerings are available, and each one has its own benefits. The quality of the materials and construction are important for a radiator. An aluminum radiator costs a minimum of $300 to $450 for a C/K, and they only go up from there.

There are a few options when it comes to ordering a radiator. The first and most simple way is to order an off-the-shelf unit with the inlets and outlets as the manufacturer placed them. New aftermarket radiators that mount in the stock location are available for the various year models.

It is also possible to save some cash by purchasing a "custom fit" radiator, typically sold in terms of dimension. For example, a four-core 33x18 radiator would notate a 33-inch-wide by 18-inch-tall radiator. Often, these radiators will fit in the stock location

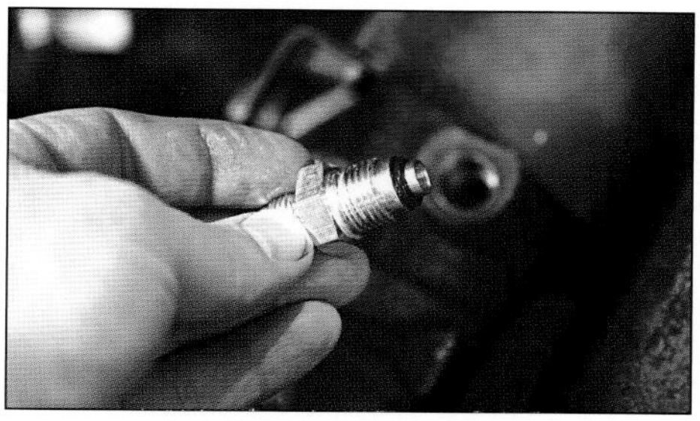

Connecting an early power-steering box to an LS pump means that some fittings are needed. There are several sizes of fittings, so verify the gearbox's threads. These are inverted flare O-ring fittings, which look a little funky. It can be tough finding these locally. The 1979-and-newer are typically 5/8-18 and 11/16-18 thread, whereas newer trucks have 16-mm and 18-mm metric threads. These are sometimes call "bump tube adapters" and are a -6 AN male fitting for the hoses.

Most hydraulic shops can make a new hose with -6 JIC and -6 AN fittings. They are the same size and flare angle, so they interchange.

using the stock or slightly modified mounting hardware, but they can cost as much as 30 percent less.

Factory Radiators

Some radiator sellers list the core dimensions, while others list the overall dimension including the tanks.

1960–1966

Unlike the later models, the early trucks have a bolt-in radiator that bolts to the radiator support. Some later models have an upper and lower clamshell-style mount like the newer trucks. The early models are downflow, so the inlet is in the upper center of the radiation with a passenger-side lower outlet. The downflow radiators measure 26.5 inches wide x 25 inches high x 3 inches and are copper-brass. The core is 21.75 inches wide x 19 inches high, and do not have automatic transmission cooler options. The upper inlet is 1.57 inches, and the outlet is 1.8 inches.

In 1963, General Motors switched to the clamshell-mount radiators, which have an upper driver inlet and lower passenger outlet. These measure 24.5 inches wide x 22.5 inches high x 3 inches, with core dimensions of 22.750 inches x 17.4 inches. The upper hose is 1.5 inches, and the lower is 1.75 inches.

1967–1972

The factory V-8 copper-brass radiator measures 20.5 inches tall x 33.130 inches wide and is 2 inches thick. The core itself is 28.375 x 17 x 2 inches. The inlet is on the upper driver's side; the outlet is on the lower passenger's side. The inlet hose is 1.5 inches; the outlet is 1.75 inches.

1973–1987

The factory V-8 copper-brass radiator measures 20.5 inches tall x 33.130 inches wide and is 3 inches thick. The core is 28.25 x 17 or 19 inches, depending on the original engine. The inlet is on the upper driver's side; the outlet is on the lower passenger's side. The inlet port is 1.3125 inches ($1\frac{5}{16}$) or 1.5625 inches ($1\frac{9}{16}$), the lower is 1.5625 inches ($1\frac{9}{16}$).

1988–1998

The original V-8 radiator is an aluminum core with plastic side tanks. The unit core measures 34 x 17.25 x 1

For the 1991 1500, we ran the power-steering lines behind the accessory drive (as shown). We made some brackets to secure the lines from moving and getting rubbed by the drive.

Check the fitment and fitting orientation before having fittings compressed at the hydraulic shop. Mark the hose and fitting with a line to ensure that it is done correctly. These fittings can not be rotated once they are compressed to the hose.

inches on the upper driver's side; the outlet is on the lower passenger's side. The inlet port is 1.3125 inches (1 5/16); the lower is 1.5625 (1 9/16) inches.

Overflow Tanks

Depending on the model of vehicle, it may or may not have an overflow tank. Most LS engines function best when the radiator is coupled with a functioning overflow tank that purges excess water to the tank when hot and draws water back into the cooling system when cool. These are readily available in the aftermarket. This mainly applies to 1960–1972 trucks, as most 1973-and-newer trucks had overflow tanks from the factory.

LS Water Pumps and Necks

Depending on the engine, the water-pump outlet position varies. There are three water pumps: truck, F-Body, and Corvette. This goes along with the depth issue. The truck is the deepest, followed by the F-Body, and then the Corvette is the shortest (the pulley is closest to the block). Each of the Corvette- and F-Body-style pumps feature a forward-directed output to the upper radiator hose (passenger's side of the engine).

Truck pumps direct the output up and out at an angle. Either pump will fit most truck chassis; the biggest difference is the crank pulley and the accessory drive being used. Finding the right hoses to fit an LS swap can be a time-consuming process, as varying radiators and water pumps cause some fitment issues.

1960–1962

A custom radiator is required, which means making hoses or using trial and error.

1963–1966

If using the stock-style radiator, trial and error or custom-made hoses are required. If using an aftermarket radiator with similar dimensions to the 1967-and-later radiators, then it is okay to use the suggested hoses below.

1967–Newer

These trucks all have very similar radiator sizes and inlet/outlets. These hoses may work, but the lower absolutely requires trimming. Do not trim anything without verifying it will work. Otherwise, the hose cannot be returned.

The Gates 21439 hose may work for the upper and the Gates 20687 hose may work for the lower on LT swaps with LS-based water pumps. LT water pumps will require custom hoses.

While a plain, stock, black rubber hose may be your choice, there are alternatives, such as flexible aluminum and stainless-steel hose kits. These kits, such as the Summit Racing polished stainless-steel kit (part number SUM-390036), solves the problem of both fitment and accessory clearance as well as brings a good look to the engine bay. The hoses can be painted, polished, powder coated, or even anodized to match the rest of the underhood trim. The tubing is bulk length and cut to fit the application. Because it is bendable, it can be reused if a later change is necessary.

For the 1966 GMC Suburban featured here, we used a non-direct-fit radiator (1967 Mustang aftermarket to be exact). We used a couple of different hoses from NAPA for the lower and fabricated an upper hose using silicone elbows and a section of 1.5-inch aluminum tubing. This looks really good and is rigid enough to not need any supports.

The stock cast-aluminum water neck points at a 90-degree angle toward the passenger's side. The heater-hose fittings point straight toward the passenger-side inner wheel well with plenty of room for the hoses to connect without any modification.

Several aftermarket alternatives to the stock cast water neck are available, so go that route. Two such options are a straight unit (which is the best unit for the early Corvettes), and a 360-degree swivel with either a 45-degree or 15-degree outlet. Each water neck must match the water-pump design: 1998–2003 or 2004-and-newer. Since there is no mechanical fan to get in the way, you can easily run a lower radiator hose to the driver-side outlet on the radiator to save having to buy a new radiator.

Steam Lines

A unique design feature on LS engines is a pair of steam lines that route from the cylinder heads through the throttle body and on to the radiator. This line circulates warm coolant through the throttle body to

The steam lines connect from the throttle body to the top of each head (as shown here).

warm the intake charge on cold days and ensures that no air is in the cooling system. It must also be routed to the return tank on the radiator. There are three ways to accomplish this.

The first is to use a traditional routing pattern and run a line from the driver-side cylinder head to the return tank on the radiator. The second is to drill and tap the top of the water pump with a 1/4-inch tap, install a 90-degree pipe fitting, and route the steam lines to the top of the water pump. This option certainly results in a cleaner look, but

Steam Line Installation

Steam lines are a necessary component of an LS engine swap. The problem is that they often look less than stellar with barbed fittings and rubber lines. A great alternative to the stock setup is to convert to AN-style lines. Aftermarket plumbing involves Army/Navy (AN) fittings, which were developed by the aerospace industry.

Each AN size directly correlates with a specific outside diameter of metal tubing. Each size is listed as -X with the number after the hyphen, indicating a 1/16-inch increase in size. Therefore, a -3 fitting would be 3/16 inch, -4 would be 1/4 inch, and so on.

Selecting which components to use depends on your budget and desired level of performance. Earl's Performance Plumbing offers several different types of fittings and hoses to suit each system's needs. This install uses the Ano-Tuff hard-anodized fittings that resist corrosion and wear better than the more common red and blue anodizing.

These are Swivel-Seal hose ends, which keep the hose from twisting when assembling the lines in the car. Otherwise, they can collapse. The steam line adapters are from Trick Flow and have -6 male ends for the hose connections. ■

1 *The factory steam lines don't look nice and are kind of clunky. Several replacement options are available. (Photo Courtesy Blane Burnett)*

2 *AN conversion mounts, such as these from Trick Flow, allow swappers to run braided hose to the radiator or water pump for a clean look. (Photo Courtesy Blane Burnett)*

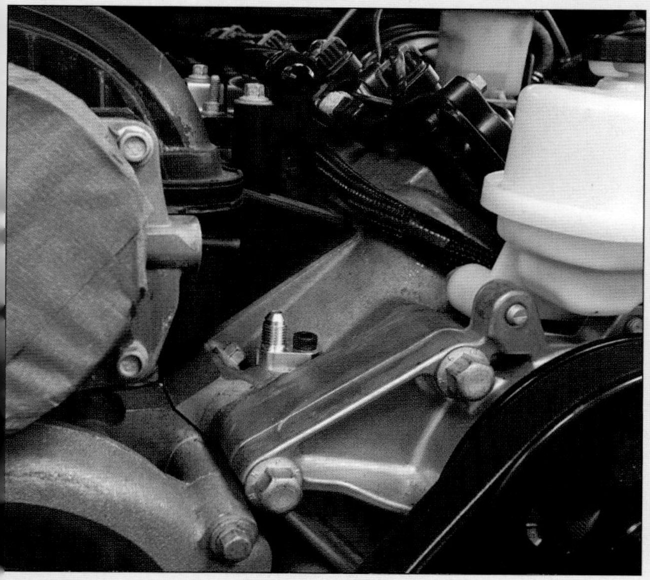

3 *The installed fittings (in satin aluminum) are a perfect fit. (Photo Courtesy Blane Burnett)*

4 *Using a few 90-degree fittings, the driver-side steam line is run under the throttle body to the passenger's side via braided Earl's line. (Photo Courtesy Blane Burnett)*

5 *The passenger's side is connected with a T-fitting. (Photo Courtesy Blane Burnett)*

6 *The radiator came with a barbed hose fitting. The -6 AN replacement fitting is on the right. (Photo Courtesy Blane Burnett)*

7 *With the fitting threaded into the radiator, a straight Earl's AN fitting was connected. The only thing that is left is to cut a piece of braided hose. Then, the steam lines are done. (Photo Courtesy Blane Burnett)*

There is a hardline (metal tube under the red wire) that runs from the passenger-side head to the driver's side. These can be replaced with some trick AN-style fittings and hoses or you can keep them stock. The only difference is the appearance.

it requires some more work. As a bonus, if aluminum or stainless-steel hard line is used, the lines could be polished, adding some flash to a very utilitarian function. The other is to splice a T-fitting into the heater hose, routing the steam line to it instead of the radiator.

Several companies are now offering steam line kits, such as Holley Performance and Summit Racing. These kits include aluminum block mounts and AN hoses and fittings to eliminate the factory lines. This allows customization of the routing for installation.

LT1 Cooling Systems

The Gen V LT1-series engines are a little bit different from the Gen III and Gen IV engines in terms of the cooling system. There are no steam lines on the LT1, so don't stress out struggling to find them; they are not there. Secondly, the factory temperature gauge mounts in the water pump itself.

Electric Fans

An electric fan must be used because Gen III and Gen IV (except for 5.3L 1999–2005 Vortec) engines do not have provisions for a mechanical fan. There are many options for electric fans, both stock and aftermarket, and each fan requires custom fitment to the radiator. For the budget-minded builder, reusing stock radiator fans is an inexpensive option. Most salvage yards give the stock fans (and maybe the radiator) for free when you are buying a complete engine. Since the Gen III/ Gen IV platform is relatively new, there will be plenty of life left in the fan motors. Of course, new fans have guarantees and can be configured as needed.

With electric fans, correct installation is essential. If the electric fans are not installed correctly (with an electric fan shroud), the fans are not able to draw air through the entire radiator, which means they will lose efficiency. The engine reaches operating temperature much faster, maximizing fuel economy because electric fans are set to run at a determined temperature.

The electric fan may also operate when the engine is off so that the coolant in the radiator cools while the vehicle is sitting. This helps keep the engine in its optimal temperature range when on cruise nights or just general driving and parking. When shopping for an electric fan, make sure to purchase a fan designed for high-performance engines that has a fan shroud to maximize efficiency. Some leading electric fans for LS engines include Spal, Maradyne, Flex-a-Lite, Griffin, Auto-Loc Zirgo, and Perma-Cool.

Adapters

If you are planning on running aftermarket gauges, install an adapter into the block to convert the sending unit to SAE threads. The block has a 12-mm plug on the rear passenger-side head that can be removed to provide the coolant-temperature-sender location. Drill and tap for pipe threads or fit a simple adapter to the head for converting from 12-mm to 1/8-, 1/4-, 3/8-, or 1/2-inch pipe thread. This will need to be done before installing the engine in the vehicle. Otherwise, it will be extremely difficult to install the adapter.

If it is too late to install the adapter, Flex-a-Lite offers an inline adapter to be installed in the upper radiator hose. Designed to fit 1½-inch and 1¾-inch hoses, these adapters have two 1/4-inch NPT threaded holes and a brass plug. This makes for a simple way to keep tabs on the coolant temperature.

AutoMeter offers an LS adapter kit (part number 5284) for use with its gauges. This kit has the correct fittings for the sensors to thread into the LS engine ports as well as a step-down resistor to provide the extra voltage needed to drive an aftermarket tach (see Chapter 6 on wiring).

TRANSMISSIONS

One of the best parts of swapping a Gen III–V engine into your truck is that you can use just about any GM transmission—from a 2-speed Powerglide to the newest 10-speed automatic. You just need to use the right parts between the engine and the transmission.

For late-model transmissions originally fitted to Gen III–V engines, such as a 4L60E or a 6L80, the engine bolts up directly. Using any older transmission, including SBC-mounted 4L60E transmissions, an adapter or different flexplate is required. All Gen III–V engine blocks share the same basic bolt pattern for bellhousings, with the Gen III–IV having one fewer bolt location and the Gen V blocks with an additional bolt at the top of the pattern. This is not an issue when using older transmissions with the standard GM V-8 bolt pattern.

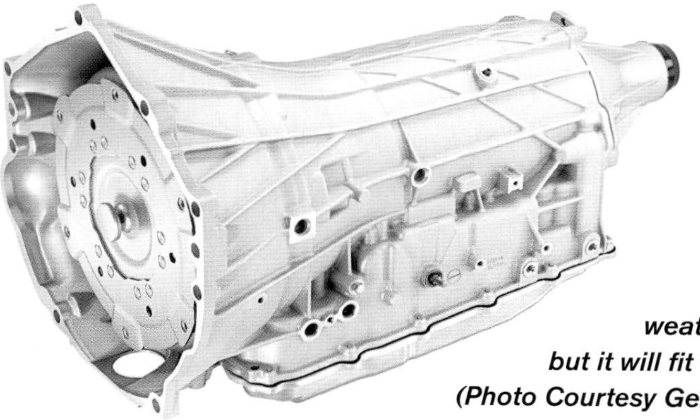

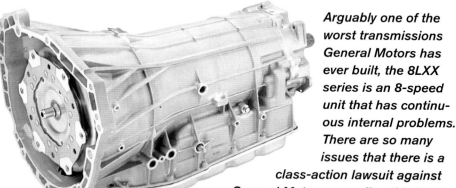

The newest GM transmission is the 10LXX series, which was co-developed with Ford. This 10-speed transmission is very smooth when warm but very clunky in cold weather. It is also large, but it will fit under most trucks. (Photo Courtesy General Motors)

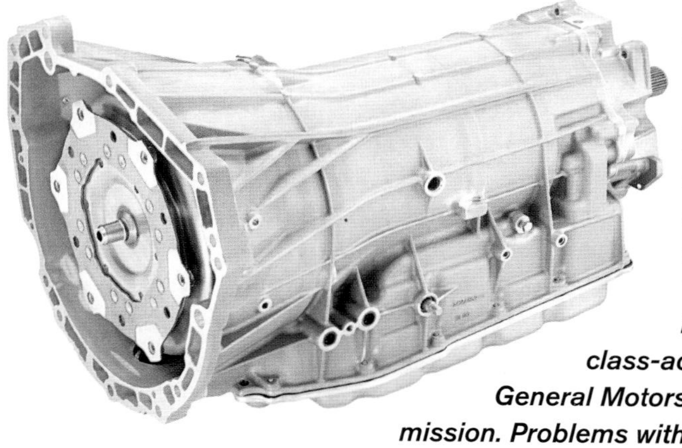

Arguably one of the worst transmissions General Motors has ever built, the 8LXX series is an 8-speed unit that has continuous internal problems. There are so many issues that there is a class-action lawsuit against General Motors regarding this transmission. Problems with this transmission include hard clunking, erratic shifting, and heavy vibrations between 50 and 75 mph. If you want a new transmission, the 10LXX or 6LXX are better options. (Photo Courtesy General Motors)

Automatics

The Gen V LT-series engine uses four specific transmissions from the factory: the 6-, 8-, and 10-speed automatics and the Tremec TR6060 6-speed manual. It isn't necessary to stick with one of these factory offerings, and thankfully so. Like the LS platform before it, the Gen V LT-series engine uses the standard SBC bolt pattern for the transmission bellhousing, allowing swappers to use just about any GM SBC-based transmission.

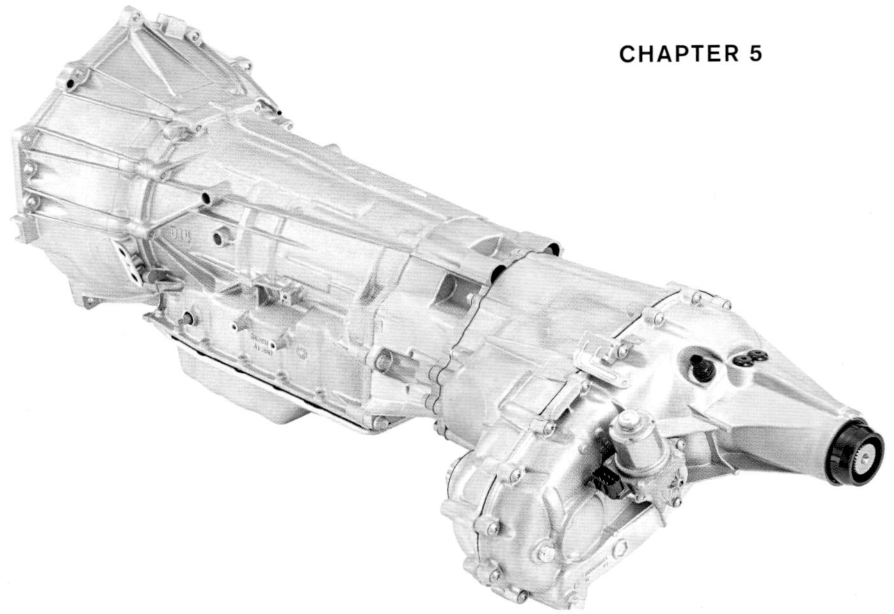

The 6LXX is a good transmission, with six speeds and a smaller case than the 8LXX and 10LXX units. These are very finicky in their own right. They need to be serviced every 50,000 miles, otherwise wear from the torque-convertor clutch can clog up the pump, which destroys the entire transmission at around 120,000 to 150,000 miles. It is cheaper to buy a low-mileage, used 6LXX transmission than it is to rebuild one, so keep that in mind. (Photo Courtesy General Motors)

It might be tempting to stick with the factory automatic transmission for your swap. Under normal circumstances, this would be a good plan. Unfortunately, there are some serious issues with both the 6- and 8-speed transmissions to know about before attempting to use one of these automatic transmissions in your swap. While the 6LXX units are good when properly maintained, the 8-speeds have some very serious internal problems to the point that class-action lawsuits have been filed against General Motors on these transmissions. The 6- and 10-speeds are a far better swap choice over the 8-speed.

10LXX

This is the newest transmission to be fitted to the Gen V LT-series engine, and it is a collaborative effort between Ford and General Motors. This transmission has been used in GM vehicles since 2018, supporting 650 hp worth of power handling in the 10L90 version, and 425 hp in the 10L80.

Shifts are incredibly smooth, much better than with the beleaguered 8-speed. There are three overdrive gears: 0.854, 0.689, and 0.636. This can be felt when driving 80 mph and punching the throttle to pass a car. You feel it drop a gear, pull hard, and you never really feel the upshift. It is *that* smooth.

This transmission is a radical departure from traditional automatic architecture. There are two hydraulic pumps, neither of which are integrated into the main input shaft, which reduces the size of the transmission. These two pumps allow the vehicle to shut down the engine for the "Auto-Stop" feature. Fuel economy is about the same compared to the 8-speed, but the shifts are much smoother and fluid, and acceleration is a little quicker.

8LXX

The Gen V LT engine is controlled by an electronic control module (ECM), and the transmission requires a separate controller. The two units talk to each other to operate efficiently. The 8-speed 8L90 Supermatic was a great idea, but the execution was flawed. The transmission performs so poorly that General Motors has been sued via class-action lawsuit over the horrendous operation of the 8-speed transmission. There are aftermarket companies that offer swap components for the 8-speed, but it is a risk.

General Motors has issued no less than 60 technical service bulletins (TSBs) on how to fix the inherent issues with the 8L90, but they often do not fix the problem. The transmission can buck wildly at low speeds, have heavy double-clunking in reverse to the point of breaking the rear differential, and shudder when cruising at part throttle. The 2017-and-newer 8LXX transmissions claimed to be fixed, but we have seen the same issues in these transmissions as well. Some swappers have successfully used these units in their swaps without issue, but it is a risk. There are better options that are safer.

6LXX

In 2006, General Motors released a couple of 6-speed automatics for its vehicles. The 6L80 and 6L90 transmissions are used in heavy-duty GM trucks and most of the performance cars. The Sigma platform, which covers the Cadillac CTS line, uses either the 5L40/5L50 5-speed or the 6L45/6L50 6-speed automatic. All LT-series vehicles use the 6LXX series of automatic transmission.

These transmissions are very stout and will perform well under most conditions, although the cases are quite large and do not fit in most passenger cars with a stock transmission tunnel. The 6L90 can handle up to 555 hp in passenger cars. In a truck, the weight reduces handling to 452 hp, and torque limits range from 530 to 550 ft-lbs. Both units are fully electronically controlled and can be tuned with programs such as HP Tuners.

The downside to the 6LXX transmissions is the longevity. These transmissions can last 200,000 or more miles, but they have a really bad habit of destroying themselves around 120,000 to 150,000 miles. This is due to a torque-convertor issue where the clutch in the convertor breaks down, sending shrapnel through the transmission, eventually killing the pump and the transmission. This can be mitigated by changing the fluid before the unit hits 100,000 miles and then every 50,000 miles or so.

It is very important with any of the GM 6LXX units to regularly check and maintain the fluid levels and flush the transmission fluid system. They will last in most cases if this is done, but buying a used 6LXX with over 130,000 miles is a serious risk. If you do, flush it before putting any road time on.

The flush procedure is not just adding a can of transmission flush in the fluid. It requires connecting the fluid system to a transmission-flushing machine that cycles the fluid without running the engine for 48 hours, draining, and refilling the transmission with new fluid. This is typically done at a transmission service shop. This is highly recommended for all GM 6LXX transmissions.

Older GM Automatics

4LXX transmissions that were built for LS-platform engines will bolt directly to an LT-series engine, provided that the right flexplate is used. The LT-series flexplate uses eight bolts instead of six, so they will not swap over. This is crucial.

Bolting an older SBC-based transmission to an LS/LT engine requires specialized spacers and flexplates because the Gen III–V engines are

The 4LXX series is the simplest option that fits in most applications without floor-pan modifications, and it bolts to the engine with ease. This is a 4-speed transmission that uses a transmission controller for tunable upgrades. The 4L60s get a bad rap for not being strong, but that is mostly due to people abusing them. There are two main types: SBC-based and LS-based. SBC-based 4LXX transmissions have an integral bellhousing (right), while the LS-based units are longer and have a removable bellhousing. Specific flexplates and torque convertors are required for each style. Go for the 4L80 if you have 600-plus hp.

The bellhousing pattern on LS engines is different from the SBC—but only in that it is missing a bolt location on the LS. An SBC bellhousing will bolt up, so older transmissions can be used with these engines.

For LT engines, the upper center bolt is shifted slightly to the passenger's side, and it is missing the second bolt to the passenger's side (like the LS).

The flexplate on the right is the adapter plate, which allows you to bolt up an early-style torque converter. The unit on the left is the stock unit. Note the dish on the stock flexplate. This is another reason that you must use an adapter flexplate for older transmissions.

shorter. If an old-style converter is simply bolted to an LS/LT engine without a spacer, it will have major problems after only a few miles of driving. The pump seal would be ruined and start to leak, causing the pump to fail. This is due to the fact that the converter won't center on the back of the crank because it does not fit.

To make up the difference, a special conversion flexplate or spacer is required. Both LS/LT engines require this. General Motors as well as many aftermarket companies offer the spacers and longer bolts over the counter. TCI has conversion flexplates for automatic transmissions and kits that include the spacer and longer bolts. A crankshaft spacer is needed, such as one from Hughes Performance, TCI, or GM, or a custom converter must be made with a longer crank hub. Bowtie Overdrives introduced its LS-swap torque converter that eliminates the need to use a spacer—it bolts directly to the stock flexplate.

This flexplate adapter from TCI allows the use of an older GM automatic transmission with a Gen III or Gen IV engine. It also provides SFI certification in case you want to go racing. This flexplate does not require a hub adapter. (Photo Courtesy TCI)

Adapting the non-electronically controlled 700-R4 and 200-4R requires a little more work. The most important component of these two overdrive transmissions is the throttle valve (TV) cable. This crucial system tells the transmission when to shift and determines the amount of pressure sent to the clutches. If this cable is off even the slightest amount, the clutches will not fully

When using an older transmission with an LS engine, an adapter ring (such as this one) is needed. This slips over the crank hub and spaces out the flexplate to accommodate the difference in interface depth for older transmissions.

The crank of the LT engines requires an adapter ring for older automatic transmissions. This one from ICT Billet fits into the crank and provides the correct spacing and diameter for the torque-convertor hub.

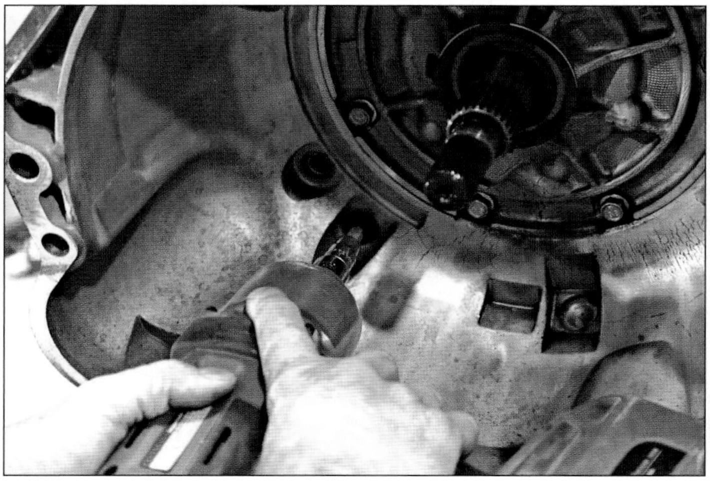

There is a specific LT bellhousing for automatic transmissions, although the SBC or LS unit still works. We removed the original from the 4L65 so that we could swap the new LT-specific bellhousing to the transmission.

The new LT bellhousing is on the left, and the LS bellhousing is on the right. The only difference we found is the additional bolt hole on the bottom left of the LT, which is actually the top left of the transmission. This is a universal housing that works for both LS and LT engines.

We installed the new bellhousing using the original bolts and torqued them to 48 to 55 ft-lbs.

An often-overlooked spec is which side of the flexplate goes to the engine side. It will be printed or etched into the steel. If you do this wrong, it won't go together.

Always use new bolts for the flexplate, as these are one-time-use torque-to-yield bolts. However, if you are upgrading to ARP reusable bolts, then there is no problem. Use medium-strength threadlocker on them.

The torquing process is 133 in-lbs on the first pass, 22 ft-lbs on the second pass, and a 45-degree turn on the final pass. Use a torque-angle gauge on the last torquing.

engage, causing the transmission to burn up and eventually fail.

Adapting the TV cable to the throttle body on an LS engine is challenging, and you need to maintain the right geometry. Doing this would require in-depth knowledge of the TV cable system, and it is not suggested for novices. There are a couple of aftermarket manufacturers, such as Bowtie Overdrives, that offer bolt-on solutions for TV cable–to–throttle body conversions.

Another viable alternative to this complicated problem is the TCI transmission valve body that removes the pressure regulation from the TV system. This valve body keeps the transmission at full-line pressure all the time, ensuring the clutches won't burn up from slipping. The TV cable is then relegated to serve as a speed control for shift points only. Fabricating a mount for the TV cable with the precision of the original style is no longer needed, making it much easier.

Many of the Gen III and Gen IV LS-series engines found in the salvage yards, swap meets, and internet sales sites already have a transmission attached. In most cases, the transmission will be an automatic. The most common GM automatic is the 4L60E or the 4L65E variant (they are the same dimensionally, but the 65 version has an extra pinion gear internally), whether the engine came from a car or a truck. The larger Vortec engines were typically mated to the 4L80E and 4L85E variant automatic transmission.

These transmissions require computer controls that are contained in the factory ECM. They can also be purchased separately through the aftermarket for carbureted LS conversions or when an aftermarket EFI controller is used.

In most cases, an adjustable shifter arm is needed for the transmission. These come with most aftermarket shifters or can be bought as accessories. This allows you to get the shifter in the car to match the detents on the transmission. If these don't match, bad things happen.

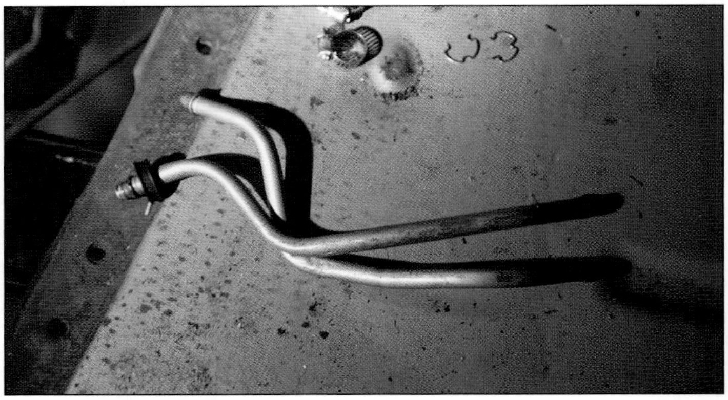

Automatic transmissions require cooling the fluid, and modern 4LXX-and-newer units have push-lock fittings such as these. You can cut the stock line and flare the end for a cheap solution.

These lines just push into the special fittings on the transmission and lock in place with a little spring clip.

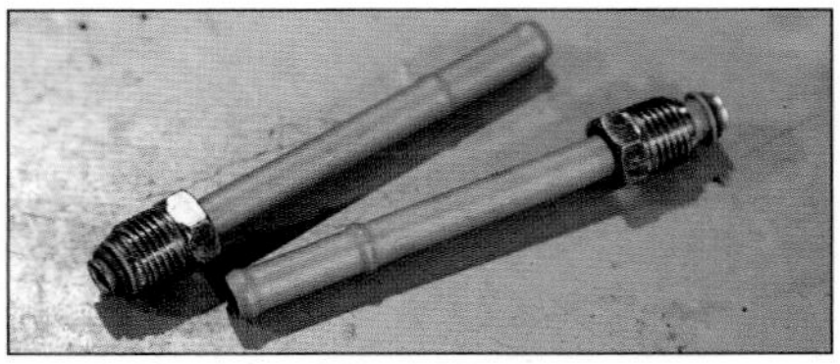

Another solution is a set of these thread-in adapters. The transmission needs inverted flare O-ring fittings, otherwise it will leak.

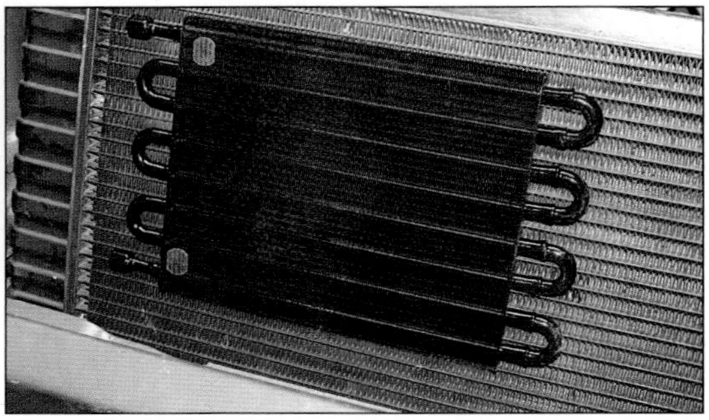

If the radiator does not have a built-in cooler, add one (such as this) to the front of the radiator. An internal cooler in the radiator is better, as it maintains the temperature more consistently than an external cooler.

Manual Transmissions

The most commonly used manual transmission for any swap is the Tremec T56 6-speed. This is a Magnum T56 that was rebuilt by American Powertrain. The other 6-speed is the TR6060, which has an integral bellhousing.

Mating a T56 to a 5.3L LT engine requires a 3/8-inch spacer. Without it, you get a giant split on the back of the engine block. The crankshaft is not machined for an input shaft on all 5.3L Gen V engines.

Using the spacer requires adding longer dowels in the transmission case. This conversion to the spacer plate is a semi-permanent install.

The 6-speed T56 manual is the most popular transmission used in LS/LT engine swaps. Formerly offered with LS engines in the 1998–2002 F-Body and GTO, the T56 bellhousing, flywheel, and clutch pack are readily available. Later-model T56 units and subsequent TR6060s use a hydraulically actuated clutch, while the earlier 1993–1997 T56 units use an external-clutch slave cylinder. The later 1998-and-newer units use an internal slave cylinder.

The 1998-and-newer T56 transmission is better suited for the Gen III–V engines with the correct bolt pattern and input shaft. McLeod offers components that will adapt older T56 transmissions to the later engines. Early T56 transmissions (1993–1999 LT1-compatible units) can be converted to mate to an LS or 2014-and-newer Gen V LT-series engine with a different input shaft. The input shaft is fairly simple to change.

While the T56 is traditionally the favored 6-speed manual gearbox, Tremec has replaced it with an updated version. Actually, there are two versions: the Super Magnum T56 which is the best option available in the aftermarket and Chevrolet Performance, and the TR6060.

The Super Magnum T56 is capable of managing 700 ft-lbs of torque. The gearing is set at 2.66, 1.78, 1.3, 1.00, 0.80, and 0.63 dual overdrive. This will hit your wallet pretty hard, at more than $4,500. However, it is the strongest 6-speed manual.

The T56060 is essentially an original T56 case with some beefier gears. Those larger guts take up a lot of room. Because the case had to stay the same size, the extra room had to be taken from somewhere. The result leaves a little to be desired from the TR6060. Tremec's solution was to use smaller synchronizers. They are very fragile, and grinding the gears even once can wreck the synchro for that gear.

Eventually, the synchro will be completely useless, and the gears themselves will start burning up. Because of this, the TR6060 is not the best candidate for an LS swap. It will certainly function, but be aware that these transmissions are prone to

We had to use a slide hammer with Vise-Grips welded on to remove the dowel. Either buy this tool or make it like we did.

To keep the spacer lined up, we installed a few bolts in the case to secure the spacer in position.

Then, we drove the dowels in with a small sledge hammer. Be careful, as you do not want to mushroom the dowel, but it does take some effort to install these dowels.

There are two types of pilot bushings for LS/LT engines. This is the larger LS7-style bushing, which sits in the rear-most cavity of the crank. The early-style bearing is much smaller and sits on the inner ring of the crank.

It is a press-fit, so use a large socket or a bearing driver to tap it into the crank.

On the Gen V 5.3L cranks, the crank bore is not quite sized correctly, so we used a modified cylinder hone to clean up the inner surface so that the bearing would press in.

failure. If using a TR6060 in your swap, make sure to use Red Line D4 automatic transmission fluid or Royal Purple SynchroMax. These oils have been reported to reduce cold-shift grinding and provide better overall shifting feel for the TR6060.

Hydraulic Clutch System

Adapting a manual clutch pedal to operate a hydraulic system is simple. Adapt the factory pedal to operate a firewall-mounted master cylinder to control the hydraulic release bearing in the transmission. If you are not using a factory clutch pedal, American Powertrain offers a complete kit to swap in its Hydramax release bearing system into a C10.

The American Powertrain unit keeps the master cylinder under the dash for a clean firewall. Just run the lines to the transmission, which can be done inside the cab, so there are not even any lines in the engine bay. The American Powertrain kits are available for 1960–1994 C10s, and they are available in complete kits for T56 and TKO TKX 5-speeds or just the pedal component without the Hydramax release bearing.

Hydramax Hydraulic Bearing

The Hydramax hydraulic bearing uses a stack of shims to set the depth of the bearing. This allows for a perfect mesh for the clutch diaphragm. The hydraulics are relatively simple to install. The kit comes with a Wilwood master cylinder and can be bolted directly to the firewall where the stock pushrod comes through. The supplied bracket for the master cylinder is adjustable for the angle.

Using the stock pushrod linkage hole will increase the pedal effort on the clutch. By raising the pickup point on the pedal, the effort needed to disengage the clutch will be greatly reduced. This is called pedal ratio, which is the difference in length between the pivot (fulcrum) of the pedal to the pushrod hole (Y) and the fulcrum to the center of the brake pedal (X).

A hydraulic master system should be between 5:1 and 7:1. Consider this: a master cylinder with a 1-inch bore and a pedal ratio of 6:1 with 100 pounds of pedal pressure yields 600 pounds of pressure at the master cylinder. Cut that pedal ratio to 4:1, and the pressure at the master drops to just 400 pounds. That is a significant difference and increases your effort by 33 percent. You can use the stock hole in the stock pedals, but it will absolutely be more difficult to operate.

Installing a Hydraulic Clutch System

1 *The T56 requires using a hydraulic clutch bearing, such as this Hydramax kit from American Powertrain. It is the simplest version and works like butter.*

2 *Install the base slide for the release bearing onto the transmission input shaft. The silver post is the locating pin. You need the longest one for this application.*

Installing a Hydraulic Clutch System *continued*

3 *Next, the release bearing is lubricated with some DOT3 brake fluid. This keeps things sliding like they need to.*

4 *Then, slide the bearing over the locating post and the main slide.*

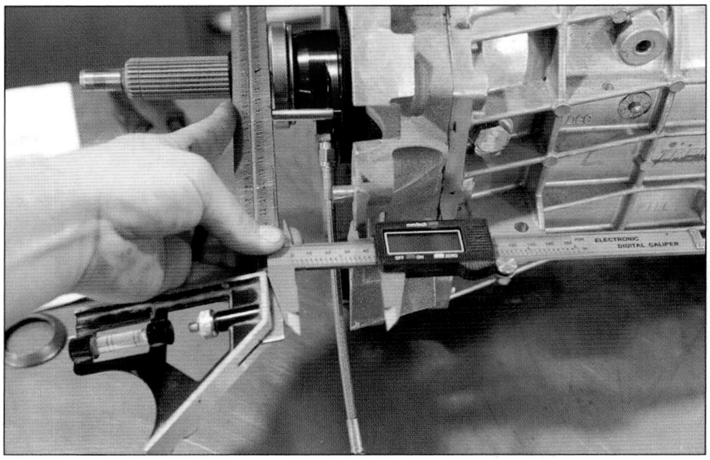

5 *Now is the tricky part. Using a straightedge and a set of calipers, measure the spacing from the bellhousing flange on the transmission to the end of the release bearing. We did this three times at three different places (3, 9, and 12 o'clock) and averaged the measurements. This is measurement B.*

6 *Install the American Powertrain clutch and pressure plate to the flywheel using some new ARP bolts. Don't forget to use the required clutch-alignment tool. Note the gold spacer on the back of the engine block—this is required, do not forget it.*

7 *Next, install the QuickTime bellhousing to the block. This is an LS bellhousing; it is not LT-specific.*

8 *Using the straightedge and calipers, take three more measurements at three different positions on the bellhousing to the fingers of the diaphragm. These are averaged as well.*

9 ***Do the math. We determined that we needed six spacers between the bearing and the slider post. Before mating the engine and transmission together for the final time, make sure the feed line and the purge line are fully installed on the bearing. It is really difficult to install it once the engine and transmission are together.***

10 ***You can use a hydraulic release bearing on older transmissions too, such as this M21 Muncie with a Hydramax bearing from American Powertrain.***

Manual Clutch Linkage

It is possible to adapt an LS/LT engine to use a manual clutch linkage. If installing an LS/LT and manual transmission in a GM vehicle originally available with a manual clutch setup, linkage, clutch, Z-bar, and related components are needed. The Gen III–V blocks are not drilled for the Z-bar, which makes it difficult to adapt the LS engine to a manual linkage. Fabricating a simple bracket that locates off the bellhousing bolts and attaches to the Z-bar is the best solution.

Another popular manual swap is the 5-speed Tremec TKO 500 or TKO 600, and the newest version: the TKX. These 5-speed manual transmissions are very popular among the GM muscle builders and offer excellent performance. American Powertrain offers complete kits for installing the TKO (and T56) for C10 trucks. These kits feature hydraulic clutches, the bellhousing, and all of the components to make the installation simple and easy. The TKO transmissions use a top-mounted shifter as well.

The new Tremec TKX was designed specifically for the aftermarket; it is not installed as a factory transmission in any vehicle. It was created to fit in more vehicles without floor-pan modifications and is more compact. Power handling is 600 ft-lbs of torque, and it can handle 8,000 rpm and shift at 7,500 rpm. There are three shifter locations and a single 0.68 overdrive. This transmission fits all GM C10 trucks.

For 1960–1972 trucks that did not come with a 4-speed manual from the factory, the transmission hump is too short. They need either the tall factory hump, a custom-built one, or an aftermarket hump, such as the fiberglass unit sold by American Powertrain.

Stock Manual Gearbox

For reasons varying from nostalgia, economy, personal taste, simplicity, or originality, some builders prefer to keep the stock manual gearbox in the truck when swapping in a Gen V LT-series engine. These swaps bolt up similarly to the automatic transmissions, but they require a few specialized pieces. There are a few ways to do this swap as well.

The input shaft is too far from the crank with a stock bellhousing, which is the same situation as with the pre-LS automatic transmissions. There are two ways to remedy this problem. The first and best way is to use a retrofit bellhousing and flywheel package. General Motors sells these components individually through its GMPP dealers, such as Pace Performance. The GMPP retrofit bellhousing features thick-wall titanium-aluminum alloy construction and CNC machining, including spot-faced mounting holes, precision dowel-pin holes, and bores that yield a precise fit.

This bellhousing bolts to all GM Gen V LT-series V-8 engines for the installation of the Muncie, T-10, Saginaw, Richmond, Tremec TKO, Tremec T56-011, and other specially built transmissions. This bellhousing works with stock clutch linkage and hydraulic-clutch actuators. It includes a steel inspection cover and mounting hardware, and it is designed to use a 168-tooth flywheel and standard GM starter. This bellhousing is lightweight, weighing only 15 pounds, and uses all factory linkage parts, including clutch forks, Z-bar, rubber dust boot, etc. According to GMPP, you must use the LS truck flywheel (part number 12561680), 12-inch clutch and pressure plate (part number RAM88744), and six metric pressure-plate bolts (part number 12561465).

621 BBC Bellhousing

An original big-block Chevy manual bellhousing can also be used instead of buying a new one. The specific part needed is the 621 big-block Chevy (BBC) bellhousing. This will fit C/K truck chassis and the LS engine without issue. The SBC and truck bellhousings have clearance issues. The flywheel will need to fit the LS and have a standard SBC clutch bolt pattern. A PRW conversion flywheel (part number 1634680) works well for this swap. For the pilot bearing, the LS7 bearing (part number 12557583) fits the LS flywheel. It costs less than the extended conversion bearings and works just as well.

The clutch depends on which transmission is being used. There are 10- and 26-spine input shafts. Make sure to have the right clutch for the transmission. Beyond that, any SBC clutch will work, provided that the flywheel has the SBC clutch pattern. The 26-spline transmissions can use a stock truck LS manual flywheel with a matching LS clutch.

If you are using the conversion flywheel, the stock length (1.25-inch) throw-out bearing works great. For stock flywheel and clutch combinations, an extended throw-out bearing is required. General Motors offers a

Bolting the Muncie to this LS1 is pretty simple. We are even using the stock bellhousing for the Muncie.

The T56 has several electrical connections that are important. On the passenger-side front is the reverse light switch.

On the passenger-side rear below the shifter is the vehicle speed sensor (VSS) for an electronic speedometer.

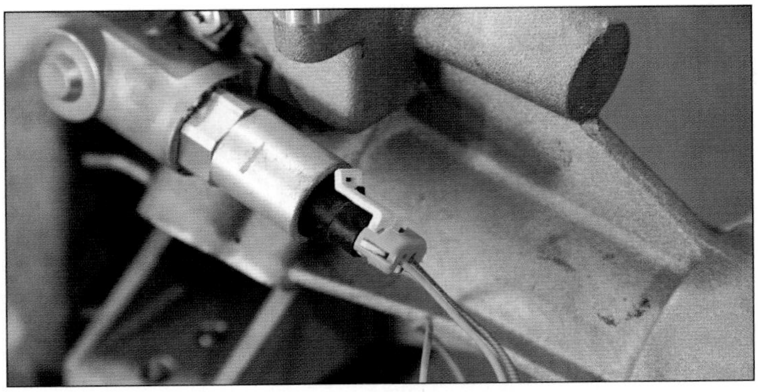

On the driver's side below the shifter is the reverse lockout solenoid. This must be connected to make reverse shifts easier. There is a special control box from American Powertrain that makes this safe. Otherwise, you could end up hitting reverse by mistake, and that would be bad.

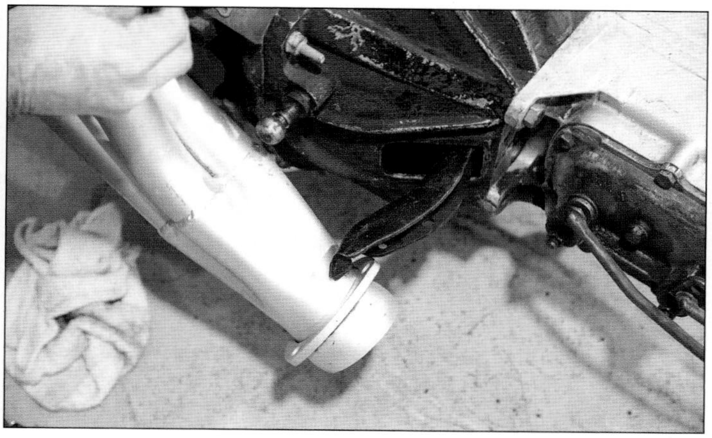

If using a mechanical release, there can be some interference issues (like this). Most LS/LT headers sweep back along the bellhousing, which causes issues for the clutch fork.

LS/LT engines do not have pivot points on the block, so use a bellhousing with a pivot. Even then, the stock manifolds get in the way. It is best to use a hydraulic release bearing.

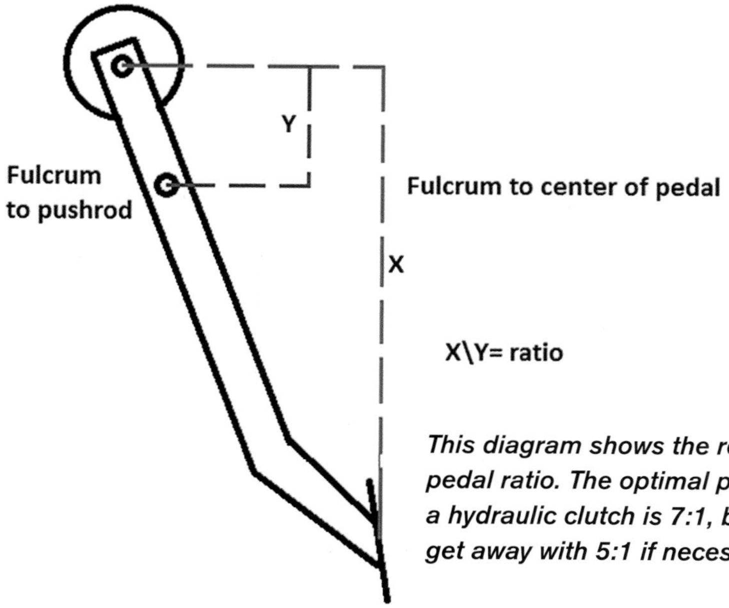

This diagram shows the relationship for pedal ratio. The optimal pedal ratio for a hydraulic clutch is 7:1, but you can get away with 5:1 if necessary.

1.75-inch-length bearing (part number PT614037) for these applications. This will require using the stock mechanical pushrod clutch linkage.

Aftermarket Versions

Aftermarket versions of these parts in complete kit from are available from McLeod and Advance Adapters. These clutch kits are designed to adapt the Gen III–V engines to early-style GM manual transmissions, such as the M21/M22, SM420, SM465, and NV4500. Additionally, these kits allow the installation of Richmond Gear manual transmissions, such as the ROD 6-speed. The Advance Adapters clutch kits typically include a custom flywheel, 11-mm flywheel bolts, an 11-inch Centerforce pressure plate and disc, pilot bushing spacer, throw-out bearing, collector gasket, 10-mm bellhousing bolts, 10-mm lock washers, and XRP dowel bolts.

If you are assembling your own parts, the key is to match the flywheel and clutch to the engine, making sure the splines on the clutch disc match the transmission. GM transmissions use 10- and 26-spline input shafts, the early manuals (before 1971) typically have 10 splines, and the later units have 26 splines. With that being said, some other aftermarket manual transmissions have either 10 or 26 splines. The 26-spline shaft is more durable than a 10-spline shaft because it distributes the input load better.

The other option is to use an extended bearing. This option allows the use of the original old-style bellhousing. Match the clutch to the engine and use a longer bearing to make up the difference for the shorter crank flange. Several companies manufacture these bearings. McLeod (part number 8617) has an extended bearing, as does General Motors (part number 12557583). The old-style bellhousing should have a provision for the Z-bar and be able to run a manual clutch setup.

Transfer Case

If you are swapping an LS/LT into a 4WD truck, there is the transfer case to deal with. There are a few ways to do this, but it depends greatly on the year of the truck. All GM 4WD trucks with straight-axle front drives have right-hand-drop transfer cases. Because the differential is on the passenger's side of the truck, a passenger-side-drop transfer case must be used.

All GM 4WD trucks from 1960 through 1987 (1988 for SUVs) have straight-axle front drives. In 1988 (1989 for SUVs), the independent front suspension (IFS) front drive came out for 1/2-ton trucks. It wasn't until 1991 that the 3/4-ton and 1-ton trucks got the IFS system. On these trucks, the differential moved to the driver's side, meaning the transfer case switched to a left-hand drop. This is not interchangeable without changing to a straight axle on the 1988-and-newer 4WD trucks.

This matters because they are the only trucks that can use the factory LS/LT-series transfer cases. There are several different units depending on the year and model, but they are all left-hand drop. The real question here is what you want from your truck. Because there are so many variables when building a 4WD truck, it is impossible to cover all of the options here.

The simplest way to LS/LT swap a 1960–1987 K10 truck is to keep the original transmission and transfer case by adapting the engine to the transmission. This keeps the transmission and transfer case in the stock or current position. An LS/LT transfer case cannot be used in any GM truck with a straight axle—only 1988 and newer with IFS.

All GM 4WD trucks came with married transfer cases, meaning the transfer case is bolted directly to the transmission body. They are part of the transmission. There are options here; they are just not as simple as keeping the original driveline. For 1960–1987 trucks, the options are switch to a divorced transfer case split, use your original (or currently used) transfer case from the original transmission, or use an adapter to bolt it to a 4WD late-model transmission. There are benefits to each option.

A divorced transfer case allows you to use any transmission. This can be done multiple ways, including using an aftermarket Atlas transfer case. You simply build an intermediate driveshaft to connect the two units. Off-roaders and rock crawlers love a divorced case because it allows adjustment for driveline angles, and this is especially important for large lifts. The drawback is that it requires a lot more fabrication.

Adapting a current transfer case to a newer transmission requires specialty parts. Advance Adapters is the main supplier for these kits, which cover most GM transmissions, including 4LXX, 6LXX, and 8LXX. The 10-speed 10LXX is a little too new to have any adapters at this time. Most of the late-model transmission support for transfer case adapters covers the 4LXX and 6LXX models.

The adapters are fairly pricey, currently between $650 and $800, but it is a relatively simple solution. In this situation, you will need either rear-biased or adjustable motor-mount adapters to ensure than the engine is mounted where the transmission can be bolted to the transfer case.

If you are swapping a 1988–1998 GMT400 truck with 4WD, then the newer transfer cases can be used. In 2007, General Motors switched from the New Venture transfer cases to Magna Powertrain MP units. There are three models: manual shift (NQG), electric shift (NQF), and auto (NQH). The manually shifted transfer case is relatively simple to swap—just mount a shifter for the transfer-case controls.

The electric models are a bit tougher. Until recently, there was no good way to swap these units without a lot of electrical knowledge. However, someone has figured it out and is now making a wiring kit. Swap Time USA has developed a wiring harness and module to control the NQH and NQF. This harness comes with a modified control module, a control knob to mount in the dash, and the required wiring harness for the transfer case.

The 2007-and-newer transfer cases fit quite well into the 1988–1998 trucks. In fact, the entire driveline (engine, transmission, and transfer case) can be loaded into the chassis at once without removing the transfer case, which is something that is very difficult to do with the factory transfer case.

In the case of the 1991 1500 that is featured in this book, we used a set of Holley LT-swap engine mounts with the rearward bias. These mounts allow for the entire drivetrain to swap into the chassis without any modification to the crossmembers. The transmission crossmember bolted into the factory location and met up with the new 6-speed transmission. It even allowed the use of the original 1991 rear driveshaft and the 2018 front driveshaft to the front axle. The original 1991 front driveshaft is not compatible with the 2007-and-newer transfer case, as the newer transfer case uses a slip yoke, and the 1991 transfer case used a bolt-on flange mount.

CHAPTER 6

Wiring a C10 LS/LT Swap

The wiring stage is the most complex and frustrating component of any LS/LT swap. No matter how you go after this part of the build, there are complexities that must be dealt with to make the engine run in your truck. Some swaps are more complicated than others, but all LS/LT engines require a complete engine harness and ECM of some type.

While most swap enthusiasts are familiar with fabrication and problem solving, the anxiety level reaches its peak even for seasoned builders when it comes to wiring. Do not be afraid, as this is a tamable beast. From giving a factory harness a "wire diet" to installing an aftermarket harness, this chapter will help you get through the spaghetti and back to eating asphalt in no time.

LS/LT engines have a lot of wires, especially in stock form. This is the complete 2018 Silverado L83 engine with its original wiring harness. We need to remove the harness to send it to standaloneharness.com to redo it for us.

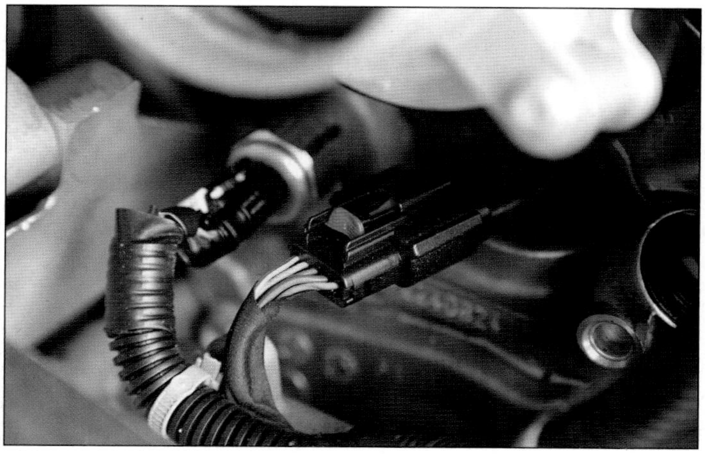

These plugs can get a little brittle, but moreover, each plug has a little locking tab that is perfect for breaking fingernails off. A small screwdriver or a pick is a big help.

LS Engine Harness Considerations

LS engines have a few options based on the year and trim level of the vehicle. Some of these parameters can be changed easily, and some are more invasive. These will be discussed in greater detail later, but the basics are throttle actuation (cable versus wire), crank sensor type (24 versus 48 tooth), cam sensor location, oxygen sensors, and MAF sensor.

If you are using a take-out engine, make sure to get every possible component from the donor vehicle. This includes the wiring harness, the ECM, the underhood fuse/relay box, the throttle pedal and TAC module (if equipped), the air intake with the MAF sensor, and the oxygen sensors.

These engines have many grounds, but don't cut them. Just unbolt them and put the bolt back where it came from for safekeeping. If even one ground is missed, strange issues will plague the setup.

The newer transmissions, such as this 6L80, use a spin lock. As the lock ring rotates, it pushes the harness plug out of the terminal. Unlike the 8- and 10-speed transmissions, the transmission controller is built into the case. The 8- and 10-speed units have separate controllers.

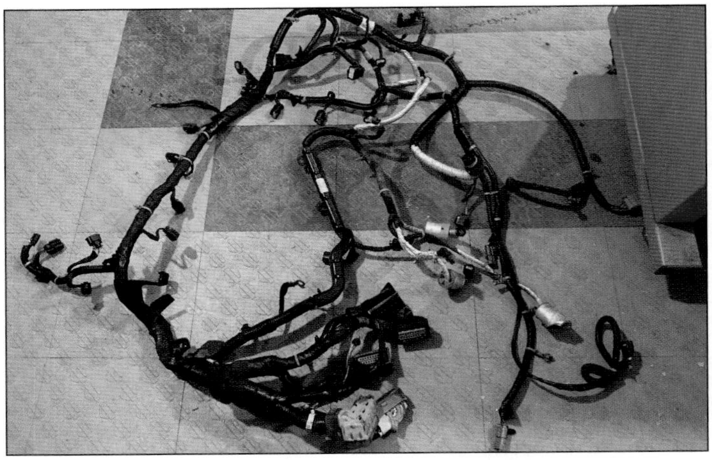

This is the stock L83 harness. If a plug breaks, don't stress because standaloneharness.com has replacements.

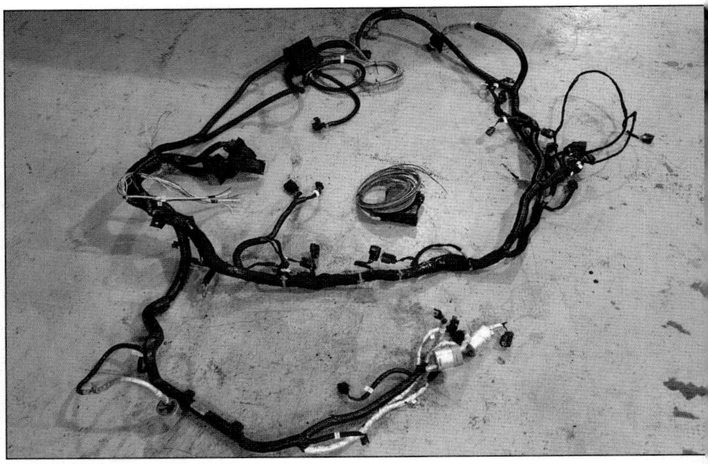

There is a reduction in wiring compared to the original. All the necessary components are here without extra wiring.

If you cannot get these items or you are using a crate or rebuilt engine, purchase these items new. This provides some options to match with the ECM and harness. The harness determines a lot of these items; as sensor connectors change, so must the plug on the harness.

Cam Sensor Locations

There are two locations for the cam sensor on LS engines. The Gen III engines use a rear-mounted cam sensor on the back of the block behind the intake. A long cam sensor reads the back of the camshaft. The later-model Gen IV engines use a different cam sensor mounted in the timing cover. It reads the cam position off of the timing gear. The placement is interchangeable, but the correct cam and gear are needed for your ECM.

Retrofitting the stock wiring harness is seemingly complex and perhaps overwhelming, but it really is not that difficult. With the proper diagrams and instructions, the stock wiring harness can be modified to greatly simplify the process of wiring the engine. The majority of the wires in the stock harness are not needed in a retrofit application. The following is a basic guideline for an LS1 stock retrofit wiring harness. There are more ways to skin this cat; this is just one of them. The pinout guide on page 83 is from a 1999 LS1.

1999–2000 LS1 PCM Plug 1

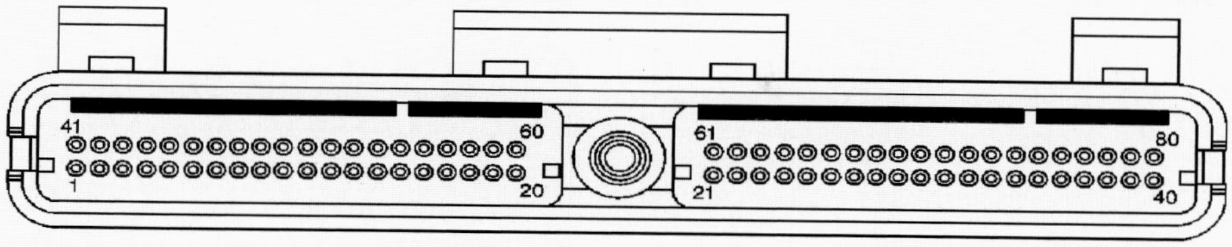

Connector Part Information	PCM Connector C1 Assembly 12191489		
	TPA (BLU) 12176408		
	Connector Cover 12191108		
Pin	**Wire Color**	**Circuit No.**	**Function**
1	BLK	451	PCM Ground
2	LT GRN	1867	Crankshaft Position Sensor B+ Supply
3	PNK/BLK	1746	Injector 3 Control
4	LT GRN/BLK	1745	Injector 2 Control
7	--	--	Not Used
8	GRA	596	TP Sensor 5V Reference
10	--	--	Not Used
11	LT BLU	1876	Knock Sensor Signal Rear
12	DK BLU/WHT	1869	Crankshaft Position Sensor Signal
13-16	--	--	Not Used
17	DK BLU	1225	Transmission Range Signal B
18	RED	1226	Transmission Range Signal C
19	PNK	439	Ignition Positive Voltage
20	ORN	340	Battery Positive Voltage
21	YEL/BLK	1868	Crankshaft Position Sensor Reference Low
22	--	--	Not Used
23	GRA	720	Fuel Tank Pressure Sensor/Fuel Tank Sender Ground
24	--	--	Not Used
25	TAN	1671	HO2S Signal Low Bank 2 Sensor 2
26	TAN	1667	HO2S Signal Low Bank 2 Sensor 1
27	--	--	Not Used
28	TAN/WHT	1669	HO2S Signal Low Bank 1 Sensor 2
29	TAN/WHT	1653	HO2S Signal Low Bank 1 Sensor 1
30-31	--	--	Not Used
32	GRY	48	Clutch Pedal Position Switch Signal
33	PPL	420	TCC Brake Switch
34	ORN/BLK	434	PNP Switch Signal
35	--	--	Not Used
36	BLK	1744	Injector 1 Control
37	YEL/BLK	846	Injector 6 Control
38-39	--	--	Not Used
40	BLK	451	PCM Ground
41	BLK	407	EGR Pintle Position Sensor Ground
42	DK GRN	335	Engine Cooling Fan Relay 1 Control
43	RED/BLK	877	Injector 7 Control
44	LT BLU/BLK	844	Injector 4 Control
45	GRA	474	A/C Refrigerant Pressure Sensor 5V Reference

Pin	Wire Color	Circuit No.	Function
46	GRA	474	Fuel Tank Pressure Sensor 5V Reference
47	GRA	416	EGR Pintle Position Sensor 5V Reference
48	GRA	416	MAP Sensor 5V Reference
49-50	--	--	Not Used
51	DK BLU	496	Knock Sensor Signal Front
52	--	--	Not Used
53	BLK	407	Transmission Temperature Sensor Ground
54	ORN/BLK	407	MAP Sensor Ground
55	BRN	1456	EGR Pintle Position Sensor Signal
56	--	--	Not Used
57	ORN	340	Battery Positive Voltage
58	DK GRN	1049	Serial Data
59	--	--	Not Used
60	BLK	452	TP Sensor Ground
61	PNK/BLK	632	Camshaft Position Sensor Reference Low
62-64	--	--	Not Used
65	PPL	1670	HO2S Signal High Bank 2 Sensor 2
66	PPL	1666	HO2S Signal High Bank 2 Sensor 1
67	--	--	Not Used
68	PPL/WHT	1668	HO2S Signal High Bank 1 Sensor 2
69	PPL/WHT	1665	HO2S Signal High Bank 1 Sensor 1
70	BRN	1174	Low Oil Level Switch
71-72	--	--	Not Used
73	BRN/WHT	633	Camshaft Position (CMP) Sensor Signal
74	YEL	410	Engine Coolant Temperature (ECT) Sensor Signal
75	--	--	Not Used
76	BLK/WHT	845	Injector 5 Control
77	DK BLU/ WHT	878	Injector 8 Control
78	--	--	Not Used
79	GRA or WHT	587 or 687	Skip Shift Solenoid Control (M/T) or 3-2 Shift Solenoid Control (A/T)
80	BLK	407	Engine Coolant Temperature (ECT) Sensor Ground

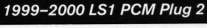

1999–2000 LS1 PCM Plug 2

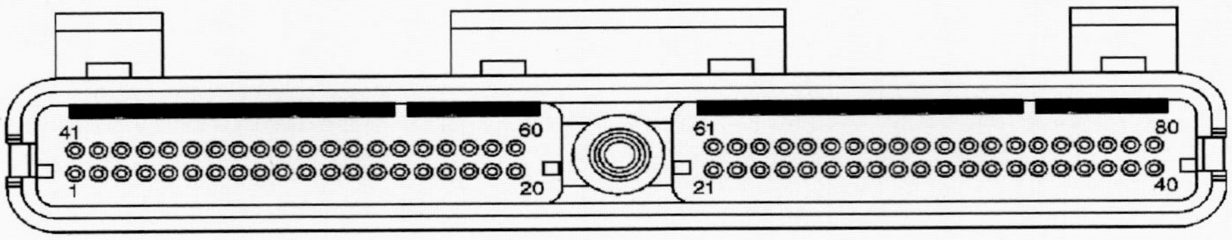

Connector Part Information		PCM Connector C2 Assembly 12191488	
		TPA (RED) 12176410	
		Connector Cover 12191108	
Pin	**Wire Color**	**Circuit No.**	**Function**
1	BLK	451	PCM Ground
2	BRN	418	TCC Control Solenoid
3	--	--	Not Used
4	PPL	421	AIR Solenoid Relay Control
5	--	--	Not Used
6	RED/BLK	1228	Transmission Fluid Pressure Control Solenoid High
7	RED	1676	EGR Control
8	LT BLU/ WHT	1229	Transmission Fluid Pressure Control Solenoid Low
9	DK GRN/ WHT	465	Fuel Pump Relay Control
10	WHT	121	Engine Speed (Tach) Output Signal
12	--	--	Not Used
13	WHT	85	Cruise Control Enable Signal
14	RED/BLK	380	A/C Refrigerant Pressure Sensor Signal
15	RED	225	Alternator L Terminal
16	--	--	Not Used
17	DK GRN/ WHT	762	A/C Request Signal
18	DK GRN	59	A/C Status Signal
19	--	--	Not Used
20	LT GRN/ BLK	822	Vehicle Speed Sensor (VSS) Reference Low
21	PPL/WHT	821	Vehicle Speed Sensor (VSS) Signal
22-23	--	--	Not Used
24	DK BLU	417	TP Sensor Signal
25	TAN	472	IAT Sensor Signal
26	PPL	2121	Ignition Control 1
27	RED	2127	Ignition Control 7
28	LT BLU/ WHT	2126	Ignition Control 6
29	DK GRN/ WHT	2124	Ignition Control 4
30	DK BLU	229	VTD Fuel Enable Signal
31	YEL	492	MAF Sensor Signal
32	LT GRN	432	MAP Sensor Signal
33	DK BLU	473	Engine Cooling Fan Relay 2 and 3 Control
34	DK GRN /WHT	428	EVAP Canister Purge Valve Control
35	--	--	Not Used
36	BRN	436	AIR Pump Relay Control
37	DK GRN	83	Cruise Control Inhibit
38	--	--	Not Used

Pin	Wire Color	Circuit No.	Function
39	RED	631	Camshaft Position Sensor B+ Supply
40	BLK	451	PCM Ground
41	GRA	435	EGR Position Sensor Ground
42	TAN/BLK	422	TCC Enable Circuit
43	DK GRN /WHT	459	A/C Clutch Relay Control
44	LT GRN	1652	Reverse Inhibit Solenoid Control
45	WHT	1310	EVAP Canister Vent Valve Control
46	BRN/WHT	419	Malfunction Indicator Lamp (MIL) Control
47	YEL/BLK	1223	Transmission Shift Solenoid B
48	LT GRN	1222	Transmission Shift Solenoid A
49	--	--	Not Used
50	DK GRN /WHT	817	Vehicle Speed Output Circuit
51	YEL/BLK	1227	Transmission Temperature Sensor Signal
52	--	--	Not Used
53	GRA/BLK	1687	Spark Retard Signal
54	PPL	1589	Fuel Level Sensor Signal
55-56	--	--	Not Used
57	PPL	719	IAT Sensor Ground
58-59	--	--	Not Used
60	BRN	2129	Ignition Control Reference Low Bank 1
61	BRN/WHT	2130	Ignition Control Reference Low Bank 2
62	--	--	Not Used
63	PNK	1224	Transmission Range Signal A
64	DK GRN	890	Fuel Tank Pressure Sensor Signal
65	--	--	Not Used
66	PPL/WHT	2128	Ignition Control 8
67	RED/WHT	2122	Ignition Control 2
68	DK GRN	2125	Ignition Control 5
69	LT BLU	2123	Ignition Control 3
70-75	--	--	Not Used
76	LT GRN/WHT	1749	IAC Coil B High
77	LT GRN/BLK	444	IAC Coil B Low
78	LT BLU/BLK	1748	IAC Coil A Low
79	LT BLU/WHT	1747	IAC Coil A High
80	--	--	Not Used

Factory ECM Pinouts

The factory pinouts changed over the years, so a complete guide would fill this book if we included them all. However, we are including a couple of the common early Gen III pinouts here.

The 1997–1998 LS1 wire harness is different from the 1999–2002 models, and the Vortec truck harnesses are different from that. These guidelines do not include wiring for AIR injection, AC, traction control, or cruise control.

The following guide is for 1997–1998 LS1 engines.

Connectors for 1997–1998 LS1 Engines

The 1997–1998 LS1 wire harness is different from the 1999–2002 models, and the Vortec truck harnesses are different from that. These guidelines do not include wiring for AIR injection, A/C, traction control, or cruise control. (Provided by LS1Tech.com & Daniel Polcyn)

Connector C100

Connector and Description

A. This is the power for the odd fuel injectors; route it to IGN 1 15A fuse
B. Not used
C. Not used
D. Not used
E. Not used
F. Not used
G. Engine control power; route to IGN 3 15A fuse
H. Cooling fan 2/high-speed relay; route to terminal 86 of cooling fan 2 relay
J. Cooling fan 1/low-speed relay; route to terminal 86 of cooling fan 1 relay
K. Not used

Connector C101

Connector and Description

A. Not used
B. Power for even coils; route to IGN 2 15A fuse
C. Not used
D. Output for fuel-pump relay; route to terminal 85 of fuel-pump relay
E. Computer power; route to IGN 4 15A fuse
F. Not used
G. Constant computer power; route to BAT 1 10A fuse
H. Not used
J. Not used
K. Not used

Connector C105

Connector and Description

A. Not used
B. Engine sensor power; route to IGN 5 20A fuse
C. Not used
D. Not used
E. Serial data signal; route into car to Data Link Connector terminal 9 (or OBDII port)
F. Not used
G. Not used
H. Not used

Connector C220

Connector and Description

A. Generator warning light negative (-) side. If your vehicle already has a generator light, it should plug in and work. If your vehicle had an internal regulated alternator, connect this to the wire that connected to terminal 1 on the alternator. If you need to add a generator light, wire this to one side of the light's terminals and the other side of the light's terminals to an ignition 12-volt fuse. The same wire with a 20-amp fuse can power all of the warning lights.
B. Oil-pressure output. If using the LS1 oil-pressure sender with the stock gauge, connect this wire to the oil-pressure gauge. The most common procedure is to use an aftermarket oil-pressure sending unit, and delete this wire. The same wire with a 20-amp fuse can power all warning lights.
C. Low-oil-level warning lamp ("–" output, this is a negative trigger). This one is also an optional accessory. If you want a low-oil light, attach this wire to one terminal of a light and the other to a 12-volt ignition source (fused, of course). The same wire with a 20-amp fuse can power all warning lights.
D. Not used
E. Not used
F. Not used
G. Vehicle speed sensor (VSS) output from computer. This is a 4,000-pulse-per-mile square-wave output: it works for GM electronic speedometers, as well as some aftermarket speedometers.
H. Not needed
J. Not needed
K. Temperature gauge output. This signal may work with older GM electronic temperature gauges, but it might not be as accurate. Most builders opt to install an aftermarket sending unit on the back of the block.

Connectors for 1997–1998 LS1 Engines CONTINUED

Connector C230

Connector and Description

A. Not used

B. This is the fabled "Service Engine Soon" light, and it is a negative trigger output. Route this wire to one terminal of a 12-volt lightbulb and the other terminal of the bulb to an ignition 12-volt fuse. The same wire with a 20-amp fuse can power all warning lights.

C. Not used

D. Tachometer output. This is a 4-cylinder, two-pulse-per-revolution output. The tach must be able to be set to 4-cylinder or be a compatible GM tachometer.

E. VATS (vehicle anti-theft system) fuel enable. This wire is not needed if the VATS has been deleted in the computer, or it could be retained and a VATS bypass box added for the extra security. Most builders remove the VATS system as it is not very user friendly.

F. Not used

G. Not used

H. To brake torque converter clutch switch. A switch that provides 12 volts to this wire must be provided when the vehicle is running. It cuts power when you press the brake pedal. There may be a cruise control switch that does this already, or one may have to be added. Adding a micro-switch (like those used in nitrous kits) from any electronics parts store will work. Build a small bracket to hold the switch behind the brake pedal lever so the switch is depressed when the pedal is at rest but opens when the brake pedal is pushed down. One terminal needs to be connected to 12-volt ignition power, and the other to this wire. This is only for automatics.

J. Park neutral position switch, negative trigger. If this switch is not wired, the vehicle is able to be started in gear, which is bad. The stock shifter may have this already. If not, one needs to be added. The process is the same as the brake converter switch above. The terminals are wired to ground instead of power. This is only for automatic transmission vehicles.

K. Serial data output to the diagnostic link connector (DLC) or OBDII connector terminal 2. This is for an OBDII port for engine diagnostics and tuning.

Relays for 1997–1998 LS1 Engines

Based on the use of 30-amp Bosch-style automotive relays, relays 1, 2, and 3 can be combined if you use one 80-amp relay. Keeping them separate simplifies any troubleshooting, plus 80-amp relays are expensive. (Provided by LS1Tech.com & Daniel Polcyn)

Relay 1

Terminal No. and Description

85 To conversion vehicle wiring (a wire that is hot in run and start modes). This wire is typically used to power the original coil. The ballast resistor must be removed.

86 To ground

30 Direct to battery voltage

87 To two 15A fuses (IGN 1 and IGN 2); route IGN 1 fuse to pin A of C100 connector, and IGN 2 fuse to pin B of C101 connector

Relay 2

Terminal No. and Description

85 To conversion vehicle wiring (a wire that is hot in run and start modes). This wire typically powers the original coil. The ballast resistor must be removed.

86 To ground

30 Direct to battery voltage

87 To two 15A fuses (IGN 3 and IGN 4); route IGN 3 fuse to pin G of C100 connector, and IGN 4 fuse to pin E of C101 connector

Relay 3

Terminal No. and Description

85 To conversion vehicle wiring (a wire that is hot in run and start modes). This wire is typically used to power the original coil. The ballast resistor must be removed.

86 To ground

30 Direct to battery voltage

Relays for 1997–1998 LS1 Engines CONTINUED

87 To one 20A fuse (IGN 5); route IGN 5 to pin B of connector C105

Relay 4 Fuel-Pump Relay

Terminal No. and Description

85 To pin D of connector C101
86 To ground
30 Direct to battery voltage
87 To one 20A fuse, then to the fuel pump

The cooling fans can use two relays or one, depending on the radiator fan setup. Two fans that run at the same time can be on one circuit, or the two fans can be wired to separate circuits, as with the factory unit. One fan functions as a low-speed fan while the other is a high-speed fan, which comes on in the event the engine is not cooling down. Use the low-speed fan relay if running only one fan.

Relay 5 Cooling Fan 1/Slow-Speed Fan

Terminal No. and Description

85 To conversion vehicle wiring (a wire that is hot in run and start modes). This wire is typically used to power the original coil. You must remove the ballast resistor.
86 To pin J of connector C100
30 Direct to battery voltage
87 To one 20A fuse or larger, depending on the cooling fan requirements

Relay 6 Cooling Fan 2/High-Speed Fan

Terminal No. and Description

85 To conversion vehicle wiring (a wire that is hot in run and start modes). This wire is typically used to power the original coil. The ballast resistor must be removed.
86 To pin H of C100 connector
30 Direct to battery voltage
87 To one 20A fuse or larger, depending on the cooling fan requirements

The last wire to connect is the starter wire. If the conversion vehicle is a GM model, this is a large purple wire. Simply route this to the starter solenoid.

Connectors for 1999–2002 LS1 Engines

The later 1999–2002 LS1 wiring harnesses are a little different because the connections are different and there are more circuits. The following is a basic guide to a later LS1 retrofit harness. Most of the wires are the same, although the placement might be different. This does not include wiring for traction control, cruise, or A/C. (Provided by LS1Tech.com & Daniel Polcyn)

Connector C100

Connector and Description

A. This is the power for the odd fuel injectors; route it to IGN 1 15A fuse
B. Not used
C. Not used
D. Not used
E. Not used
F. Not used
G. Engine control power; route to IGN 3 15A fuse
H. Cooling fan 2/high-speed relay; route to terminal 86 of cooling fan 2 relay
J. Cooling fan 1/low-speed relay; route to terminal 86 of cooling fan 1 relay
K. Not used

Connector C101

Connector and Description

A. Not used
B. Power for even coils; route to IGN 2 15A fuse
C. Not used
D. Output for fuel-pump relay; route to terminal 85 of fuel-pump relay
E. Computer power; route to IGN 4 15A fuse
F. Not used
G. Constant computer power; route to BAT 1 10A fuse
H. Ground this wire
J. Not used
K. Not used

Connectors for 1999–2002 LS1 Engines *CONTINUED*

Connector C105

Connector and Description

A. Not used
B. Engine sensor power; route to IGN 5 20A fuse
C. Not used
D. Not used
E. Not used
F. Not used
G. Tachometer output. This signal is a 4-cylinder, two-pulse-per-revolution output. The tach must be able to be set on 4-cylinder or be a compatible GM electronic tachometer.
H. Not used on a 1999. For a 2002 harness, this is the exhaust gas recirculation (EGR) valve. The EGR is typically bypassed for conversions.

Connector C220

Connector and Description

A. Oil-pressure output. This signal can be used for a GM electronic oil-pressure gauge. If it does not work, install an aftermarket sending unit.
B. Clutch pedal position switch on a 6-speed transmission. This is obviously not used on an automatic.
C. Power supply to torque converter clutch (TCC) stop lamp switch. This is not used in a 6-speed vehicle or if the vehicle already has a TCC stop switch. If the vehicle does not have a stop lamp switch, use this to feed power to the switch.
D. To brake torque converter clutch switch. There must be a switch that provides 12 volts to this wire when the vehicle is running and then cuts power when the brake pedal is depressed. There may be a cruise-control switch that does this already, or one may have to be added. Adding a micro-switch (such as those used in nitrous kits) from any electronics parts store works. Build a small bracket to hold the switch behind the brake pedal lever so the switch is depressed when the pedal is at rest but opens when the brake pedal is pushed down. One terminal needs to be connected to 12-volt ignition power, and the other to this wire. This is only for automatic transmissions
E. This wire must be grounded
F. Not used
G. Reverse light switch for 6-speed transmissions; not used in an auto
H. Park/neutral position switch, negative trigger. If this switch is not wired, the vehicle can be started in gear, which is bad. The stock shifter may have this already. If not, one needs to be added. The process is the same as the brake converter switch above. The terminals are wired to ground instead of power. This is only for automatic transmission vehicles.
J. Not used
K. VSS output from computer. This is a 4,000-pulse-per-mile square wave output; it works for GM electronic speedometers, as well as some aftermarket speedometers.

Connector C230

Connector and Description

A. Not used
B. This is the fabled "Service Engine Soon" light. This is a negative trigger output. Route this wire to one terminal of a 12-volt lightbulb and the other terminal of the bulb to an ignition 12-volt fuse. The same wire with a 20-amp fuse can power all of the warning lights.
C. Not used
D. Not used
E. VATS fuel enable. This wire is not needed if the VATS has been deleted in the computer, or it could be retained and a VATS bypass box added for the extra security. The best way is to delete VATS altogether.
F. Not used
G. Not used
H. Not used
J. Not used
K. Serial data output to DLC or OBDII connector terminal 2

Relays for 1999–2002 LS1 Engines

Based on the use of 30-amp Bosch-style automotive relays, relays 1, 2, and 3 can be combined with an 80-amp relay. However, keeping them separate simplifies any trouble-shooting, and 80-amp relays cost quite a bit. (Provided by LS1Tech.com & Daniel Polcyn)

Relay 1

Terminal No. and Description

85 To conversion vehicle wiring (a wire that is hot in run and start modes). This wire is typically used to power the original coil. The ballast resistor must be removed.
86 To ground
30 Direct to battery voltage
87 To two 15A fuses (IGN 1 and IGN 2); route IGN 1 fuse to pin A of C100 connector, and IGN 2 fuse to pin B of C101 connector

Relay 2

Terminal No. and Description

85 To conversion vehicle wiring (a wire that is hot in run and start modes). This wire is typically used to power the original coil. The ballast resistor must be removed.
86 To ground
30 Direct to battery voltage
87 To two 15A fuses (IGN 3 and IGN 4); route IGN 3 fuse to pin G of C100 connector, and IGN 4 fuse to pin E of C101 connector

Relay 3

Terminal No. and Description

85 To conversion vehicle wiring (a wire that is hot in run and start modes). This wire is typically used to power the original coil. The ballast resistor must be removed.
86 To ground
30 Direct to battery voltage
87 To one 20A fuse (IGN 5); route IGN 5 to pin B of connector C105

Relay 4 Fuel-Pump Relay

Terminal No. and Description

85 To pin D of connector C101
86 To ground
30 Direct to battery voltage
87 To one 20A fuse, then to the fuel pump

The cooling fans can use two relays or one, depending on the radiator fan setup. Two fans that run at the same time can be on one circuit, or the two fans can be wired to separate circuits, as with the factory unit. One fan functions as a low-speed fan while the other is a high-speed fan, which comes on in the event the engine is not cooling down. Use the low-speed fan relay if running only one fan.

Relay 5 Cooling Fan 1/Slow-Speed Fan

Terminal No. and Description

85 To conversion vehicle wiring (a wire that is hot in run and start modes). This wire is typically used to power the original coil. The ballast resistor must be removed.
86 To pin J of connector C100
30 Direct to battery voltage
87 To one 20A fuse or larger, depending on the cooling fan requirements

Relay 6 Cooling Fan 2/High-Speed Fan

Terminal No. and Description

85 To conversion vehicle wiring (a wire that is hot in run and start modes). This wire is typically used to power the original coil. The ballast resistor must be removed.
86 To pin H of C100 connector
30 Direct to battery voltage
87 To one 20A fuse or larger, depending on the cooling fan requirements

In order to tune the computer, you need a DLC or an OBDII port. These can be taken from any DLC- or OBDII-equipped vehicle; the salvage yards are full of them. They can be mounted anywhere inside the vehicle. The pins on the port are typically labeled 1 through 16, starting at the top left with 1, and proceeding sequentially with the bottom right pin being 16. The port should be wired as follows:

Pin 2: Serial Data line (purple)
Pin 4: Ground (black)
Pin 5: Ground (black/white)
Pin 9: DLC Serial Data Line
Pin 16: Constant 12 volts (not ignition) (orange)

LT Engine Harness Considerations

The Gen V LT engine family has a few more issues when it comes to the wiring harness than the LS series. For starters, the Gen V engines are all designed to use a pulse width modulation (PWM) fuel pump and cooling fans. Swappers cannot simply wire the ECM to a 12-volt fuel pump or cooling fan and expect it to work. In fact, doing so can cause major damage.

General Motors makes running changes to the wiring and sensors, so verify what plugs are on your engine harness before ordering sensors (if you don't get all of the sensors with the take-out engine). Just like the LS series, it is imperative to get all of the components possible from the donor vehicle. All Gen V engines are drive by wire, and the pedals are different among the truck and car harnesses, so pay attention to that.

Another concern for the LT-series engines is that none of the ECMs have transmission controllers built in. They are separate units, so if you are taking the transmission from the donor vehicle, get the transmission harness and transmission control module (TCM) as well.

Note that only 2014–2018 Gen V LT-series ECMs can be easily

Some plastic wire reliefs and guides were left in place. If you will change the accessory drive, these have to be removed.

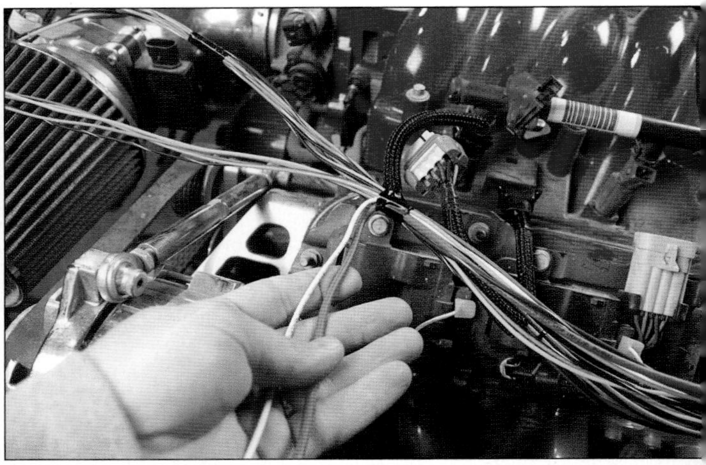

Some aftermarket harnesses require you to do all of the wire break-out and looming, such as this one. This gives th swapper more control over the routing and layout, which can be nice if you will be changing drives and sensors.

The traditional plastic wire loom tends to get old quickly, so we use PowerBraid from Painless Performance. It is clean, flexible, and easy to work with.

A pre-made harness, such as this one from Chevrolet Performance, makes this otherwise-daunting task easy. All of the terminations are made, and it even comes with an OEM fuel block. This is all OEM stuff packaged by General Motors for swaps.

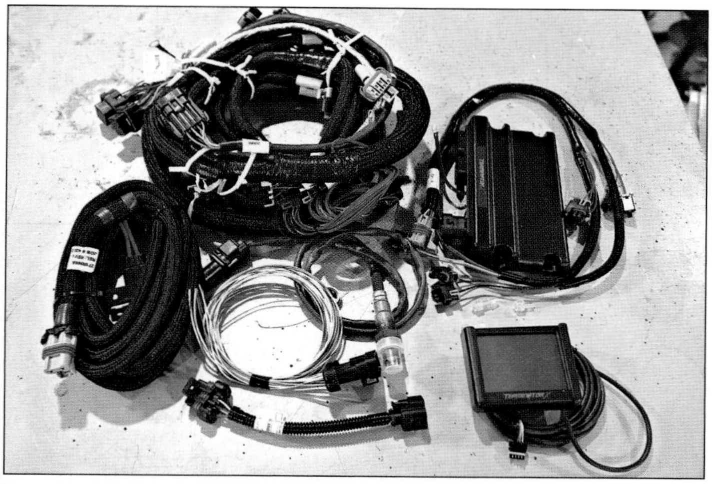

If you choose to forego using the factory ECM, the Holley Terminator ECM system is a great option. It simplifies the installation and tuning and comes with everything that is required.

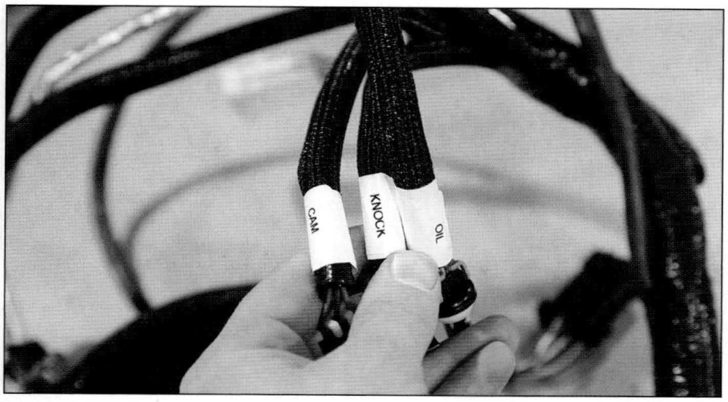

Most harnesses are labeled with the function of each terminal, but many retrofitters for stock harnesses don't label the terminals. Just match up the plugs.

reprogrammed. All 2019-and-newer Gen V ECMs have internal hardware that must be replaced to be used in a swap. It is possible to use an earlier ECM and harness with the correct sensors or an aftermarket ECM on 2019-and-newer engines. Otherwise, send the ECM to HP Tuners to be modified for tuning.

In most cases, the factory harness for Gen V LT-series engines can be retrofitted for a swap if the time is taken to give it a proper wire diet. However, the problem with this is that the plugs are quite brittle and break easily, so take great care when removing the factory plugs from the engine. If you are using an LT-series engine as a take-out from a vehicle, getting every piece from the donor vehicle is very helpful.

The following is the pinout for a 2014–2016 LT1, which is very similar to the L83/86 truck harness with a few exceptions, namely that the pedal and throttle-body reference and signal wires may be reversed.

The wiring harness calls for a brake-pedal-pressure switch, but on a swap, all you need to do is wire pin 57 white/d-blue (blue X1 plug) to the brake-light switch. Gen V ECMs need to see 12 volts with brakes applied, which is opposite of the Gen III and Gen IV engines. The brake-pedal sensor is not needed.

K20 Engine Control Module X1 (Blue)

Code	Color
BK	Black
BN	Brown
BU	Blue
D-BU	Dark Blue
GN	Green
D-GN	Dark Green
GY	Gray
RD	Red
PU	Purple (darker than violet)
WH	White
YE	Yellow
VT	Violet (lighter than purple)

PIN	Color	Function
1	Not occupied	–
2	D-BU/WH	Fuel Line Pressure Sensor Signal
3	Not occupied	–
4	YE/WH	Throttle Inlet Absolute Pressure Sensor Signal
5	WH/RD	Throttle Inlet Absolute Pressure Sensor 5V Reference
6	GN	AC Refrigerant Pressure Sensor Signal
7	Not occupied	–
8	BK/YE	Fuel Line Pressure Sensor Low Reference
9	D-BU/WH	Fuel Tank Pressure Sensor Signal
10	YE/RD	Fuel Tank Pressure Sensor 5 Volt Reference
11	Not occupied	–
12	Not occupied	–
13	D-BU/GY	Outside Ambient Air Temperature Sensor Signal
14	WH/RD	Accelerator Pedal Position 5 Volt Reference (1)
15	YE/WH	Accelerator Pedal Position Signal (1)
16	Not occupied	–
17	Not occupied	–

PIN	Color	Function
18	Not occupied	–
19	Not occupied	–
20	Not occupied	–
21	BN/RD	AC Pressure Sensor 5 Volt Reference
22	BK/BN	AC Refrigerant Pressure Sensor Low Reference
23	Not occupied	–
24	BN/RD	Fuel Line Pressure Sensor 5V Reference
25	D-BU/VT	Primary Fuel Level Sensor Signal
26	BK/GN	Fuel Level Sensor Low Reference
27	Not occupied	–
28	Not occupied	–
29	Not occupied	–
30	BK/D-BU	Accelerator Pedal Position Low Reference (1)
31	Not occupied	–
32	WH/GY	AC Compressor Clutch Relay Control
33	BN/RD	Accelerator Pedal Position 5 Volt Reference (2)
34	GN/WH	Accelerator Pedal Position Signal (2)
35	Not occupied	–
36	D-BU/BK	High-Speed GMLAN Serial Data (+)(3)
37	WH	High-Speed GMLAN Serial Data (-)(3)
38	WH	Fuel Temperature/Composition Signal
39	D-BU	High-Speed GMLAN Serial Data (+) (1)
40	WH	High-Speed GMLAN Serial Data (-) (1)
41	Not occupied	–
42	Not occupied	–
43	Not occupied	–
44	GY	Fuel Pump Controller Data Out Signal
45	Not occupied	–
46	BN/WH	Check Engine Indicator Control
47	WH	Brake Apply Sensor Supply Voltage (location has two wires)
47	GY/RD	Clutch Apply Sensor Voltage Reference
48	D-BU/YE	Brake Apply Sensor Signal (location has two wires)
48	YE	Clutch Apply Sensor Signal
49	Not occupied	–
50	Not occupied	–
51	VT/GN	Run/Crank Ignition 1 Voltage
52	RD/BN	Battery Positive Voltage
53	BK/PU	Accelerator Pedal Position Low Reference (2)
54	Not occupied	–
55	Not occupied	–
56	Not occupied	–
57	WH/D-BU	Cruise/ETC/TCC Brake Signal
58	Not occupied	–
59	BN/YE	High-Speed Cooling Fan Relay Control
60	YE/WH	Four-Wheel-Drive Wheel Lock Indicator
61	GY/BK	Four-Wheel-Drive Low Signal
62	VT/D-BU	Powertrain Main Relay Fused Supply (2)
63	YE/BK	Starter Enable Relay Control
64	Not occupied	–
65	Not occupied	–
66	WH	EVAP Canister Vent Solenoid Control
67	VT/D-BU	Powertrain Main Relay Fused Supply (3)
68	BK/BN	Brake Apply Sensor Low Reference (location has two wires)
68	BK/GY	Clutch Apply Sensor Low Reference
69	Not occupied	–
70	VT/YE	Accessory Wakeup Serial Data
71	Not occupied	–
72	YE	Powertrain Relay Coil Control
73	VT/D-BU	Powertrain Main Relay Fused Supply (1)

K20 Engine Control Module X2 (Black)

PIN	Color	Function
1	Not occupied	–
2	Not occupied	–
3	BK/GN	Fuel Rail Pressure Sensor Low Reference
4	Not occupied	–
5	GY/BK	Output Speed (Digital) 5V Sensor Reference
6	VT/WH	Vehicle Speed Sensor Signal
7	BK/GN	Vehicle Speed Sensor Low Reference
8	GN	Output Speed (Digital) Signal (location has two wires)
8	BN/WH	Output Speed High (Replicated TOS) Input Signal
9	Not occupied	–
10	VT/GY	Heated Oxygen Sensor High Signal Bank 1 Sensor (1)
11	VT/WH	Heated Oxygen Sensor High Signal Bank 2 Sensor (1)
12	VT/D-BU	Heated Oxygen Sensor High Signal Bank 1 Sensor (2)
13	VT/GN	Heated Oxygen Sensor High Signal Bank 2 Sensor (2)
14	Not occupied	–
15	GY/D-BU	Humidity Sensor Signal
16	BN/WH	Throttle Actuator Control Close
17	Not occupied	–
18	BN/RD	Fuel Rail Pressure Sensor (5) Volt Reference
19	D-BU/WH	Fuel Rail Pressure Sensor Signal

PIN	Color	Function
20	Not occupied	–
21	WH	Output Speed (Digital) 5V Sensor Return
22	Not occupied	–
23	GN/WH	Reverse Switch Signal
24	Not occupied	–
25	Not occupied	–
26	WH/BK	Heated Oxygen Sensor Low Signal Bank 1 Sensor (1)
27	YE/WH	Heated Oxygen Sensor Low Signal Bank 2 Sensor (1)
28	WH/YE	Heated Oxygen Sensor Low Signal Bank 1 Sensor (2)
29	YE/D-BU	Heated Oxygen Sensor Low Signal Bank 2 Sensor (2)
30	Not occupied	–
31	Not occupied	–
32	YE	Throttle Actuator Control Open
33	Not occupied	–
34	BN/RD	Throttle Position Sensor 5 Volt Reference
35	Not occupied	–
36	VT/GY	Knock Sensor Signal (1)
37	WH/GY	Knock Sensor Signal (2)
38	Not occupied	–
39	Not occupied	–
40	VT/D-BU	Crankshaft Position Sensor Replicated Signal
41	GY/WH	Heated Oxygen Sensor Heater Low Control Bank 1 Sensor (1)
42	GY/WH	Heated Oxygen Sensor Heater Low Control Bank 1 Sensor (2)
43	GN/WH	Manifold Absolute Pressure Sensor Signal
44	GY/RD	Manifold Absolute Pressure Sensor 5 Volt Reference
45	Not occupied	–
46	Not occupied	–
47	Not occupied	–
48	Not occupied	–
49	WH/D-BU	Induction Air Temperature Sensor Signal
50	Not occupied	–
51	GN/D-BU	EVAP Canister Purge Solenoid Control
52	GN/WH	Mass Airflow Sensor Signal
53	BN	Charge Indicator Control
54	BK/BN	Throttle Position Sensor Low Reference
55	GY	Generator Field Duty Cycle Signal
56	BK/YE	Knock Sensor Low Reference (1)
57	BK/GY	Knock Sensor Low Reference (2)
58	WH/GY	Transmission Park/Neutral Signal (1)
59	D-BU	Oil Pump Command Signal
60	BN/GN	Oil Level Switch Signal
61	GN/YE	Heated Oxygen Sensor Heater Low Control Bank 2 Sensor (1)
62	WH/BN	Heated Oxygen Sensor Heater Low Control Bank 2 Sensor (2)
63	BK/GN	Manifold Absolute Pressure Sensor Low Reference
64	Not occupied	–
65	BK/D-BU	Outside Ambient Temperature Sensor Low Reference
66	Not occupied	–
67	Not occupied	–
68	Not occupied	–
69	WH/YE	Throttle Inlet Absolute Pressure Sensor 5V Return
70	D-BU/WH	Throttle Position Sensor (SENT1) Signal
71	Not occupied	–
72	Not occupied	–
73	BL/WH	Signal Ground

K20 Engine Control Module X3 (Gray)

Pin	Color	Function
1	YE/BN	Oil Pressure Sensor Signal
2	WH/RD	Oil Pressure Sensor 5 Volt Reference
3	BN/YE	Fuel Rail Pressure Sensor 2 Signal
4	Not occupied	–
5	Not occupied	–
6	Not occupied	–
7	Not occupied	–
8	D-BU	Engine Coolant Temperature Sensor Signal
9	Not occupied	–
10	VT/D-BU	Crankshaft 60X Sensor Voltage
11	GN/D-BU	Ignition Control (3)
12	YE/D-BU	Ignition Control (4)
13	D-BU/GY	Ignition Control (5) (location has two wires)
13	D-BU/WH	Ignition Control (2)
14	BN/D-BU	Ignition Control (6) (location has two wires)
14	GN/D-BU	Ignition Control (3)
15	BK/GY	Ignition Control Low Reference Bank 2
16	YE	High-Pressure Fuel Pump Actuator High
17	BK/PU	Oil Pressure Sensor Low Reference
18	Not occupied	–
19	Not occupied	–
20	Not occupied	–
21	Not occupied	–
22	Not occupied	–
23	Not occupied	–
24	BK/BN	Coolant Temperature Sensor Low Reference
25	BK/PU	Crankshaft 60X Sensor Low Reference

Pin	Color	Function
26	GN	Crankshaft 60X Sensor Signal
27	D-BU/WH	Ignition Control (2) (location has two wires)
27	YE/D-BU	Ignition Control (4)
28	GN/GY	Ignition Control (7) (location has two wires)
28	D-BU/GY	Ignition Control (5)
29.	VT/WH	Ignition Control (8) (location has two wires)
29	BN/D-BU	Ignition Control (6)
30	D-BU/VT	Ignition Control (1)
31	BK/D-BU	Ignition Control Low Reference Bank 1
32	VT/BK	High-Pressure Fuel Pump Actuator Low - Control
33	YE/VT	Camshaft Position Intake Sensor (1)
34	GY/D-BU	Camshaft Position Intake Sensor Supply Voltage (1)
35	Not occupied	–
36	Not occupied	–
37	Not occupied	–
38	Not occupied	–
39	VT/BN	Camshaft Phaser Intake Solenoid (1)
40	Not occupied	–
41	Not occupied	–
42	Not occupied	–
43	GY	Cylinder Shutoff Solenoid Control (3)
44	YE/D-BU	Cylinder Shutoff Solenoid Control (4)
45	GY/D-BU	Direct Fuel Injector (DFI) High-Voltage Control Cylinder 4
46	GY/D-BU	Direct Fuel Injector (DFI) High-Voltage Control Cylinder 4 (location has two wires)
46	D-BU	Direct Fuel Injector (DFI) High Voltage Control Cylinder 2
47	GN	Direct Fuel Injector (DFI) High-Voltage Control Cylinder 3 (location has two wires)
47	PU/GN	Direct Fuel Injector (DFI) High-Voltage Control Cylinder 6
48	GY	Direct Fuel Injector (DFI) High-Voltage Control Cylinder 8 (location has two wires)
48	PU/GN	Direct Fuel Injector (DFI) High-Voltage Control Cylinder 6
49	GN	Direct Fuel Injector (DFI) High-Voltage Control Cylinder 1
50	YE/GY	Direct Fuel Injector (DFI) High-Voltage Control Cylinder 7 (location has two wires)
50	WH/GN	Direct Fuel Injector (DFI) High-Voltage Control Cylinder 5
51	D-BU	Direct Fuel Injector (DFI) High-Voltage Control Cylinder 2
51	WH/GN	Direct Fuel Injector (DFI) High-Voltage Control Cylinder 5
52	BN	Direct Fuel Injector (DFI) High-Voltage Control Cylinder 1
53	BK/GN	Camshaft Position Intake Sensor Low Reference (1)
54	Not occupied	–
55	Not occupied	–
56	Not occupied	–
57	Not occupied	–
58	Not occupied	–
59	BK/BN	Cam Phaser with Return Low Reference
60	Not occupied	–
61	Not occupied	–
62	Not occupied	–
63	D-BU	Cylinder Shutoff Solenoid Control (1)
64	GN	Cylinder Shutoff Solenoid Control (2)
65	D-BU/WH	Direct Fuel Injector (DFI) High-Voltage Supply Cylinder 4
66	D-BU/WH	Direct Fuel Injector (OFI) High-Voltage Supply Cylinder 4 (locations has two wires)
66	D-BU/GY	Direct Fuel Injector (DFI) High-Voltage Supply Cylinder 2
67	GN/GY	Direct Fuel Injector (DFI) High-Voltage Supply Cylinder 3 (locations has two wires)
67	PU/GY	Direct Fuel Injector (DFI) High-Voltage Supply Cylinder 6
68	PU/GY	Direct Fuel Injector (DFI) High-Voltage Supply Cylinder 6 (locations has two wires)
68	GY/WH	Direct Fuel Injector (DFI) High-Voltage Supply Cylinder 8
69	GN/GY	Direct Fuel Injector (DFI) High-Voltage Supply Cylinder 3
70	WH/YE	Direct Fuel Injector (DFI) High-Voltage Supply Cylinder 7 (locations has two wires)
70	GN/WH	Direct Fuel Injector (DFI) High-Voltage Supply Cylinder 5
71	GN/WH	Direct Fuel Injector (DFI) High-Voltage Supply Cylinder 5 (locations has two wires)
71	D-BU/GY	Direct Fuel Injector (DFI) High-Voltage Supply Cylinder 2
72	BN/WH	Direct Fuel Injector (DFI) High-Voltage Supply Cylinder 1
73	BK/WH	Signal Ground

X84 Data Link Connector Circuit

Pin	Color	Function
1	GN	Low-Speed GMLAN Serial Data
2	Not occupied	–
3	Not occupied	–
4	BK	Ground
5	BK/WH	Signal Ground
6	D-BU	High-Speed GMLAN Serial Data (+) (1)
7	Not occupied	–
8	Not occupied	–
9	Not occupied	–
10	Not occupied	–
11	Not occupied	–
12	D-BU/YE	High-Speed GMLAN Serial Data (+) (2)
13	WH	High-Speed GMLAN Serial Data (-) (2)
14	WH	High-Speed GMLAN Serial Data (-) (1)
15	Not occupied	–
16	RD/WH	Battery Positive Voltage

Several service providers will take a harness, delete all of the nonessentials, and send it back. These typically cost less than $1,000, and we have seen this service for as little as $600. For the 1991 OBS 4x4 seen in this book, we used standaloneharness.com to retrofit our 2018 harness. There are multiple great things about this service: any broken plugs will be replaced, you will receive a very clean factory-looking harness, and it is less expensive than ordering a new harness. The drawback of this method is that there is not an option to extend the harness for ECM placement or longer lengths on any specific sensors. However, there is the option to choose what pedal you are using to ensure that the harness is correctly pinned.

Aftermarket Harnesses

The nicest part of aftermarket harnesses is that they are customizable. The factory engine harnesses are not very long, so the ECM and other components must be installed wherever you can. This always means that the ECM will be under the hood (there is no hiding it), and choices are limited in terms of where sensors are located on the engine. This is okay as long as the donor engine and harness is from the same vehicle. However, if you are converting the engine to a different accessory drive, certain items will have to be relocated. That may mean extending wires, which can be tricky on low-voltage sensor wiring.

With an aftermarket harness, it can be ordered for any style of engine and any adjustments for length. If an extra 6 feet is needed for the ECM terminals, that is possible. The other benefits are that they come with all the wires needed and none of the extra ones, it is all new wiring, and they are well labeled. Factory harnesses are not labeled at all, and it can be really tricky sorting out all of the plugs, especially when many of the plugs are the same.

Several companies offer harnesses for Gen V engines, including Current Performance, Speartech, Howell, and Chevrolet Performance. For the most part, they are all similar. The key is finding the functions that you need at the price you want to spend. The cheapest runs about $800, and most are in that price range, but they can cost more than $2,000 with options

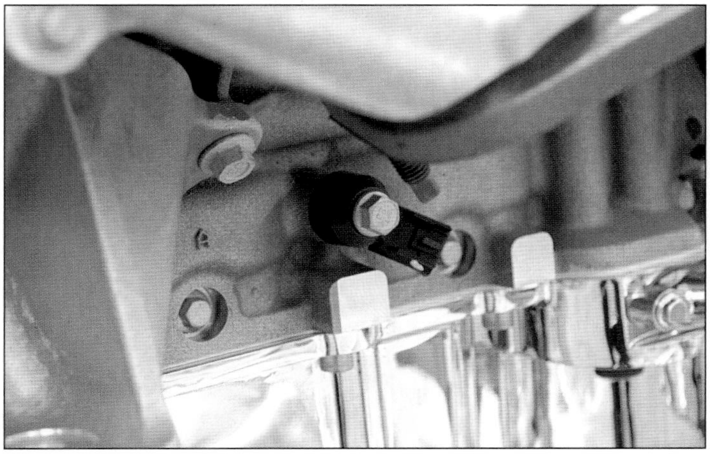

When doing an LS swap, you need to know if you have a 24x or 48x reluctor wheel on the crank, as the harness must match. The black crank sensor shown here is a 24x, while the gray crank sensor is a 48x.

There are three types of LS fuel injector plugs. Shown (from the left) are the flex-fuel Z style, old-style STD, and Delphi 45 T style. Flex-fuel engines have the Z style, and the other two were used on other engines.

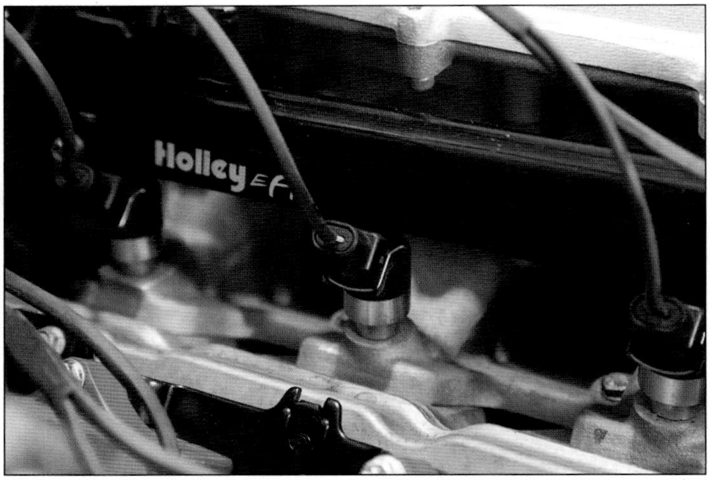

The injector plugs on the harness need to match the injector type for the engine. If yours do not match, you will have to use adapters or install the correct connectors to the harness. This is a common issue for performance engines when aftermarket injectors are used.

that include tuned ECMs, sensor kits, and transmission controls. Ordering a custom harness usually takes a few weeks to receive.

Some companies delete the fuel-system components from their harnesses, which requires using a standard electronic fuel pump and regulator. This creates a very serious runtime issue for Gen V engines, particularly at start up, idle, and wide-open throttle (WOT).

The problem is that the ECM must know the precise pressure in the fuel system so that it can compensate on the injector side. All Gen V LT-series engines are direct injected, so the fuel pressure is absolutely critical. A non–pulse width modulation (PWM) fuel system can be used, but the ECM must have the fuel-pressure sensor installed in the fuel line and that requires the fuel control module. At this point, you only need the correct pump to operate the engine. There is absolutely no good reason to not use the correct PWM-controlled fuel pump with a Gen V LT-series engine.

The only loose wires to deal with are battery voltage, ignition, and grounds. The rest of the wires are pre-terminated and plug directly into each component. Even the starter on Gen V engines uses a plug instead of wire studs. The main battery wire for the starter is a threaded stud, however. All of the terminals on the harness are Metri-Pack terminals with small silicone O-rings, nylon molex plugs, and small crimp-style pins. To replace one of these, a special crimping tool is needed.

Gauges

Getting the information from the ECM to the gauges is a critical piece of the puzzle. In most cases, a swap will use aftermarket gauges with the exception of GMT400 (also referred to as OBS) trucks. Because these trucks were EFI from the factory, General Motors actually kept the same signals through the current LT-series line. This means that you can actually wire up the outputs from the ECM to the factory gauges, and they will work. This is a serious boon for LS swaps in these later-model trucks, as gauges tend to be a pricey upgrade. The downside is that for Gen V LT-series engines, the speedometer and tachometer are harder to deal with.

Factory Harness Integration

Swapping an LS/LT engine into a truck or SUV built before 1988 (trucks) and 1992 (SUVs) does not require any factory harness integration, as these trucks had separate engine harnesses. For 1988-and-later GMT400 series trucks, the factory integrated critical non-engine circuits into the ECM wiring harness. Because of this, when swapping an LS/LT engine into one of these trucks, the factory ECM harness is retained and integrated into the new engine harness.

While you could leave the mass of unused wires in the harness, only a few of the original wires are needed. The best and cleanest option is to remove the factory ECM harness (*do not cut!*), delete the unnecessary wires, and re-loom it.

Routing Wiring Harnesses

1 ***On the 1991 1500, we needed to get the new LT harness into the car in two places. On the driver's side is the stock opening for the clutch mechanism. Since this is an automatic, we chose to cut this out.***

Routing Wiring Harnesses *continued*

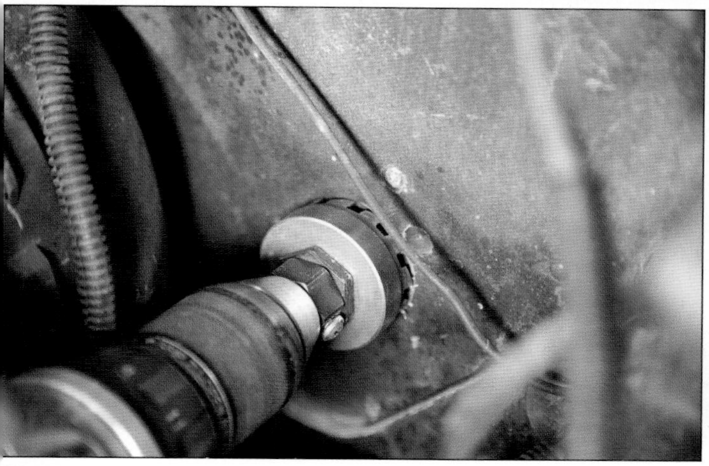

2 ***Use a hole saw to cut open the firewall. Some areas of the firewall are double-walled, so be prepared.***

3 ***To protect the wires, use a rubber-boot grommet that secures to the firewall. Ours used four screws.***

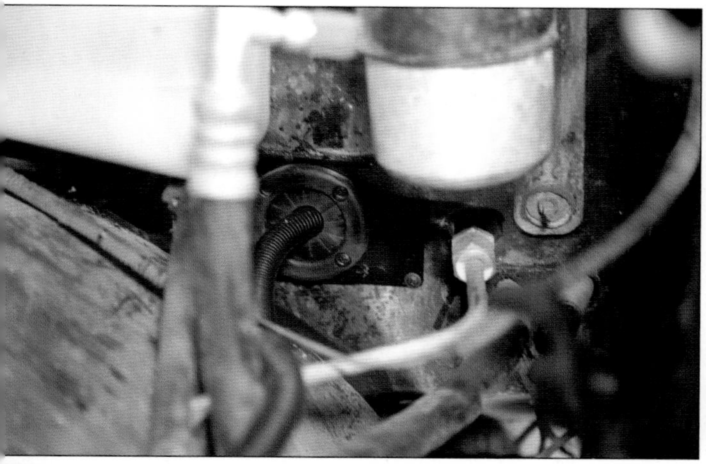

4 ***Do the same on the passenger's side under the air-conditioner drier to bring wires in and out from behind the glove box. We made a steel plate to cover the large rectangular opening that was used for the stock ECM.***

5 ***On the 1991 truck, the factory wiring is very convoluted. There are necessary wires on both sides of the engine, and there is no rhyme or reason as to why they run the way they do. Just don't cut anything on GMT400-series trucks until you know for sure that the wiring isn't needed.***

Which wires are removed depends on the engine and gauge package being used. Below is a list of factory ECM harness wires that you will use for LS/LT swaps, some of which are optional.

Note that these wires are for a 1991 C1500 4WD truck. General Motors changed the colors of these wires several times, so verify your wiring with a correct wiring diagram for the vehicle's specific year. Some vehicles have one-year-only wiring diagrams. Additionally, 1988–1992 truck models were changeover years, and both C10 and GMT400 models were being built at the same time, so it is possible to find a GMT400 model with an earlier harness.

The following wires are technically one harness, but one side enters the cab on the passenger's side (ECM/HVAC/convenience center), and the other side connects to the body plug on the driver-side firewall. This is confusing and easy to get mixed up. It took two days to sort out the wiring and get them routed as needed to match up to the 2018 L83 harness we

Weather-Pack and Metri-Pack Terminals

Beginning in the 1970s, General Motors began using a specialized weather-resistant terminal design called Weather-Pack. Designed by Packard Electrical Division (now known as Delphi or Delphi-Packard), the modular terminal system seals the wires and terminals, preventing corrosion and ensuring a good connection.

In the 1990s, Weather-Pack gave way to the upgraded version called Metri-Pack, which is a similar modular terminal design with some key improvements. LS/LT wiring harnesses are all made with Metri-Pack terminals, while 1973-and-newer C10s have Weather-Packs, and OBS trucks switched along the way to Metri-Pack. The 1992 1500 featured in this book still had Weather-Packs. By 1996, all GM vehicles had Metri-Pack terminals.

The Weather-Pack terminal is always inline, meaning that the connectors are in a flat line and are a uniform shape. They only connect to each other (male and female halves) and not directly to component terminals. All Weather-Pack terminals are round with a male pin and a female barrel. Another limitation of Weather-Pack terminals is that the small terminal size limits the amp rating to 20 amps (anything more runs the risk of melting the pack itself). Weather-Pack terminal blocks come in sizes from 1 to 7 wires.

Components for Weather-Packs are ridiculously cheap, so repairs or custom connections are cheap and easy. Every shop should have an assortment of generic Weather-Pack terminals and blocks for repair and custom work. A Weather-Pack terminal on your starter, or other components that might get removed or replaced, often makes removal and replacement much easier.

Metri-Pack terminals use flat blades and rectangular female terminals in a metric size, which is where the "Metri" name comes from. Most of the Metri-Pack terminals are sealed, but not all, as interior connectors don't need to be sealed. The biggest improvement in modular termination with the Metri-Pack design is the connector block itself. There are tons of shapes and styles, with inline, double stack, and more variations in different series.

The 150 series uses 1.5-mm terminals and is rated at 14 amps. The 280 series uses 2.8-mm terminals and services up to 30 amps. The 480 series has a (are you ready for this?) 4.8-mm terminal rated at 42 amps, and the 630 series services 46 amps with 6.3-mm terminals. Metri-Pack terminal blocks are often product specific, such as throttle pedals or sensors. There are generic Metri-Pack blocks available for building your own quick-connects for various projects.

Assembling these types of terminals requires a few special tools. The main tool is a pair of barrel-style crimping tools, preferably with ratcheting action that does not unlock the tool until the crimp is completed. The ratcheting tools are fairly expensive, but there are non-ratcheting tools available. The second tool is a small-diameter pick that is used to disassemble the terminals from the block.

The key to crimping Weather-Pack and Metri-Pack terminals (and the earlier GM modular plug terminals as well) is to use the right size of terminal for the wire and not to under-crimp or over-crimp the terminal. Under-crimping will leave a loose-fitting connection and over-crimping can actually cut the terminal in half. When assembled correctly, these terminals are very durable and ensure the best connection. Just be patient when crimping, as the terminal pins can roll in the tool, ruining the crimp. ■

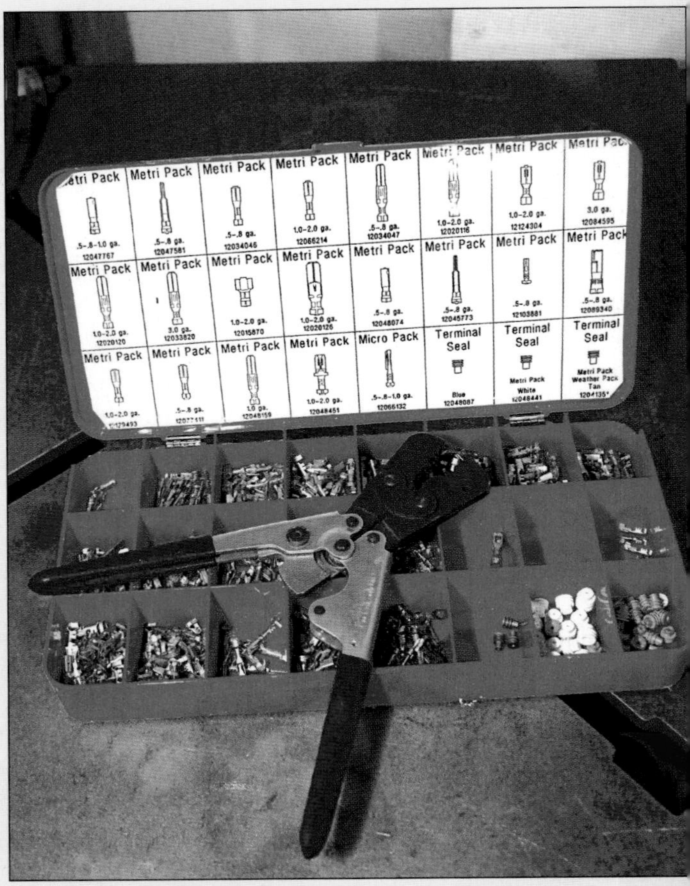

1 ***Metri-Pack terminals come in various sizes for different gauges of wire. A selection like this isn't necessary, but it is nice to have them on hand when one is needed.***

2 The main components are the terminal, the sealing boot, and the pin itself. There is also an optional sealing boot for the back of the wire/terminal.

3 A special crimp tool is required for these terminals. Do not use a standard crimper. These crimpers apply the exact correct pressure and automatically release when the crimp is complete.

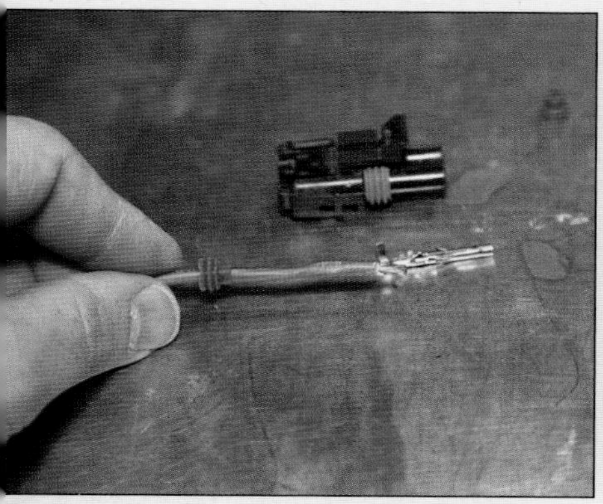

4 Slide on the wire seal. Then, strip a short section of wire to prepare for crimping.

5 The terminals can roll inside the crimper, so be careful to ensure that they don't. The crimpers can't over-crimp the terminal when it is properly inserted.

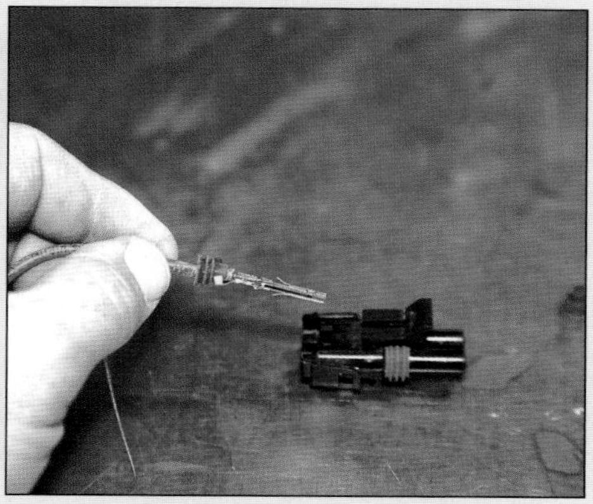

6 Slide the sealing boot to the end of the terminal.

7 Using the correct jaw on the tool, crimp the sealing boot to the terminal.

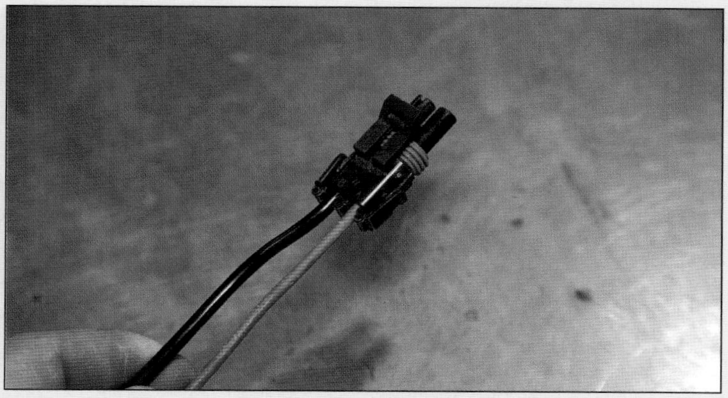

8 Then, the terminal gets pushed into the terminal block until the locking pins click into place.

were using on the 1991 C1500 truck. Take your time on this project, leave the wires long, and don't finalize the loom work until making sure all the wires are run where they need to go. Do not cut any plugs until function is verified.

Some of the wires crisscross the engine bay (and behind the firewall), and there are a lot of redundant wires that are unnecessary with an LS/LT swap. The following guide illustrates the origin/destination point for the side of the wire needed. A wire may not originate through the firewall where you think it should. For instance, there are about four purple brake-switch wires that run to a diode box. Only the single purple wire is needed in Position A on the brake-switch-diode box, which is on the passenger-side firewall plug and connects to the white 14-pin plug that is behind the glove box. This is the actual wire that goes to the brake switch, which runs to the interior passenger's side of the truck, instead of out the firewall in the driver-side body plug. Before you cut any wires, make sure you have the right one.

Repurposing a Factory Wiring Harness

1 *We spent two days sorting through wiring on the factory ECM harness for the 1991 truck. General Motors changed the wiring color and location every year from 1989 through 1996. You need the year-specific wiring diagram to do this properly. If you just chop the ECM harness, you will create weeks of work to fix it.*

2 *The factory ECM plug is this nasty, sticky block of wires in a plastic separator that is covered in a molded rubbery block. It is ugly and awful. We used some side cutters and spent about 30 minutes cutting the block away from the harness without cutting the wires. It could be left, but there will be a lot of cut wires and you still need a new hole on the passenger-side firewall, so cutting this out is best.*

3 *This is what the block looks like inside. It is a messy and tedious job.*

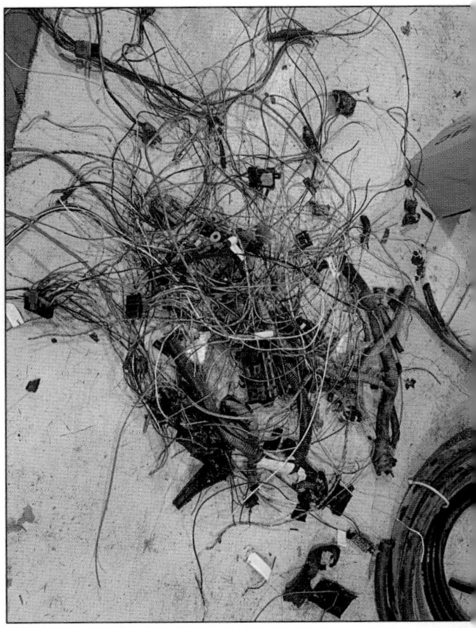

4 *We removed about 10 pounds of wiring from the factory ECM harness.*

Repurposing a Factory Wiring Harness *continued*

5 *There are about six brake-switch wires in the harness, and they all run to this diode box. This box is not needed, but you must trace the wires to the brake-light switch. Strangely, the brake-light switch wire runs from the brake pedal to the passenger's side, out the firewall, and back to the driver's side of the engine bay.*

6 *The body plug on the driver-side firewall received a good wire diet. We traced all of the wires, labeled them, and cut them. The wiper motor wires are part of the engine body plug, so be careful.*

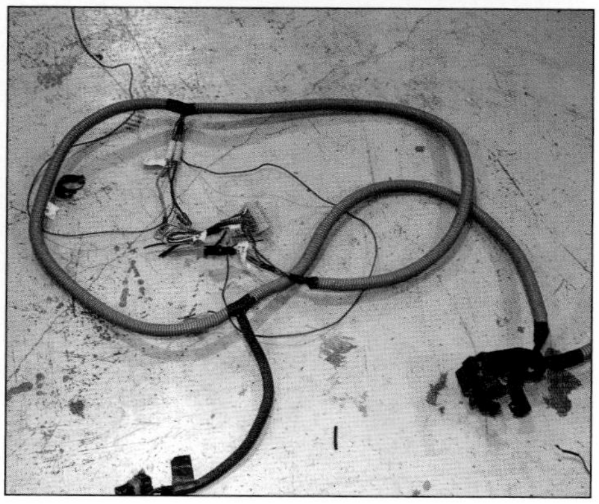

7 *This is the finished factory harness from the body plug to the passenger-side firewall pass-through. GMT400s have very complicated wiring, as they were just starting to integrate with the ECM.*

1991 GMT400 C1500 4WD
Factory ECM Harness Side GT101 Plug
(Entrance to cab located on passenger-side firewall below AC drier)

Circuit	Purpose	Color	Plug Position
Brake Switch	TCC Control	Purple	L C200 15-Pin
AC Compressor	To Pressure Switch	Light Green	HVAC Plug C
CEL	Check Engine Light	Brown/ White	M C200 15-Pin
Speed Sensor Hi	Speedo	Purple/White	3-Pin Plug
Speed Sensor Lo	Speedo	Light Green/ Black	3-Pin Plug
Grounds	Ground	Black/White	N C200 15-Pin
Fusible Links	Headlamps	Red with Black Link	A C202 4-Pin

1991 GMT400 C1500 4WD
Factory Body Engine Harness C100 Plug
(Located on driver-side firewall)

Circuit	Purpose	Color	Plug position
Tachometer	Tachometer Signal	White	–
Oil Pressure	Oil Press Gauge	Tan	E2
Coolant Temperature	Temperature Gauge	Dark Green	C2
Grounds	Ground	Black	B1
Ignition	+12v In "Run" and "Start"	Pink/Black 12g	G3
Starter	+12V "Start" Only	Purple 10g	A1
Alt Large Lug	+12v All Time Fuse Link	Red 10g, Has a Rust Color Fusible Link	H1
Alt Trigger	+12v In "Run"	Brown	D2
Fusible Links	+12V Constant	–	C1

Retained Circuits with Terminal Blocks

Circuit	Details
Wiper Motor	Cluster of five wires in a Metri-Pack connector. Wire colors: purple, gray, white, gray, black/light blue.
ABS module	Cluster of eight wires in a six-pin block, can be deleted if the ABS valve is removed. Wire colors: black (2), brown, orange, white, tan/white, purple/white, purple.

Sensors

When it comes to monitoring LS/LT engines, there are two ways to do it: either run aftermarket gauges and sensors or pull the data from the ECM. Adding sensors to these engines is not difficult with one exception: the tachometer. LS engines with a stock ECM have a tachometer wire, but it is a two-pulse-per-revolution signal.

To make this work for a tachometer, either switch to an aftermarket tachometer to read a 4-cylinder engine or alter the signal in the tune to be a V-8 signal (this needs to have a program like HP Tuners to do so). Additionally, the signal is very weak, requiring a "pull-up" resistor to beef up the voltage so that it can register with the tachometer. To beef up the voltage, wire a 1000-ohm to 5000-ohm resistor to a +12-volt ignition source (fuse protected) and cross the other side of the resistor to the tachometer in line with the tachometer feed wire. The resistor will provide additional voltage to the signal without interfering with the signal.

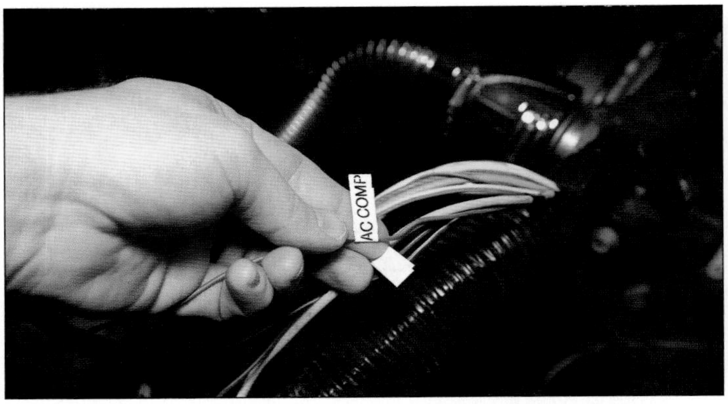

The standaloneharness.com L83 harness has a few loose wires that are labeled for connection to the vehicle, such as the AC compressor wiring. This is the trigger wire from the HVAC controls to turn on the compressor clutch.

We also reused the factory L83 battery lugs, which are OEM quality and work. It is nice to save yourself from unnecessary work.

We added some extra grounds from the head and block to the body and frame. LS/LT engines are very sensitive to ground loops.

A large 4-gauge alternator charging wire was added to ensure that we had ample capacity to charge the battery.

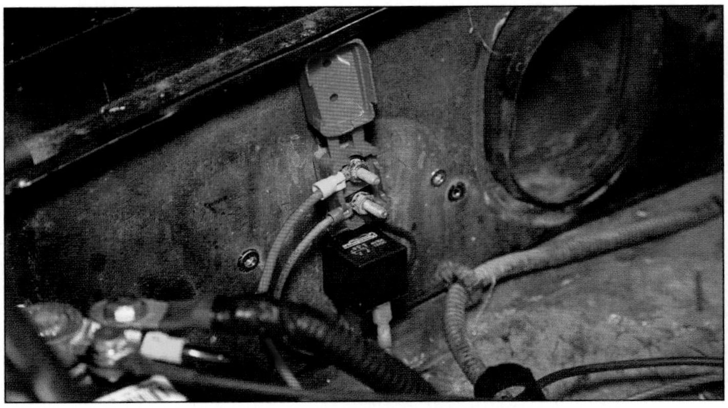

All electrical components need fuse protection. For the electric fans, we opted for an auto-reset circuit breaker. This was placed next to the battery on the passenger-side fender for minimal distance between the battery terminal and the circuit breaker.

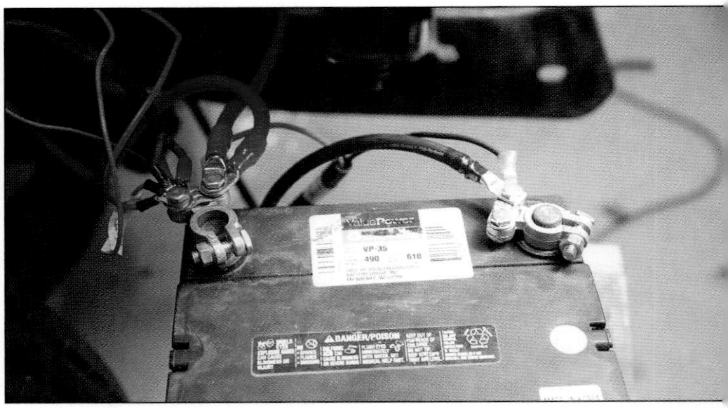

These modern engines need power tied directly to the battery, so there tends to be a lot of wires on the battery terminals. All ECMs and TCMs must be directly connected to the battery, but auxiliary wiring can be run to a distribution block on the fender or core support.

The coil packs for the Gen III and Gen IV engines are in very good condition, so there is no need to replace them at all. The failure rate is low on these coils, so replacing them just isn't necessary. You would be hard pressed to find a dealer that has seen any failed coils. A coil from a 1999–2004 car or a 1998–2003 truck is on the left, and a coil that was used on 1999–2006 4.8L, 5.3L, 6.0L trucks or 2003–2006 Hummers is on the right. Not shown are 2005-and-newer car and truck coils. The terminals are different on all three.

This LS1 harness does not match to these Vortec truck coils. This can be a costly mistake, as coils are not cheap.

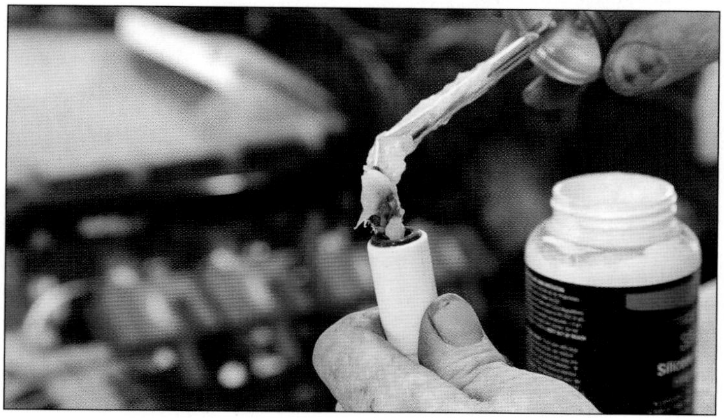

Don't forget to put some silicone dielectric grease inside the spark-plug terminals to protect them from seizing onto the spark plugs.

Gen V engines don't always have a usable tachometer signal coming from the engine or ECM at all. Instead of a tachometer signal, there is a camshaft signal on the black X2 connector, pin 39 (white wire). Because it is a camshaft sensor reading, it may or may not be able to be read by the tachometer, which has to be set to "4-cylinder" and requires a pull-up resistor just like on LS engines.

Many LT ECMs are not even programed for this signal, and the wire may not even be in that terminal on your wiring harness. This makes adding a tachometer much more difficult. When using this signal, the tachometer may act erratic at idle, due to the fact that the signal is coming off a cam sensor. This signal output type can't be adjusted in the ECM like LS ECMs can.

If a harness is not wired for the cam signal, it can be added to the molex plug in the harness. Once the wire is installed, activate the signal in the ECM. This requires programming with HP Tuners or similar full-access tuning software. A handheld unit will not get deep enough into the ECM to activate this signal. It is not possible to adjust the signal output type like you can with LS ECMs.

One of the most unique aspects of the Chevrolet Performance Gen V swap harness and ECM is that this kit comes with the tachometer wire. The ECM is also programmed to provide a standard tachometer signal. This is something that only General Motors can do because it can create whatever it wants inside the ECM, whereas aftermarket tuners cannot alter the actual code of the ECM. This is one major benefit of the Chevrolet Performance controller kit.

If using anything other than the Chevrolet Performance controller kit (with a stock ECM), the solution comes in the form of a Dakota Digital BIM module. This module connects directly to the OBD-II port, and it pulls all of the pertinent information from the ECM, including oil pressure, water temperature, speed (when wired to the ECM from the transmission), and the tachometer signal. It is a plug-and-play unit, which really makes wiring easy. The only thing it doesn't get is the fuel level, which can be pulled from a factory GM fuel module if you are using one in the tank. It makes installing custom gauges a breeze. Dakota Digital makes various bus interface modules (BIMs) to operate its digital dash clusters or traditional gauges too.

The signals coming from the BIM module can be used to drive most aftermarket gauges, or Dakota Digital gauges can be used. Dakota Digital gauges are available in direct-fit or universal applications. What makes this nice is that extra sensors and adapters don't need to be run. The BIM module pulls the data directly from the ECM via the OBD-II data port. Should access to the data port be needed, simply remove the BIM plug and plug in the scan tool or programmer.

There are other options for pulling the tachometer signal from the ECM, including a Lingenfelter Performance CAN2-002 unit. It is similar to the BIM module, except that this one can be configured to operate aftermarket or factory gauges as long as they use analog signals.

There is one other possible solution for a tachometer signal, which is to wire the engine with the AutoMeter 9117 module. This module wires in line with the ignition coils and creates a tachometer signal from the power supply of each coil. Wiring this module into the harness of an engine will take a little bit of time and is a complicated amount of wiring, but it is a reliable method of generating the required tachometer signal for an aftermarket tachometer.

Outside of the tachometer signal, adding sensors for aftermarket gauges is not difficult. However, they will need some modifications. There are a few points available for oil pressure, which depend on what accessory drive, oiling system, and motor-mount adapters are being used. Even the factory check engine light (CEL) can be used.

1991 GMT400 Gauge Wiring

This is for a 1991 OBS 1500 with a gas engine. These may change throughout the year range of the GMT400 series, so it is a good idea to verify your wiring *before* connecting any sending units to these wires. Below are the wire colors at the gauge terminal plug behind the gauge cluster.

Item	Wire Color
Coolant Temperature	Dark Green
Oil Pressure	Tan
Tachometer	White
Fuel Level	Purple
Speedometer: Hi sense	Purple/White, Lo sense – Light Green/Black
Voltage	Pink/Blue
Check Engine Light	Brown/White or Yellow

Installing a Transmission Controller

1 ***For the 1966 Suburban, we selected a Quick 4 transmission controller from US Shift. This is an incredibly simple install (mostly plug and play), and we have control of the shifts from the control module itself.***

2 ***The only tricky part of the install is splicing into the TPS signal wire on the ECM. Splice this in and solder the wires together.***

3 ***Wrap the wire in high-quality 3M Super 33+ electrical tape. Don't use cheap tape on important wiring.***

Installing a Transmission Controller *continued*

4 *Integrate the TCM wiring harness into the Holley Terminator harness and tape it at the T-junction. This is where the cheaper tape can be used.*

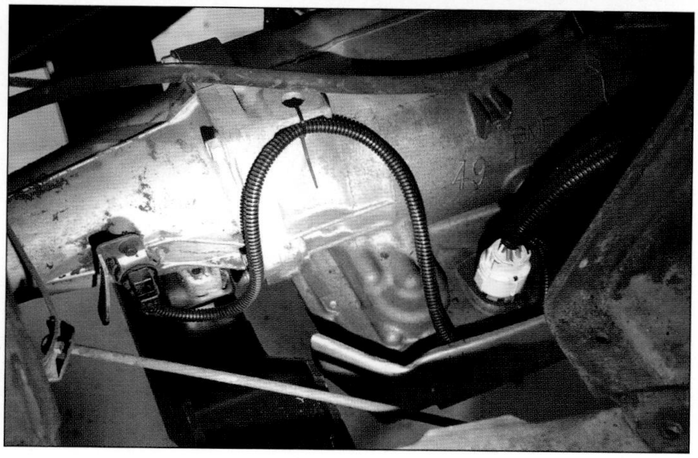

5 *Run the transmission harness to the transmission and plug in both sections. Don't forget to secure the harness to the case with some zip ties to avoid it flopping around and getting damaged by road debris.*

Oil Sensors

There are a few options for installing an aftermarket oil-pressure/temperature sensor on LS/LT engines. The one that can actually be used depends on several factors. For LS engines, the simplest option is the oil-cooler bypass cover on the oil pan. For Gen V engines, there are three available ports for pressurized oil: in front of the driver-side bellhousing above the oil cooler port, the oil cooler port itself, and the top oil port for the factory vacuum pump (truck engines).

LS- and LT-Series Engines

The oil pan on both LS- and LT-series engines has a port for an external oil cooler. Unlike the LS engines, most LT engines actually use this port. The LT1 car engines use a large oil-to-water cooler that bolts to the block. This is not usable on most swap applications because it is too large to clear the steering box or frame. Some trucks have an air-to-oil cooler mounted to the radiator with a junction block and hard lines mounted to the oil pan. You may choose to use this for your LT swap, or you may choose to eliminate it.

The first option is to keep the cooler and add a port block. Several companies make adapter blocks for the oil port cover, including Holley, ICT Billet, and Dirty Dingo. These blocks allow the oil to pass through the block and continue to the oil cooler. They are available with or without an oil-pressure boss. Clearly, the block with the port is the better way to go because it has the port

This is the control module for the 2018 NQH transfer case that we used in the 1991 1500 truck. We received this unit and harness from Swap Time USA. At the time of publication, this is the only place that has figured out how to retune these modules to allow the NQH to work in swaps.

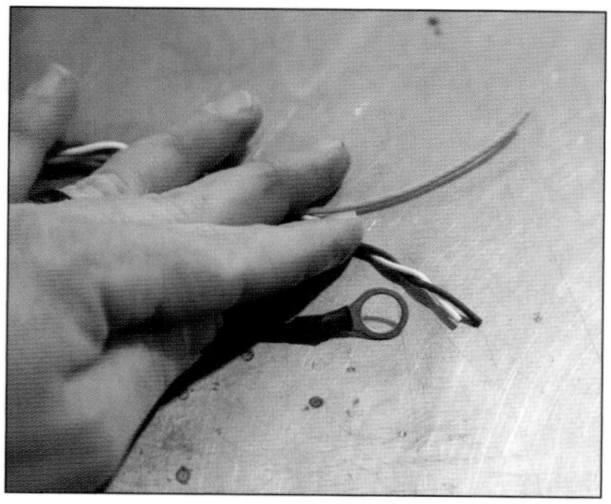

These are the only loose wires for the module. Pink is switched power, and the black ring terminal is the ground. The blue and white wires splice into the OBD-II port: blue to pin 6, white to pin 14.

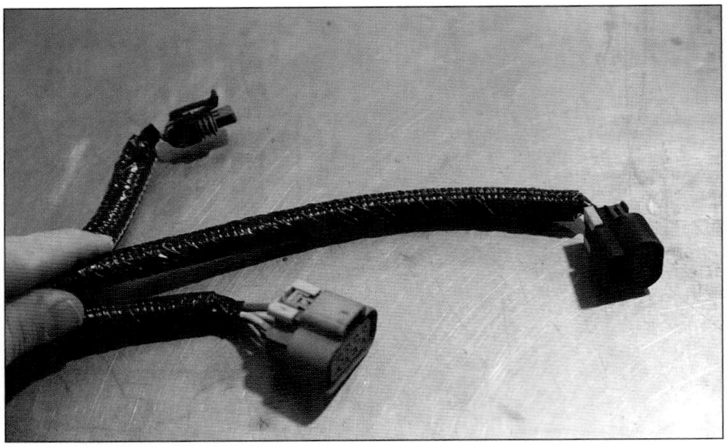

The rest of the harness is plug and play to the transfer case itself.

There are three terminals on the transfer case. The harness is long enough to reach from under the dash to the rear of the case.

Our 1991 1500 truck was missing all of the wiring for the front axle, so we had to make a new harness. The red is power, and the black is ground. This will run to a relay controlled by a switch on the dash to engage the front differential.

you need. This option allows the use of an oil cooler and picks up the oil pressure/temperature.

If the engine does not have the cooler or it is not being used, the next option is to block off the cooler ports. There are several options, including the factory GM bypass cover or one of the many aftermarket covers. The factory cover is a domed piece, which can be drilled and tapped (similar to LS bypass covers), but the cap is rounded, so be really careful so that it does not leak.

For Gen V engines, make sure to get the correct bypass cover because General Motors was including the wrong cover in its bypass kit. This may have been rectified, but you should check the part numbers just in case. The following part numbers are the factory components: 12630766 for the cover, 12623359 for the gasket, 11562426 for the bolt (x2), and 11611351 for the plug. The plug is only needed if you have the factory water-to-oil cooler.

The aftermarket covers are typically billet aluminum and may or may not have an oil port already drilled and tapped. It just depends on the cover. It can always be drilled if necessary.

Gen V Engines Only

For LT-series engines, there a few other options for oil-pressure/temperature sensors, which are to block the pressure port and the oil feed for the vacuum pump. Most LT swaps will not use the vacuum pump, as it is there for emissions purposes and located where most accessory drives put the power-steering pump. If you are using a truck version of the LT (L83/84/86/87 engine codes), that will need to be eliminated. If you are running a car version (LT1/LT4), it is already plugged from the factory.

The upper port is a 12 mm x 1.75 thread. A standard adapter to 1/8-inch NPT threads right in, giving all the oil pressure–related goodness that is needed. However, this location may not work, depending on the engine mount adapters that are being used. Most will clear, but deep setback or sliding mounts, such as those from Dirty Dingo, will not clear the upper port with a standard adapter. This port can still be used if you make a hard-line adapter (GM part number 11546665) so that the sensor can be relocated around the adapter plate. These adapters have a small head that allows you to torque down the plug for a secure seal.

Block Oil Port

There is a large plug on the rear driver's side of the block, just in front of the bellhousing flange and above the oil ports on the pan. This is a pressurized oil port. The threads are M16 x 1.5, and adapters are available to convert this port for a sensor. It may or may not be positioned well enough to use a standard barrel-type oil sensor, so use elbows or a hardline adapter to make the sensor fit.

Any one of these ports can be used for oil pressure or oil temperature if you have the necessary clearance for the sending unit.

Coolant

Locating a coolant port on LS/LT engines is typically done at the water pump. For most swaps, either drill and tap the water pump or use an adapter between the water pump and block, depending on what accessory drive is being used.

LT-only Engines

There are two water ports on the Gen V engine: the factory sensors port on the water pump and the large drain plug on the driver's side of the block. The drain plug (part number 11611351) is used for the water-to-oil cooler, which is plugged off when not using that cooler. There is not currently an adapter fitting for this port, though it would not be difficult to make one.

The factory sensor cannot be replaced because the ECM requires this input. This requires getting creative. There are a few options, and it all depends on the accessory drive.

Installing a Swap Time USA Module

1 ***The Swap Time USA module uses the factory transfer-case switch. Take the switch apart so that it can be molded into the dash.***

2 ***Cut a piece of ABS plastic that matches the ashtray under the gauge cluster. There is a hole for a rocker switch and a bezel for the transfer-case knob.***

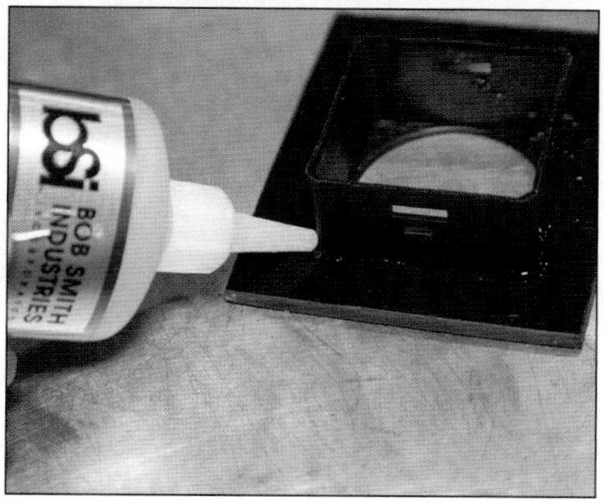

3 ***Glue the bezel in place with super glue and allow it to cure.***

4 ***Sand it down and smooth it out with some pinhole glaze.***

5 ***Once the plate is textured and painted, install it into the ashtray. It will close if the metal frame above the tray is trimmed away.***

LS and LT Engines

If you are using a factory accessory drive, then the best option is to drill and tap the water-pump housing itself. In most cases, it is possible to drill and tap the pump near the factory sensor. A standard 1/8-inch NPT sensor requires an 11/32-inch drill bit and a 1/8-inch NPT tap. Make sure that there is enough room in the water port for the sensor to seat and not hit the backside. Remove the pump (best method) or stuff the port with a greased towel to catch any shavings. Then, vacuum out the pump afterward to be sure.

Many aftermarket accessory drives use LS-style water pumps that require spacers on LT-series engines. Some kits come with a second port for a water temperature sensor, but some do not. It is easy to drill and tap a spacer as described to accommodate a second sensor. Another option is to drill and tap the top of the water pump in the same manner, which is a common solution for LS swaps.

The last option is to install a temperature sensor in the radiator hose or in the radiator itself. These are not as accurate as engine-mounted sensors, but they are an option.

While it may feel unnerving to drill into the water pump, it is quite simple and a very effective solution. As with any project like this, take your time, research your project's components to determine which solution will fit your application best, and be patient. When drilling and tapping, ensure that no metal shavings are left in the engine.

Installing Dakota Digital Gauges

LT swapping the late-model Chevy trucks comes with some issues, particularly for the gauges. Unlike the Squarebody and previous models, installing aftermarket gauges into an OBS interior is not as simple. This is because these trucks were all ECM-controlled, so they don't have traditional sending units. Luckily, for swappers, the factory gauge signals are the same as LS/LT signals, so the factory gauges can be reused—up to a point.

1 ***This 1991 Chevrolet 1500 GMT400 has been LT swapped with a 2018 Silverado drivetrain. We could have reused these gauges, but we opted to swap them out for a set of Dakota Digital HDX gauges. First, remove the old ones. The gauge pod itself has several small Allen-head screws holding it in place. Save these screws for reuse.***

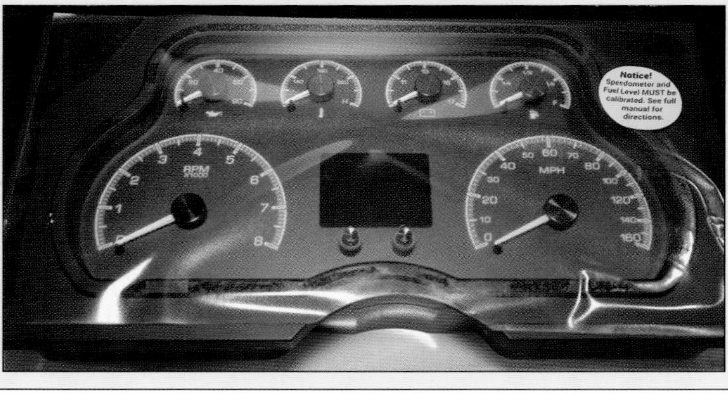

2 ***Insert the new Dakota Digital HDX gauges into the factory location and screw them down using the original screws.***

3 *There are two plugs on the back, but only use the one at he top.*

4 *This is the factory gauge cluster terminal pod. Pull it out of the pocket to access the wires.*

5 *Use a few of the factory wires for the high-beam lights, turn-signal indicators, and the brake lights. These wires were located, cut, and labeled. These wires change by year, so make sure to use the correct diagram for your year and model of truck.*

6 *To get the new cluster to fit, trim away a section of the actory plug pocket.*

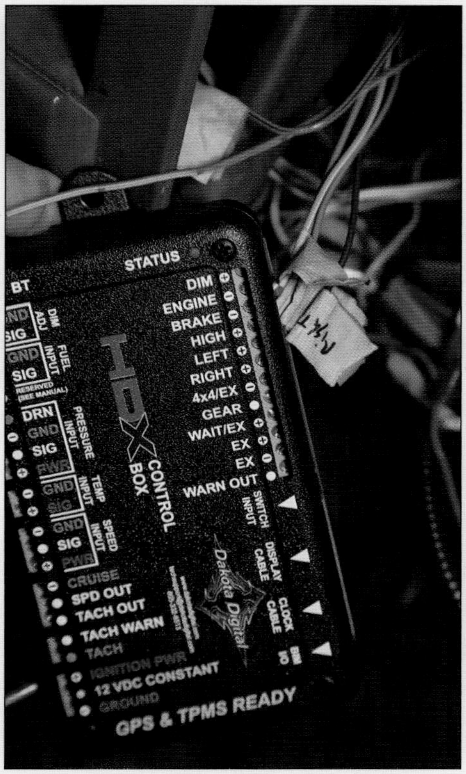

7 *Under the dash, wire up the HDX module. These gauges can be used with any engine and wire from the sensors, but we used the Dakota Digital OBD-II port adapter to pull the info from the ECM itself.*

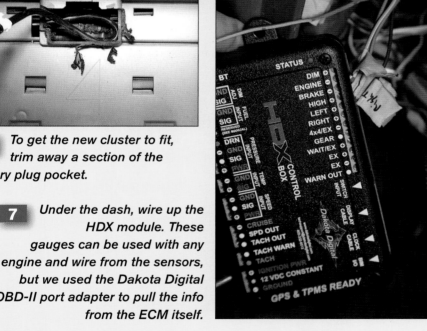

8 *Don't forget the ground.*

9 *This is the OBD-II port. If access is needed to the port, simply pull off the plug, run the tuner or code scanner, and then put this plug back on when you are done. Of course, the gauges won't work while this is disconnected.*

Installing Dakota Digital Gauges *continued*

10 ***The new gauges look so much better than the stock ones, and accurate engine details are shown straight from the ECM. LT engines do not have a good tachometer signal, so this solves that issue.***

LS swaps are simple. Simply wire up the gauges behind the dash to the signal outputs from the ECM.

LTs require a few more steps. The factory gauges can be used, but the speed sensor has to be sourced from the transmission control module (TCM) and either not run a tachometer or run an aftermarket tachometer, which depends on the gauges in an OBS truck.

To solve this issue, we went with Dakota Digital's direct-fit HDX series of gauges, which have traditional needles and look amazing in the dash. Combined with the bus interface module (BIM), the entire system installed in just a couple of hours with minimal wiring. This gauge setup can be used with the original engine too; it does not have to be a swap.

The installation is very straightforward. A wiring diagram for the factory gauge cluster is needed but does not come with the kit, so you will need some basic Google searching skills to find what you need based on which gauges you want to connect. The control module can read the factory warning lights as well as the turn signal, high-beam, cruise, etc. All of the trigger wires are in the two factory terminals.

We selected the wires we wanted to use (turn signals, high-beam, and parking brake), cut them from the plug, and then taped up the terminals for safety. We ran a new fuel-level wire, as the original had been chewed up by rodents. The terminals can be removed altogether, but it is not necessary. For the 1991 GMT400 truck, the wires are as follows:

Item	Wire Color
Right-hand turn signal	Dark blue
Left-hand turn signal	Light blue
High-beam indicator	Light green
Parking brake	Tan with white stripe

Everything else we need comes from the BIM module, which we secured under the steering column trim cover. If access is needed to the OBD-II port for tuning or checking codes, simply disconnect the BIM module plug. Installing the Dakota Digital gauge cluster is likely the simplest gauge install available; it really is that fast and easy. The only wires not available from the factory terminals are ground (which are available in the terminal, but we didn't trust the wire size) and battery power, which we pulled from the fuse box.

Installing the gauge panel into the truck requires a little bit of trimming to the factory gauge terminal pocket. The kit comes with a handy guide, but in the end we just eye-balled it. This new gauge cluster really freshens up the looks of the interior of the truck and makes us want to clean up the rest of interior even more. Once the engine is running and the vehicle is ready to drive, the gauges themselves can be set up and tuned. ■

ECMs AND INITIAL SETUP

The hardware portion of the swap process is a matter of turning wrenches, but the software part is a little bit different. Depending on what route is taken, it can be plug and play or it may require getting inside the ECM and fiddling around with things. Stock ECMs are locked out from simply wiring it up and hitting the key. This is because the factory security system is not in the swap truck. Not to worry, as the aftermarket has this issue handled.

Aftermarket ECMs provide options that the factory ECM can't, such as boost control, nitrous timing, etc. How the LS/LT swap is controlled is based on how much you want to spend and what level of control you need. If you are simply building a daily driver or weekend cruiser, stock is just fine without the need to retune. If you are adding performance parts or plan to upgrade down the line, an aftermarket ECM or a stock ECM with a tuner might be a better option. There are unique aspects to the ECM for both LS- and LT-series engines, each depending on the year and model. In many cases, the ECM must match the engine, especially when it comes to LS engines.

LS ECMs

There are two main types of computers: 24-tooth reluctor and 58-tooth reluctor-wheel engines. The reluctor wheel is mounted to the crankshaft inside the block to the rear. The crank position (CKP) sensor is mounted to the right rear of the block, behind the starter. As the crankshaft rotates, the teeth on the reluctor wheel interrupt the magnetic field created by the sensor. This sensor records these interruptions and sends a signal to the computer,

The 1997–1998 LS1 Y-Body and F-Body computer is different from the later LS1 ECM. The pinouts are different, and the wiring harnesses are different. This shows the front and back sides of a 1998 Camaro ECM.

The later ECMs for 1999–2002 LS1s look different, and they are. The wires are in different places, so do not try to wire an early harness to a later ECM. It won't work.

The 2004–2005 ECMs were only capable of drive by wire, but several programmers have figured out how to reprogram that portion of the ECM. This allows installation of a less complicated drive-by-cable throttle body on a 2004–2005 LS engine.

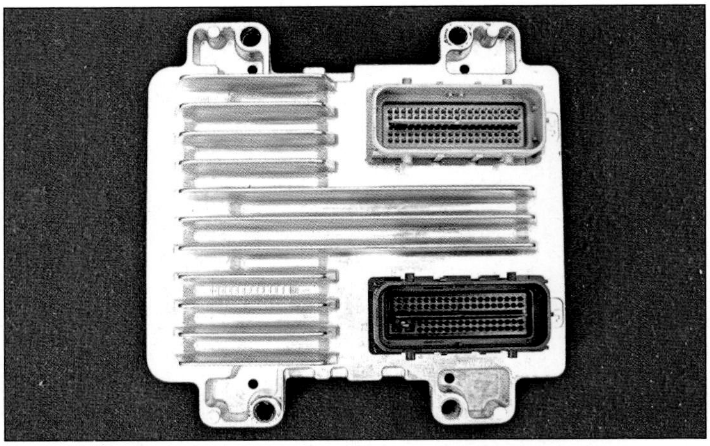

This is a 58x reluctor computer. The ancillary parts are very expensive, so make sure to get all these from the donor car. Otherwise, you will have to spend lot of money to buy these components individually.

and these signals are used to detect issues, such as misfires and detonation, with the ignition system.

It is important to know which reluctor type you have: 24x or 58x. A quick check for this is to look at the reluctor wheel sensor—a black sensor is a 24x wheel, the gray sensor was used for 58x engines. The 2014-and-newer Gen V LT-series engines all have a black 58x sensor.

The following engines came with a 24-tooth reluctor wheel: the 1997–2004 Corvette engine; the LS1 and LS6 engine (all were drive by wire); the 2005 LS2 Corvette engine; the 1998–2002 Camaro/Firebird engine; the 2004 LS1 GTO engine; the 2005–2006 LS2 GTO engine; the 2004–2006 SSR engine (LS2 and 5.3L); and the 1999–2006 4.8L, 5.3L, and 6.0L Vortec truck engines.

Engines can be drive-by-cable or drive-by-wire setups, depending on the vehicle. The 58-tooth reluctor wheel is found on drive-by-wire engines only. This reluctor wheel cannot be used with a drive-by-cable throttle body without modifications. If you are trying to run these engines with a traditional throttle cable, they need to be converted to a 24-tooth reluctor wheel along with a 2005 cam gear on the front of the engine and a 24-tooth reluctor wheel computer.

The alternative to an expensive conversion is to use a convertor module, such as the TRG-002 from Lingenfelter Performance. This electronic box converts the 58x crank signal and 4x camshaft signal into the 24x and 1x signals used by the 24x ECM, allowing the installer to use throttle by cable and to mix and match ECMs and engines.

The following engines have the 58-tooth reluctor: the 2006-and-newer Corvette LS7 engine; the 2008-and-newer Corvette LS3 engine; and the 2007-and-newer 4.8L, 5.3L, and 6.0L Vortec truck engines.

Each engine within the 24x and 58x groups uses a specific computer. The wiring harnesses are dedicated to each computer, so it's very important to get all of the components when pulling an engine from a salvage vehicle. If the proper computer is not included, one can be sourced from eBay or another retailer. Find out which computer is needed. The following is a list of service part numbers for the ECU computers.

ECU Computer Service Part Numbers

Year	Make & Model	Part Number
1997–1998	Corvette, Camaro, Firebird, and Vortec engines	16238212, 16232148 (red and blue plugs)
1999–2000	Corvette, Camaro, Firebird, and Vortec engines	09354896, 16263494
2001–2003	2001–2002 Camaro, Firebird, Vortec; 2001–2003 Corvette LS1 & LS6	12200411
2003	Vortec truck engines	12576106
2004	Corvette LS1 and LS6	12586242
2004	Vortec truck engines	12586243
2004	GTO and SSR	12598343
2005	GTO and SSR	12603892
2005	Corvette LS2	12597191, 12597883
2005–2006	Vortec truck engines	125862432
2006	Vortec truck engines	12583560, 12583561
2006	5.3L SSR	12596679
2006–2007	LS2 and LS7	12603892
2007 and newer	Vortec truck engines	12597121

The 24x ECMs can be programmed for either drive by cable or drive by wire. For instance, a 1999 F-Body LS1 with a drive-by-cable throttle body can be wired to a 2000 Corvette drive-by-wire ECM, but the ECM must be reprogrammed to reflect the drive-by-cable change.

There's a second option: convert an engine to drive by wire by reprogramming the original computer. The wiring harness must be able to plug into the particular computer. The 1998 F-Body computers and harnesses are not compatible with 1999-and-later harnesses or computers because the plugs are different. If you plan on running the stock harness and computer, make sure you get them from the donor vehicle or buy them used if you can't.

Building an ECM Mount

1 *Mounting an LS ECM is not very difficult. Mounting holes can often be drilled right into the case like this. We drilled small 1/8-inch pilot holes and then stepped up to 1/4 inch for the bolts.*

2 *Using a pair of angle brackets that we made, the ECM can be bolted to the inner fender.*

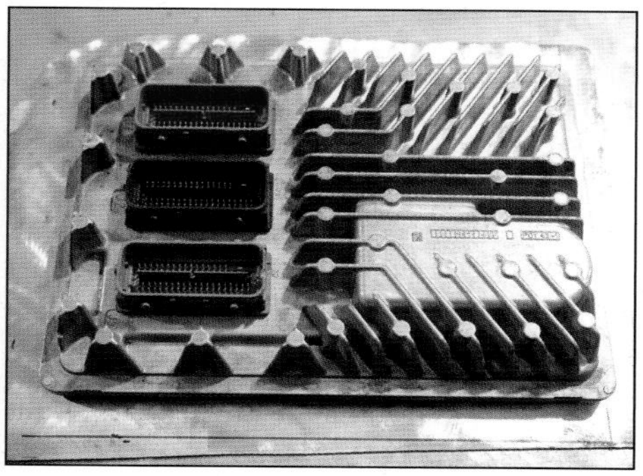

3 *The first LT-series ECM (E92 and E92A) works for all V-8 versions of the 2014–2018 Gen V engine. It needs a special mount, as there are no provisions for mounting the ECM. The later 2019-and-newer E99, E93, and E90 ECMs are hardware locked and must be shipped off to be unlocked, which is very costly.*

4 *We made a clamshell-style mount for the 1991 1500 ECM. To do so, take measurements off the ECM and transfer them to a strip of sheet metal.*

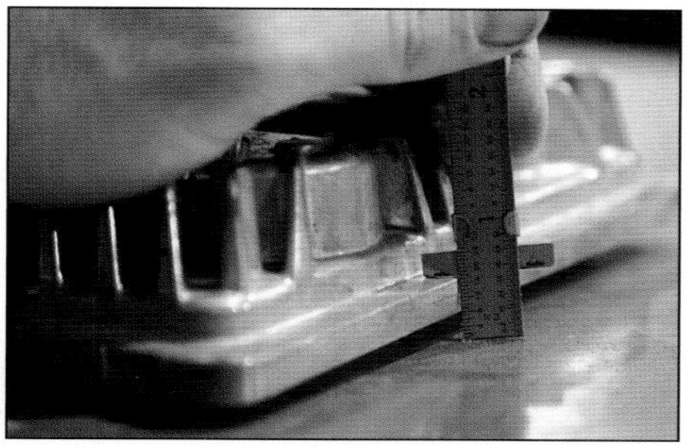

5 *The brackets will be a Z shape, so the width of the ECM flange and the height off the table are needed.*

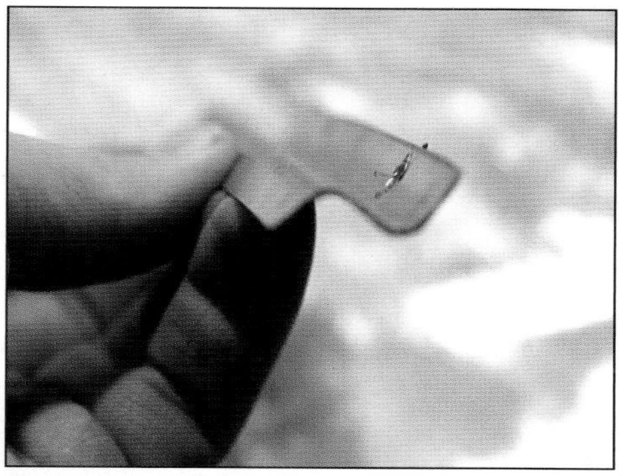

6 *Bend each bracket into a Z shape to clamp the edges of the ECM.*

7 *Next, make a plate to serve as a base for the ECM and drill some holes for the rivnuts.*

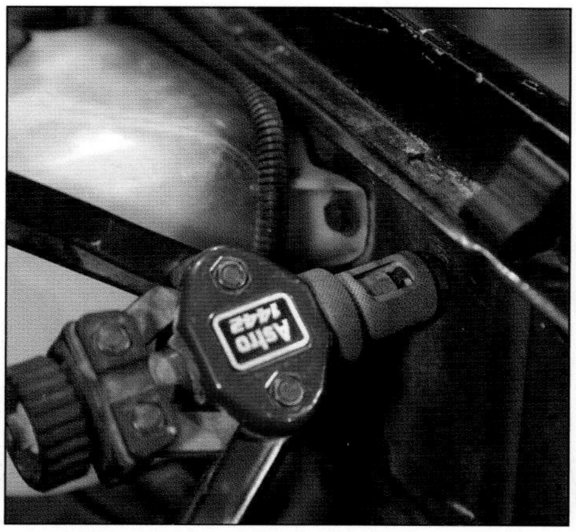

8 *If you don't want to deal with nuts and bolts, use a rivnut tool to set a threaded insert into the fender of the truck and the base plate for the ECM mount.*

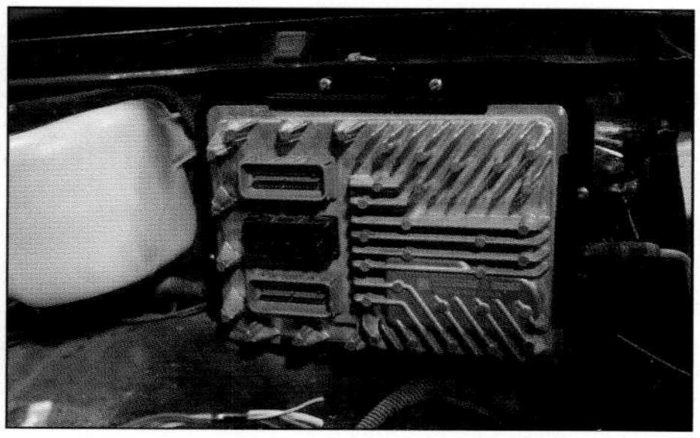

9 *The finished mount looks good, blends in with the truck, and was simple to make. It is possible to buy fancy CNC-machined mounts too.*

Drive-By-Wire to Drive-By-Cable Conversion

Information provided by Brenden Patten

The drive-by-wire system is a potentially confusing portion of the wiring conversion. Each engine that uses the drive-by-wire system requires a specific pedal, throttle body, and, in some cases, a throttle actuator control (TAC) module.

In most cases, the drive-by-wire components are not interchangeable. The pedal, TAC module, and throttle body must remain with the engine for it to work properly. The only interchangeable components are the Vortec truck modules, but the programming in the computer must be changed as well.

There are several different component packages, which vary by vehicle. The 1997–2004 Corvette uses a pedal and separate TAC module to operate the specific throttle body. In 2005, General Motors went to a drive-by-wire pedal that incorporated the TAC sensor into the pedal, so only the pedal and throttle body is needed for a swap. The same goes for the 2005–2006 GTO, which used a specific GTO pedal-only configuration. The SSR trucks use a dedicated drive-by-wire pedal with a TAC module. The Cadillac CTS-V used a pedal and TAC module up to 2004, when it was switched to a pedal only in 2005 and up. The 2007 Trailblazer used a pedal only and is different from the rest of the trucks.

The Vortec-powered trucks with the adjustable pedal system are not suitable and must be adapted for use with conversion engines. These trucks use a drive-by-wire pedal mounted on a moving platform that adjusts to the height of the driver. Of course, it is possible to simply swap to a cable-driven throttle body or a carbureted setup for one of these engines. The trucks' pedals and TAC modules are very confusing; General Motors seemed to do a lot of different things with the trucks over the years.

Drive by wire is not for everyone, but converting a drive-by-wire engine to drive by cable is not cut and dried. Some ECMs can be converted to drive by wire.

Drive by wire was first available in the trucks in 1999, and there have been many different pedals with and without TAC modules. This is why it is so important to get all of the components from the donor vehicle beforehand. If you didn't grab the pedal (not everybody would think to grab the gas pedal when doing an engine swap), they can be purchased from any GM dealer, salvage yard, or even a few aftermarket shops, but make sure to have all the details for your particular engine and ECM.

Converting a drive-by-wire ECM to operate a drive-by-cable application is possible, but not all drive-by-wire ECMs are capable of making the switch. The following ECMs are known to be drive-by-wire/drive-by-cable compliant:

First, remove the back of the ECM case to look for this section of the board.

If the ECM board does not have pins soldered into this location, then it cannot be converted.

ECM	Details
1999–2002 Serv. No. 09354896, 12200411	All blue/red connector PCMs will work with either drive by wire or drive by cable with the correct programming installed.
2003 Service No. 12576106 with Hardware No. 12570558	Most 2003 trucks use this PCM—but not all.
2004 Service No. 12586243 with Hardware No. 12583659	Most GTOs, Express vans, Cadillac CTS-Vs, and some trucks use this PCM.
2005–2006 Service No. 12589462 with Hardware No. 12589161	Found in Express vans and some trucks.
2007 Service No. 12602801 with Hardware No. 12589161	Found only in Express vans.

If the ECM does not have these numbers, check it by taking the back cover off and looking for the location on the circuit board labeled "B67U1." If that location has pins soldered to the board, then it has the controller needed to be drive by cable. If not, then it cannot be used.

The issue with going from drive by wire to drive by cable is that the drive by cable requires the controller for the idle air control (IAC) valve. The controller opens and closes the valve when needed. Most of the truck ECMs do not support drive-by-cable conversion. All drive-by-wire ECMs require reprogramming to be used for drive-by-cable applications.

Wiring the drive-by-wire computer requires adding the IAC and throttle-position-sensor (TPS) wires. The 2003-and-newer oil-pressure plug works for the TPS sensor, but the IAC uses its own plug, so that will need to be sourced.

The wire color and location shown match 2003-and-newer Express vans that had mechanical drive-by-cable throttle bodies. The oil-pressure-sensor plug can be used from a 2003-and-newer harness for the TPS. Pay attention that the 5-volt reference and low reference are opposite between oil pressure and TPS. If you are using the oil-pressure plug for TPS, either switch the black and gray wires at the TPS plug or switch the black and gray wires at the PCM. If these are not switched, the TPS will work backward. Finally, move the oil-pressure signal wire (TAN/WHT) from green 58 to green pin 24.

Note that the exact location the TPS received its 5-volt reference from does not matter; it could come from pin 7 or 8. Same goes for the low reference; it could come from pin 60 or 63. What is important is that the TPS has 5-volt reference and low reference at the correct locations at the sensor.

Throttle Position Sensor
(Factor Pin Location For 2003-and-Newer Drive-by-Cable Express Van)

Sensor Pin Location	Wire Color	Description	ECM Plug/Pin Location
Pin A or 1	Gray	5-volt Reference	Blue Pin 8
Pin B or 2	Black	Low Reference	Blue Pin 60
Pin C or 3	Dark Blue	TPS Signal	Green 24

Oil Pressure Sensor (2003-and-Newer Harnesses)

Sensor Pin Location	Wire Color	Description	ECM Plug/ Pin Location
Pin A or 1	Black	Low Reference	Blue Pin 63
Pin B or 2	Gray	5-volt Reference	Blue Pin 7
Pin C or 3	Tan/White	Oil Pressure Signal	Green Pin 58

Idle Air Controller Valve

Sensor Pin Location	Wire Color	IAC PIN Description PCM Plug	ECM Plug/ Pin Location
Pin A	Light Green/Black	IAC Coil B Low	Green Pin 77
Pin B	Light Green/White	IAC Coil B High	Green Pin 76
Pin C	Light Blue/Black	IAC Coil A Low	Green Pin 78
Pin D	Light Blue/White	IAC Coil A High	Green Pin 79

If you are converting from drive by wire to drive by cable on a red/blue harness, just add the wiring for the IAC valve and TPS.

A red/blue connector PCM can be used on a 2003-and-newer harness (green/blue connector) with cable throttle with a few simple modifications. The only other thing that needs alteration is the oxygen-sensor wiring. On the 2003-and-newer blue/green connector PCMs, the PCM supplies a ground for the oxygen-sensor heaters, and 12V-plus comes from the fuse block. In the 1999–2002, power and ground is fed directly to the oxygen-sensor heaters. The changes needed to make the 2003-and-newer blue/green harness work with a blue/red computer are as follows:

Remove the blue PCM connector pins 24, 27, 64, and 67. These should all be black with white stripes. These were extra ground wires provided to the 2003-and-newer PCM so that it could control ground to the oxygen-sensor heaters. The 1999–2002 PCM does not need these. Just pull the pins out, but don't cut anything yet. You need to hook these to a few other wires pulled out of the PCM connectors.

Next, remove the wires from the PCM connector that go to the oxygen-sensor heater control. There is one wire for each oxygen sensor. If you are only using front oxygen sensors in the conversion, omit anything to do with Sensor 2.

Drive-By-Wire to Drive-By-Cable Conversion *continued*

Bank/Sensor	Color	Details
Bank 1 Sensor 1	Black/White	Green connector pin 72
Bank 1 Sensor 2	Brown	Green connector pin 52 (after CAT O_2 sensor)
Bank 2 Sensor 1	Light Green	Green connector pin 74
Bank 2 Sensor 2	Red/White	Green connector pin 53 (after CAT O_2 sensor)

Now, it should have four ground wires and two (or four) oxygen-sensor heater control wires pulled from the PCM connectors. Locate the four tan oxygen-sensor low-reference wires going into the blue PCM connector. If you are just using front oxygen sensors, it's blue pins 26 and 29. If you are also using rear oxygen sensors, add pins 25 and 28. These wires will always be tan and may have a white stripe.

The easiest way to splice these together is to pull the pin out (note its location), remove some insulation with a stripper, solder on the new wire, and tape up the solder joint. It might be possible to use heat-shrink tubing as well. Then, reinstall the pin in its original location. Leave about 12 inches of wire loose for each wire spliced into. Do this for all the oxygen sensors.

There should be four black/white ground wires loose: two to four oxygen-sensor heater-control wires, and two to four wires going to each of the tan wires. All of these wires need to be hooked together in a big splice pack. Using a piece of 1/4-inch or 5/16-inch heat-shrink tubing, slide the tubing over all four ground wires, several inches past the ends to be soldered. Next, strip about 1 inch of insulation off all the wires. Start hooking them together end to end, solder all of these together, and slip the heat shrink over when done.

The last step is making the connectors fit inside the PCM. To do this, cut the rib off of the green plastic terminal cover so it will fit in the red PCM socket. Use oxygen sensors for a 2002 5.3L Chevy truck with a white plastic connector, and it will plug right into the 2003-and-newer harness without changing plugs. ■

LT ECMs

Gen V engines have five models of ECM: E92, E92A, E93, E99, and E90. The E92 and E92A variant are essentially the same ECM, but the E92A (referred to as the "Late" ECM) uses a three-pin fuel-pressure sensor on the fuel rail instead of the earlier four-pin that was used with E92 ECMs. These ECMs can be switched out among engines, provided that the fuel-pressure sensor is switched out and the correct harness is used for the ECM. There may be some different sensors as well, specifically the oxygen sensors, as these vary by the vehicle in which the engine was originally installed.

When changing the reluctor type (24x to 48x or vice versa), the reluctor wheel also requires changing the cam timing gear. The reluctor wheel and the cam gear work in tandem to monitor the ignition system. If they don't match, the engine won't run. You need to know this detail if you change cam gears as well.

The real problems showed up in 2019 with the E99, E93, and E90 ECMs. General Motors decided to change its ECMs from a tunable unit to a non-user-tunable ECM. These are hardware locked, meaning no amount of flashing will allow it to be tuned.

This is a bit of a misnomer, as a tune can be loaded onto them but sometime within about 30 days, the vehicle will actually reach out to talk to General Motors. These vehicles all have regular online communication with the automaker, and the system will automatically wipe the aftermarket tune and revert back to the stock tune. This is called the Factory Immobilizer Reset Service, and it is hard-coded with the vehicle's VIN. All 2019-and-newer GM LT-powered vehicles have this issue.

HP Tuners and several other tuning software companies have figured out how to delete this feature, but it is not cheap. The HP Tuners

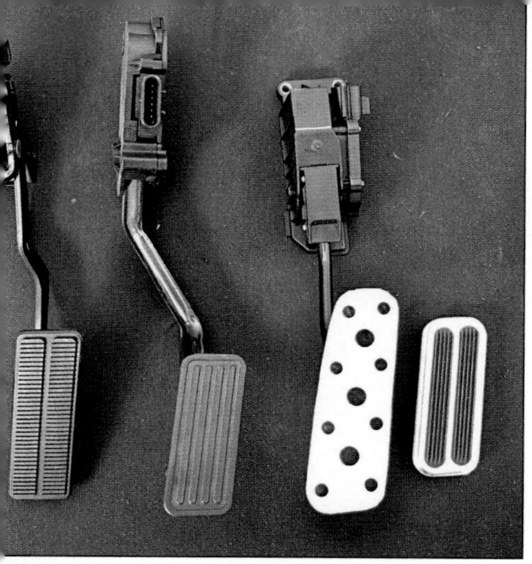

Several different drive-by-wire pedals are available, including (from left to right) a 2005-and-newer Corvette pedal, a 2005–2006 SSR pedal, a 2005–2006 GTO pedal, and the Lokar pedal replacement pad. There is also the 1997–2004 Corvette pedal, the CTS-V pedal, the 2007 Trailblazer pedal, and the rest of the truck pedals, which interchanged throughout the years.

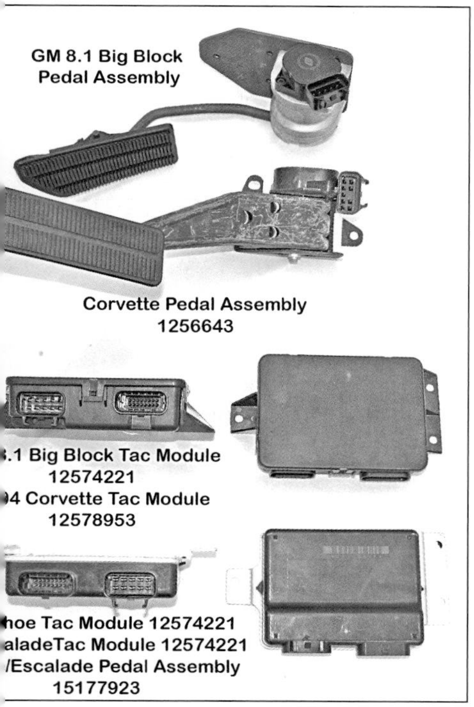

The pedals and throttle actuator control (TAC) modules for LS engines are a matched set. Both units are needed to properly operate a drive-by-wire throttle. The Tahoe/Escalade pedal assembly is not shown.

E90 exchange runs about $700 to "jailbreak" these ECMs. They also have regular intervals where the replacement ECMs are out of stock, so the ECM may or may not be able to be exchanged when needed. The jailbreak service for the E99 ECM starts at $2,000. At this time, there are no jailbreak services for the E93 ECM.

Now for the good news. It is possible to run a 2019-and-newer Gen V engine on an E92 ECM, but it has to have the right harness, and the 2019-and-newer transmissions are *not* swappable at this time. There is no transmission-control unit currently available that will work in a swap for the second-generation GM automatics. Performance Systems Integration (PSI) offers retrofit harnesses for later Gen V engines operating with an E92 ECM for as little $1,650.

Gen V LT-Series Engine ECMs		
Year	Engine	ECM
2014–2016	L83, L86, LT1, LT4	E92
2017–2018	L83, L86, LT1, LT4	E92A
2019 and newer	L84, L87	E90
2019 and newer	LT1, LT4	E92A
2019 and newer	LT5	E99
2020 and newer	LT2	E99
2020 and newer	L8T	E93

The LT ECM measures $9\frac{7}{8}$ inches long x $7\frac{1}{8}$ inches wide x $1\frac{5}{8}$ inches deep, with a 1/4-inch inset lip for mounting. There are no other provisions for mounting. You cannot drill the case at any point, so it must be mounted in a clamshell or with straps.

The factory ECM mounts are very large and can be used in trucks, but they are big chunky blocks of black plastic and are not very good looking. Dirty Dingo and ICT Billet offer aluminum mounts, or you could make your own. The ECM case is weather-resistant, as long as water does not collect and submerge any part of the unit.

Building a clamshell is a simple process. The cutout for the ECM should be 6½ x 9¼ inches. The thickness of the ECM at the flange is 1/2 inch (to the back of the case). There is a small lip on the back of the case, so make two rings and sandwich the 1/4-inch lip or make a solid base and use one ring on the front side of the ECM. Keep in mind that the plugs stand off the face of the ECM about 1½ inches, so make sure to have room for the plugs as well as the ECM in the mounting location.

Aftermarket ECMs

Where the factory ECMs are well-built and reliable, they certainly leave some potential performance on the table. A stock LS ECM can handle 1,000 hp with a really good tuner who knows these engines well, but there are some limitations. Really large cams, big boost, and other upgrades mean the stock ECM simply can't manage.

Additionally, tuning a stock ECM is not as easy as most aftermarket ECMs because the software is less intuitive. Beyond basic changes, a tune can really get screwed up if you don't have any training. Aftermarket ECMs typically come with more intuitive tuning software, with drop-down selection boxes and have tech support to help get the engine running right. Some aftermarket ECM programs have basic and advanced tuning options, while some only have the basic options.

Building a Throttle Cable

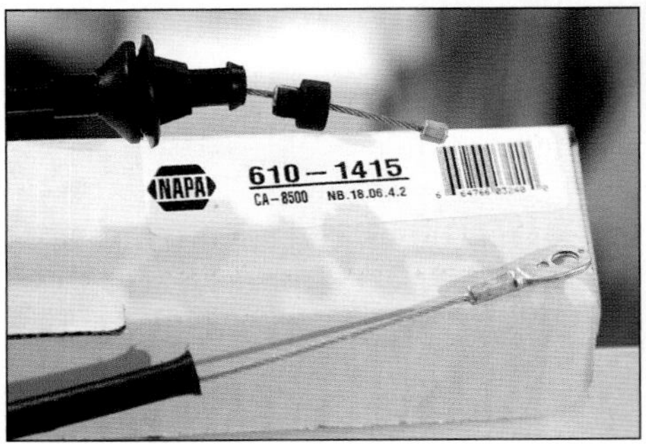

1 For the 1966 Suburban, the throttle is cable operated, so we needed to build a new cable. We could have sourced an aftermarket kit, but we wanted to use a cable that was $18 at the local NAPA store.

2 The cable fits the throttle-body blade. We just need to make an adapter for the factory pedal.

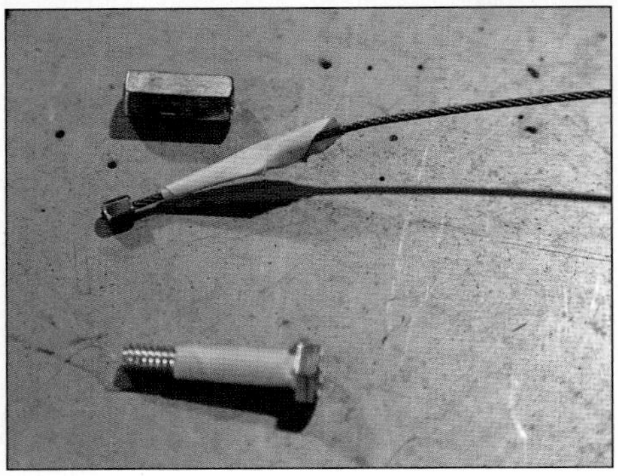

3 Make an adapter with a 1/4-inch bolt and a 1/4-inch coupler nut. Tape off the bolt and the cable end.

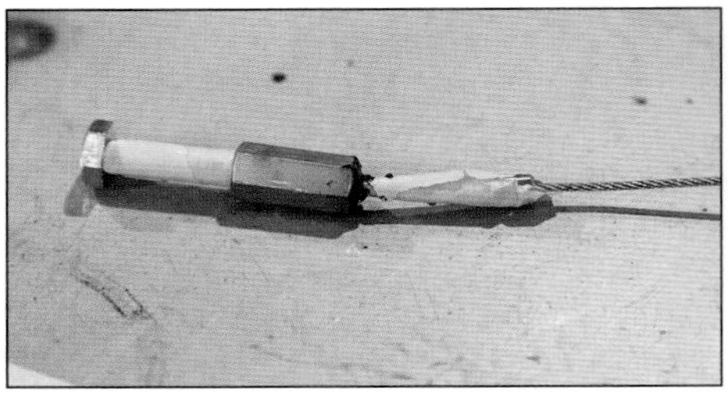

4 The bolt sets the depth of the cable end, and then you can backfill the coupler with J-B Weld. Once the epoxy begins to set up, remove the bolt so that it doesn't get locked in.

5 Make a bracket for the new cable to operate correctly. We used a piece of 11-gauge steel, marked out the square slot, drilled the corners, and used a band saw to cut out the center.

6 Bend the end upward and drill the mounting holes. This will bolt to the intake manifold in two places.

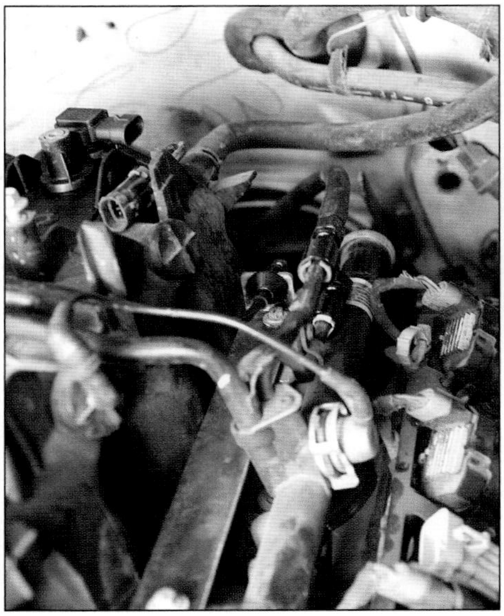

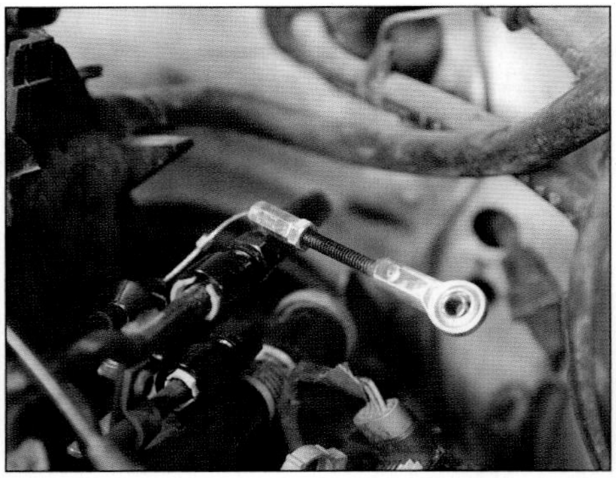

7 This shows the cable and bracket mounted to the intake. Once the fabrication is finished, the bracket will be painted black.

8 Thread a Heim joint to the coupler that was epoxied to the cable earlier. This allows the cable length to be adjusted to make sure that the throttle opens and closes correctly.

9 This cable now connects to the factory pedal arm and works like a dream.

LS ECMs: Chevrolet Performance

While these are technically factory-type ECMs, they are programmed for swaps. This means none of the OEM lockouts including VATS and active fuel management/displacement on demand are active, simplifying the initial startup and run process. There are numerous Chevrolet Performance ECMs available tuned for specific crate engines and factory take-outs.

When buying a GM ECM kit, it comes with the ECM, the harness, oxygen sensors, the MAF, the MAF boss, the drive-by-wire pedal (where applicable), and instructions. These greatly simplify the entire process and come with GM reliability, which in the world of LS swaps is a big deal. What these ECMs do not come with is any type of tuning software or on-the-fly touchscreen controller, unlike most of the other aftermarket engine management options. You also still don't get race-level controls for making really big power.

LS ECMs: Holley Terminator and Terminator Max

Holley has really hit the engine swaps hard and basically owns the market on LS/LT swaps. These controllers have all the options that you could possibly want, including support for drive by wire (Max only), transmission control (Max only), four inputs, four outputs, boost control, nitrous control, advanced tables, and datalogging all in one unit, out of the box.

The base system, Terminator X, controls the engine basics for drive-by-cable engines for 24x and 58x crank sensors. This means that if you have a 58x engine but want to run a cable throttle, you are ready to go. If you need a transmission controller built in, the Terminator X Max is the go-to option. The Max units include drive-by-wire support, as well a GM transmission controller for 4LXX transmissions. These ECMs will run out of the box, but they will not be optimized for your application and will require tuning, as they are not self-learning.

Most Terminator X and X Max systems come with a 4.5-inch touchscreen controller that provides a lot of great features, including setup, tuning, datalogging, troubleshooting, engine codes, and gauges. There is a 6.86- and 12.3-inch Pro Dash available for these controllers, so the entire dash gauges can simply be replaced with a digital screen.

The base tune is easy to set up using the handheld controller and drop-down boxes, simplifying the initial setup process. These ECMs are self-learning, and once the base tune is programmed, the ECM monitors the engine and begins tuning itself. Within just a few miles, the ECM will begin to perfect the engine's tune for maximum drivability.

LS ECMs: FAST EZ-LS 2.0

A leader in high-end racing engine management, Fuel Air Spark Technology (FAST) has an EZ-LS 2.0 that gives the ability to operate an LS swap with ease. Featuring a handheld color touchscreen interface, it is possible to set up and tune an LS swap while monitoring the engine's vitals with up to 20 different parameters. The system comes with the wiring harness and necessary components to get any LS engine up and running quickly. This is a self-learning system, so as you drive starting with the base tune, the ECM learns the engine and driving style and adjusts to optimize itself.

LT ECMs: Holley Terminator and Terminator Max

There is only one aftermarket Gen V ECM on the market (at the time of publishing): the Holley Terminator X and X Max system. Just like the LS versions, these are designed to control LT1, LT4, L83, and L86 engines. The L84, L87, and L8T are currently not covered. The Terminator X system incorporates the gasoline direct injection (GDI) and VVT systems in these engines, giving you the maximum potential for control.

The 3.5-inch handheld controller is used to set up the operation of the ECM, and it can function as a gauge as well. All of the same features from the LS Terminator X and X Max are included. This does come with a few interesting adjustments.

All Gen V engines are drive by wire, but the Terminator X is drive by cable only, so ditch the drive-by-wire throttle body and switch to a cable-operated unit. You must retain

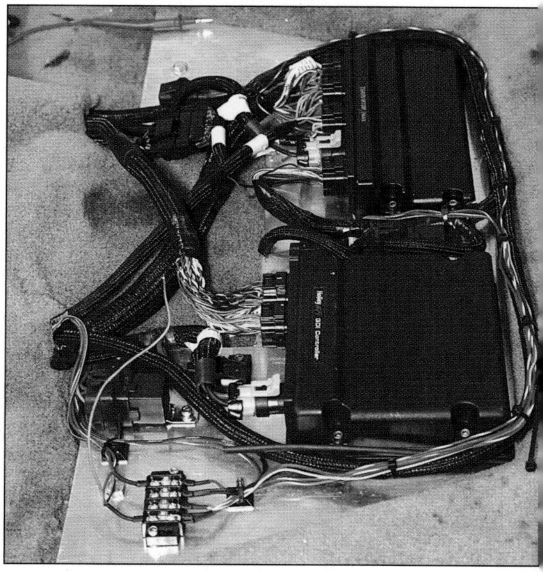

Mounting an aftermarket ECM is not too difficult because ECMs are designed to be bolted down. This is a Holley Terminator system mounted under the seat of a Squarebody C10.

The CTS-V pedal works for LS/LT engines and is the unit recommended by General Motors for LT swaps. This will bolt directly into a Squarebody C10.

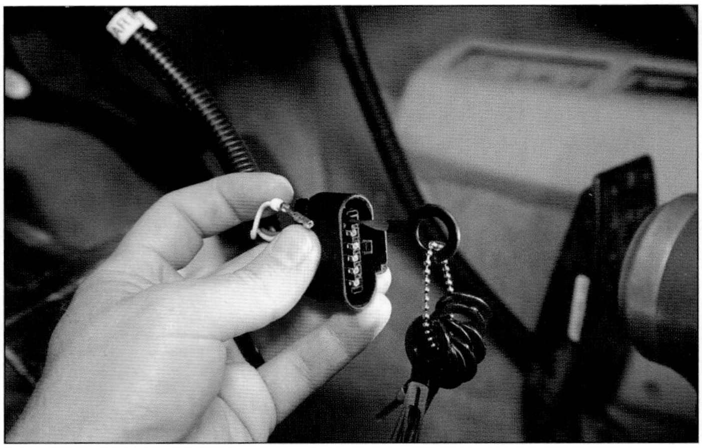

Using a set of terminal keys, we removed the white and blue wires.

the factory fuel injector harness, as this is not supplied with the system. If you want drive-by-wire or transmission control (4LXX only), the Terminator X Max has that capability.

The Terminator X and X Max system does not support the GM Gen V PWM fuel-pump system. It requires a static fuel-pressure system, 59–72 psi at 45 gallons per hour (gph), to run the engine. It also only works with factory camshaft fuel pump lobes, which is a three-wing design. Some aftermarket cams have different fuel-pump lobe designs, and these will not work with the Terminator X or X Max.

You do get the ability to have complete control over the VVT system. The software includes tables for initial setup, but it is possible to get in there and really tweak them as needed. Another interesting feature is the ability to tune the injector phasing, which is critical for direct injection, giving the detailed control needed for higher-output engines.

LT pedals have two wiring versions: car and truck. This harness came with the plug wired for a car pedal, but we are using the truck pedal, so we have to re-pin it.

The two wires are then flip-flopped. The blue goes to the last terminal, and the white wire goes to the third location. Now, the plug is wired for the truck pedal. Nothing else needs to change.

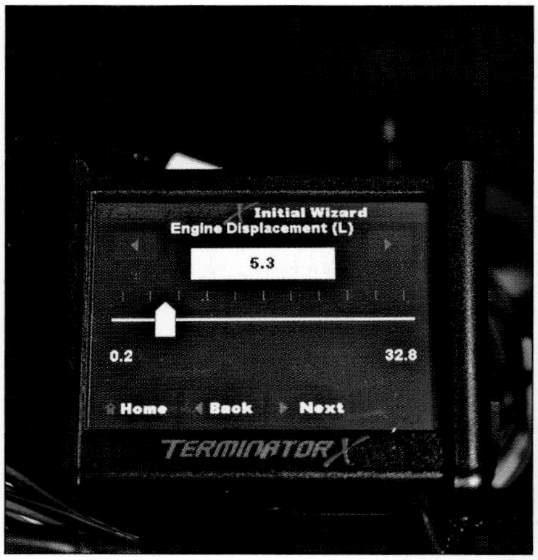

The 1966 Suburban is controlled with a Holley Terminator ECM system. This is very intuitive and easy to set up. Best of all, after the initial setup is done, the ECM will start learning and tune itself.

Displacement on Demand/ Active Fuel Management Delete

Many swappers who have completed a Gen V swap report that the factory displacement-on-demand system should be deactivated in the ECM. The common issue is that in a swap application, there are fewer chassis and drivetrain sensors, which make the displacement-on-demand system not work very well. It tends to be noisy as well. Simply turn this off on the ECM for stock engines.

If you are performing a cam swap, the displacement-on-demand system must be deactivated in the ECM and the hardware in the engine must be removed as well. This is due to the fact that most aftermarket camshafts are not designed to work with the displacement-on-demand system.

Another issue with the active fuel management/displacement-on-demand system is that they use eight regular lifters and eight displacement-on-demand lifters for 2014–2018 engines, and they have a different system for 2019-and-newer engines. There have been a lot of reports of displacement-on-demand lifter failures in LT engines—some in as little as 500 miles. While that is certainly an extreme case, the common complaint of noisy lifters occurs most often between 50,000 and 150,000 miles. The problem is that these lifters fail and that can lead to all kinds of drivability issues.

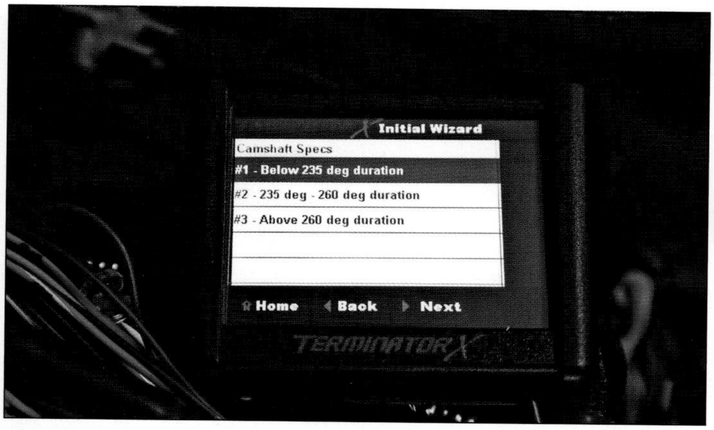

Use the basic cam settings (as shown), and the ECM will adjust as it is driven.

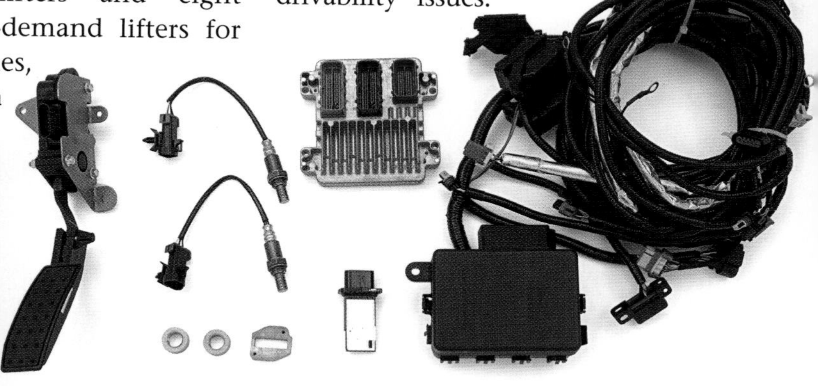

GM's Connect and Cruise ECM systems provide an OEM-quality setup for swaps. These simplify a swap for basic engine packages and run out of the box with no tuning required.

The stock gauges don't even have to be used at all, as the 4-inch screen is capable of showing everything you need unless you have a Terminator MAX with transmission control.

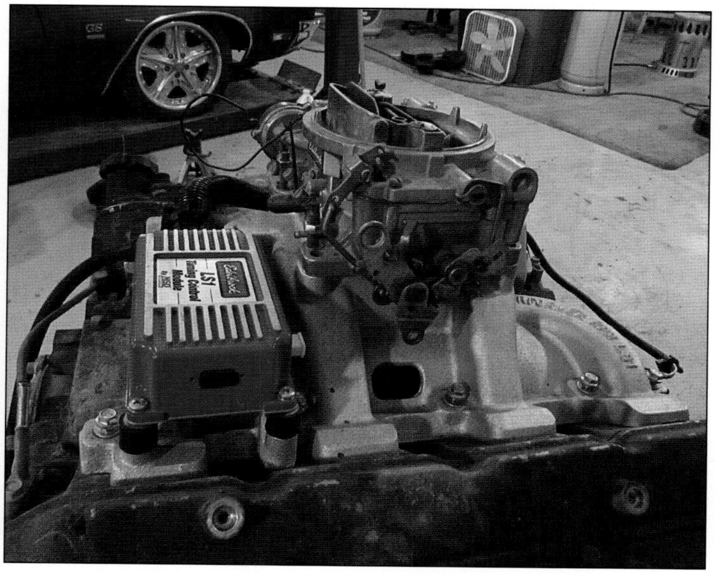

Some swappers still want to run a carburetor. This carbureted intake and controller from Edelbrock comes with a controller from MSD that mounts directly to the intake, eliminating mounting issues.

All L83/4 5.3Ls, L86/7 6.2Ls, and LT1/4 engines have active fuel management/displacement on demand. The LT5 and L8T engines do not have active-fuel-management/displacement-on-demand systems. This provides a solution for LT swappers who want to hardware-delete the active-fuel-management/displacement-on-demand system.

Some LS engines have active fuel management/displacement on demand as well. The replacements are similar but easier and cheaper, as there are more options. For LTs, there are aftermarket cams, which are expensive, and then there is the low-buck option: stock non-displacement-on-demand cams. The LT5 cam and L8T cam are non–displacement on demand, slip into any 5.3L or 6.2L Gen V block, and they are surprisingly cheap. For less than $150, you can get a stock Gen V cam to displacement-on-demand delete your LT engine. Here is what you need:

Cams

The LT5 cam (part number 12664572) is perfect for any 6.2L and will give a slight power increase over the stock L86/7, LT1, or LT4 cam. This can be used on a 5.3L as long as you swap out the valve springs and caps to the 6.2L Gen V pieces, as the LT5 cam has more lift.

The LT5 cam has 1.8:1 rocker arms, is a hydraulic roller, has a 0.551-inch lift (intake)/0.524-inch lift (exhaust), has duration at 0.050 inch of 200/207 degrees, and has a 116-degree lobe separation angle.

The L8T Cam (part number 126724690) is designed for the 6.6L iron-block truck Gen V engine. This cam is slightly bigger than the stock L83/4 5.3L cam, making it the perfect option for a stock engine. This will result in a slight increase in power and torque, and nothing else has to change for a 5.3L swap.

The L8T cam has 1.8:1 rocker arms, is a hydraulic roller, has a lift of 0.502 inch (intake)/0.494 inch (exhaust), has a duration at 0.050 inch of 193/199 degrees, and has a 114-degree lobe separation angle.

Lifters (GM part number 12499225)

Your active-fuel-management engine will have eight standard lifters and eight active-fuel-management lifters. This part gets you 16 new standard lifters.

Lifter Guides (GM part number 12595365)

These are the plastic guides that keep the lifters from rotating, keeping the roller going the correct direction on the cam lobe. These guides are different for active-fuel-management lifters, and you will need four of them.

Lifter Valley Oil Towers

Similar to the 2007–2014 Gen IV engines, an active fuel management mechanical delete requires plugging the oil towers. There is not a factory GM part to accomplish this, but the aftermarket has this covered. Replace the valley cover with a non-displacement-on-demand unit, which runs about $200, such as the displacement-on-demand delete cover from Texas Speed and Performance (part number 25-TSPG5VC-BLACK), or simply block the oil ports.

Brian Tooley Racing plugs (part number CBI/OBO) are nice-looking pieces for about $65. There are several plug options available for $35 to $100. These steel plugs are pressed into the oil towers under the factory valley cover to block the oil. Most of these plugs are threaded for removal with a slide hammer. These plugs also work in Gen IV active-fuel-management/displacement-on-demand engines.

Sensors

There are a few sensors that are required for the LT-series engine to operate correctly, and not all of these come with the engine. These include the fuel-pressure sensor (part number 13579380), MAF sensor (part number 23262343), and oxygen sensors (two required, part number 12659516).

How these sensors are installed and where they are located makes a difference in how the engine operates. The MAF sensor must be installed inline with the air intake tube with some pretty strict guidelines. Unfortunately, this is just not always possible.

GM specifications require an air-inlet tube that is 4 inches in diameter by at least 6 inches long, with the MAF mounted at least 10 inches away from the throttle body. This means that the section where the MAF sensor is mounted must be 4 x 6 with the MAF located in the center, which must also be at least 10 inches from the throttle body, meaning that the air-inlet tube must be at least 16 inches long. It is not always possible to make this work, but it needs to be as close to this spec as possible. A longer air tube is fine, but shorter is not a good idea. More details are in Chapter 9.

Transmission Controllers

LS ECMs have built-in controllers for the corresponding available transmissions from the time the engine was produced. If you are using a stock ECM, this can be configured into the wiring harness and tuned with the same software as the ECM. For LS engines, this is the simplest solution. Gen V ECMs do not have any transmission controller built in, so either a factory TCM if using a late-model transmission (6LXX, 8LXX, 10LXX) or an aftermarket controller is needed. You can always opt for an aftermarket controller for any LS transmission as well.

The Gen V–mounted 6LXX transmissions have the TCM built into the transmission itself. It just has to be wired up. If you are using a stock LT ECM, this can be configured into the wiring harness. The 8LXX and 10LXX require separate units, which are stock controllers and need a separate wiring harness.

Chevrolet Performance offers the "Connect and Cruise TC-2" TCU system for 4LXX-series transmissions. There is a kit for 4L6X/7X units and one for 4L8X transmissions. The TCU plugs into the ECM so that the two controllers can talk to each other. These transmission controllers also work with E-Rod and other Chevrolet LS ECMs. General Motors does not currently offer an aftermarket version of its 10-speed TCM.

The factory TCMs are great, but there are aftermarket versions available as well. There are several aftermarket transmission controllers, such as the TCI transmission control unit (TCU), and US Shift's Quick 4, which gives greater tuning capability of the GM electronic-controlled transmission than the factory controller. These units are compatible with most GM electronically controlled automatic transmissions. With the click of a mouse, it provides load, gear, RPM, and speed-based programming.

Transmission controllers come with the tuning software and the wiring harnesses. The software allows changes to many parameters, even allowing paddle and push-button shifting configurations and manifold pressure–based shift firmness. These features greatly add to the ability to tune the transmission far beyond the capabilities of the stock TCM or ECM.

US Shift's Quick 4 Gen2 stand-alone TCM was installed on the 1966 GMC Suburban featured in this book. This is such a simple installation and control system that it installs in less than an hour and is ready to run out of the box. You don't have to sit there and try to figure out how to tune the thing. It will control the 4L60/65, 4L70E (2008 and earlier), and 4L80/85 transmissions as well as a few Ford transmissions.

While the install is simplified, this is a full-fledged controller, giving the ability to control every aspect of the transmission, including line pressures, shift calibrations, slip detection, 4WD options, and convertor control. It even has a burnout mode and four shift presets for different driving needs.

Throttle Pedals

To control the throttle, you need a throttle pedal, or in this case, an "accelerator pedal position sensor," which is the long way to say a gas pedal. Because some LS and all Gen V LT-series engines are drive by wire, they have to run an electronic pedal. Later-model pedals for LS engines (only the 2010-and-newer CTS-V pedal and the 2010-and-newer Gen 5 Camaro) will swap to LTs.

LS Pedals

Electronic throttle pedals for Gen III and Gen IV LS-series engines can be a bit confusing. Gen IV pedals are model-specific, but the electronics inside are basically the same across all 58x platforms. These pedals use a six-pin plug and even work on LT engines. Gen III pedals are much more complicated.

Gen III pedals require a pedal and a TAC module. The pedal is a position sensor, and the TAC module does all the calculations and sends the info to the ECM. Both are needed, and they must match the ECM and wiring harness you have. These work for the 24x reluctor engines.

8.1L Big-Block Pedal

This pedal came in 2001–2006 trucks with the 8.1L big-block engine. This pedal has a classic pedal look and a flat vertical mount that is relatively easy to mount to the firewall. A TAC module (GM part number 12574221) is required.

LS1 Pedal

The most popular for Gen III swaps, the Corvette pedal (GM part number 1256643) has a classic pedal look and a simple two-bolt mount that adapts well to most trucks. This pedal requires a TAC module (GM part number 12578953).

Gen III Vortec Truck Pedal

The most common pedal is the 2003–2007 Vortec pedal (GM part number 15177923), which is identical to the Gen V truck pedal but requires a TAC module (GM part number 12574221). The far-offset plastic pedal makes it harder to mount in most trucks, but brackets are available in the aftermarket.

Gen IV Pedals

The 2010–2015 CTS-V pedal (part number 10379038) is compact and easy to fabricate mounts for. The pedal mounts through the main body to a steel bracket. The bolts run perpendicular to the pedal arm (left to right in the vehicle). This means that to use this pedal, the steel bracket must be adapted to your truck. Because it is steel, it can be welded pretty easily. This pedal is inexpensive and readily available. As a bonus, the actual foot of the pedal is removable, so any foot can be used on your pedal, including the stock pedal from most 1973–1987 C10 trucks. This also works for Gen V swaps.

The 2010-and-newer fifth-generation Camaro pedal (part number 22741799) is becoming more popular for LT swaps in trucks. These pedal mounts are built in and are directly behind the pedal arm, so this pedal can be mounted directly to the firewall in many cases without any adapters at all. For 1973–1987 C10 trucks, use the factory pedal mount and drill one extra hole. This assembly will bolt directly to the firewall and sit in the original pedal position. This also works for Gen V swaps.

LT Pedals

Several pedals are available for LT swaps.

2010-and-Newer CTS Pedal (part number 10379038)

A donor pedal from a 2014-and-newer truck, a 2014-and-newer Corvette pedal, a 2010-and-newer Camaro pedal, or the 2010-and-newer CTS pedal (part number 10379038) can be used. The CTS pedal is the unit that General Motors sells in all of its swap kits. In most cases, a bracket will have to be built to mount the pedal to the firewall. Sometimes this is simple, and sometimes it is not.

Whenever possible, try to use at least one of the original mounting points for the original pedal as a locating point for the bracket. This will ensure that the pedal is close to where it needs to be to feel comfortable when driving. Keep in mind that there are three different pedal harness configurations: truck, Corvette, and car. The difference is not the plug itself, but rather the positioning of the wires in the plug. The wires can be moved around if the harness configuration doesn't match the pedal.

2014-and-Newer Truck Pedal (part number 25832864)

If the original pedal from a 2014-and-newer donor vehicle was sourced, this is the pedal you have. While it will save a little money if you get this pedal with the engine, it doesn't work very well in swaps. One is featured in this book, as it was used in the 1991 C1500 L83 swap, and it was not worth the effort. The pedal arm has a hard right offset that puts the actual mechanism really close to the foot brake. We had to fabricate a large adapter bracket. This might work on the 1960–1972 C10s, but it is best to use a different pedal. The foot pad is also all one piece with the pedal arm, so you are stuck with the foot pad.

2014-and-Newer Corvette Pedal (part number 23417313)

Some consider this pedal to be the most customizable, as the foot pad is separate and the base has forward-facing mounts, but this is a large pedal assembly and has a rolled upper firewall mount that is not going to match well to any C10-series truck.

Tuning Software

Programming the stock ECM can be done several ways. There are computer-based programs available, such as HP Tuners and EFI Live, which are designed to work with the Gen III and Gen IV computers. Most of the aftermarket tuning modules and software are locked, meaning they lock themselves to a particular computer on the first use. To unlock them, passcodes or VINs for additional vehicles must be purchased. Some products include two passes to tune two separate vehicles. Typically, when purchasing tuning software, there is unlimited tuning capability or tunes on the same vehicle.

Do-it-yourself or computer-based tuning packages are very efficient and handy to have. They allow tuning of the engine for a multitude of parameters, help identify trouble codes, and add some personalization to the engine without getting greasy. There are some things that home-based tuning software can't do.

Most software packages can't make significant changes to the programming of an ECM, so the engine can be tuned, but the ECM cannot be changed from drive by wire to drive by cable or vice versa. The software also is not the best way to swap a computer from a different year to a different engine; this requires more significant programming beyond what the tuning software was designed for. These programs are great for what they do, which is to tune the existing programming to better suit your application and needs.

HP Tuners

This comprehensive tuning software allows swappers to tune and adjust every aspect of the stock ECM. Available in a base or pro form, the HP VCM Suite adjusts Gen III–V computers. This system works on the credit system, and it allows tuning of up to four specific vehicles, unlimited tunes for the same year and model vehicle (any 2000 Camaro LS1 for example), even unlimited Gen III–V vehicles.

Whichever option is chosen costs credits. A single vehicle license costs 2 credits, a year and model license cost 6 credits, and unlimited LS1 tunes cost 70 credits. The basic software purchase includes 8 credits, and additional credits are always available, adding to the flexibility of the software.

This software costs a good deal more than a handheld tuner or shipping a computer off, but it has much more flexibility and will likely be worth the extra cost in the end. However, the HP Tuners software cannot load programming from different model years to any given computer. Therefore, it is important to start with the right year computer for your engine application. Considered by many to be the most comprehensive tuning software publicly available, the HP Tuners software is an excellent choice.

EFI Live

EFI Live offers several versions of its FlashScan products. FlashScan and FlashScan and Tune are the main two. The tuning version allows the building of individual ECM tunes, controlling all of the aspects of the ECM programming. The FlashScan software works on a VIN licensing system, which requires each vehicle to be licensed. The main kit includes two VIN licenses while additional licenses can be purchased.

The EFI Live software is capable of tuning Gen III–V computers. The FlashScan software features more than 600 engine calibrations for the in-depth ECM tuning, as well as fixes for issues with the stock computers such as VATS, MAF, and traction-control system (TCS) fault codes. The software is constantly upgrading and evolving, ensuring the product purchased will not only serve its current purpose but it will also be up to date as the technology changes.

Handheld Tuners

These are an alternative to the computer-based software programs and offer more portability for tuning the engine. Handheld engine tuners allow tuning the computer on the fly and running diagnostics whenever the need strikes and regardless of location. The upper-end handheld tuners are typically comparable in price to the entry-level, computer-based software programmers.

Handhelds usually control the basic functions and parameters needed to tune the engines, but they only provide the basics. That means the computer-based software programs have many more variables and options. The biggest advantage of the handheld tuners is their ease of use. The simple user interface makes tuning easier than the computer-based software. There are many handheld tuners available; the market is flooded with quality viable options.

If changing from drive by wire to a throttle cable or swapping a newer ECM to an older engine, you need to work with a reprogrammer. Many shops offer mail-in reprogramming services so that the ECM can be precisely programed to your requirements. If keeping a stock or slightly modified tune in the computer, sending the stock ECM off to be reconfigured is usually cheaper than buying a tuning package. It is also the only way to make certain changes. Some wiring harness dealers, such as Painless Performance, offer complimentary basic ECM tuning with a purchase of a harness.

Fabricating a Throttle Pedal Mount

Unlike a standard cable-operated throttle pedal, the throttle-pedal-position sensor is a large block mechanism that is mounted off one side of the main unit with three bolts. New or used pedals can be purchased, and some come with the factory steel bracket and some do not. This bracket is not of much use other than to simplify the fabrication process. We used a pedal that we sourced online. It came with the steel bracket, which we used as the base to weld up the rest of the mount.

Take a lot of measurements and make notes on where the pedal sits before removing the original pedal. We used the original gas-pedal mount to make a pattern. It became the base for the new mount that we fabricated. We simply traced the base pad of the stock pedal mount onto a piece of poster board. We also marked the locations of the holes on the board. This was transferred to a piece of 1/8-inch steel that was cut and drilled.

The factory mounting bracket has tabs and extra material that gets in the way, so we trimmed away the mounting tabs (to the original vehicle), leaving only the main bracket.

Fabricating a Throttle Pedal Mount *continued*

The angle of the pedal greatly depends on the shape of the firewall and the other obstacles in the way. Be sure to take careful measurements to get the new pedal to sit how you want it.

On this vehicle, the pedal mount sat at an angle of 32 degrees perpendicular to the motion of the actual gas pedal. If we just built the pedal straight off the firewall, the pedal would run at a severe angle, making it unusable. We factored in the angle and offset the bracket to compensate.

The depth of the pedal off the firewall depends greatly on the make and model of the vehicle as well as where you would prefer the pedal to sit. These pedals only have a couple of inches of swing, so they don't move very far compared to a stock pedal. You may be tempted to put the pedal as close to the floor as possible, but that will make the driving experience frustrating. Place the throttle pedal about 1 inch or so below the brake pedal; anything more is too much. The goal is an easy transition from the throttle to the brake pedal.

With the depth of the pedal decided, we cut some 1/8-inch flat-stock steel to length and tacked the new mount together. Ensure that none of the support stands obscure any of the mounting points for the pedal or the firewall mounts. Just do a couple of tack welds on each piece to test out the fit of the pedal.

The last step of this project actually isn't about the mount but the pedal itself. The pedal comes with the same basic injection-molded pedal pad that all new GM cars use. To bring the original stealth feel to the vehicle, we wanted to reuse the original pedal pad.

We removed the pads from both throttle arms and tried to install the old one using the spring from the old pedal. It was close, but it didn't quite fit. In the end, we had to shave off about 1/8 inch from the top of the new throttle arm, add some extra material to the bottom of the arm, and then ground it all down smooth. The purpose of this was to get the right angle on the pedal. The pad has a wider slot for the pedal arm, so we had to make a spacer using some #10 screw washers. A solid spacer could easily be made by cutting a small piece of tubing.

The stock GM CTS pad does not pivot on the pedal arm. With our new modification, the original pad now looks and feels right, plus it pivots on the arm just like it did from the factory. You would never know it was not the stock pedal, even when driving the vehicle. ■

1 ***Our 1991 1500 was using a truck LT pedal, so we needed to make a bracket. First, we unbolted the factory pedal. The plan is to use the factory pedal mounts.***

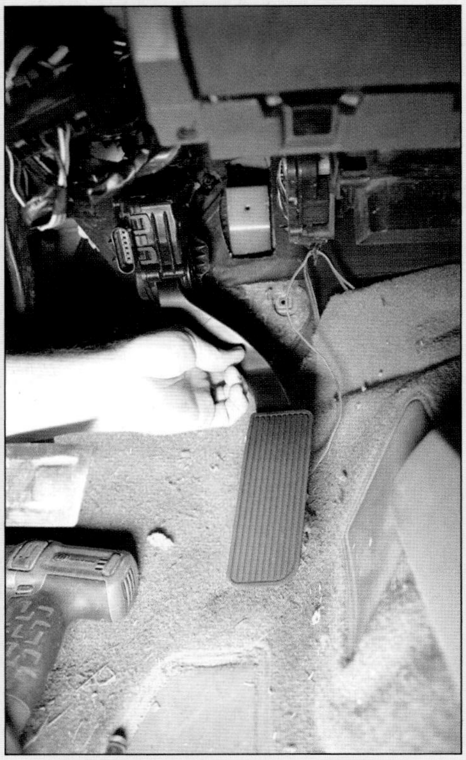

2 ***Because the truck pedal has this weird bend in the pedal, the assembly has to move toward the driver-side door.***

3 *Using 11-gauge sheet metal, trace the shape of the pedal and drill some mounting holes.*

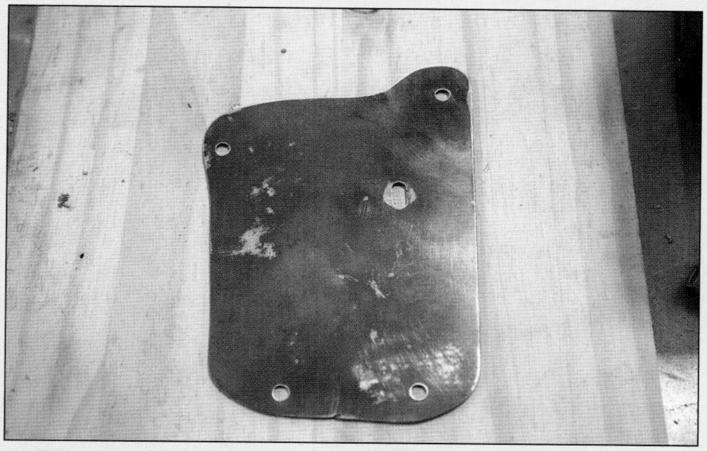

4 *This is the plate. It is a little big, but the truck pedal requires it.*

5 *Cut some pieces of square tubing at an angle to match the firewall perpendicular to the pedal flange, which needs to be vertical. Weld the tubing to the plate and drill holes for the bolts.*

6 *We used rivnuts for the pedal bolts.*

7 *The assembly bolted to the firewall and is quite sturdy with no flex. The pedal looks pretty good in the stock placement.*

ECM Initial Startup

Once the engine is swapped and all wired up, tuning the ECM is the next step. The process of tuning LS/LT engines is very complex, and we simply can't even begin to cover even the most basic of tunes here. However, we can show the basics of getting a stock ECM prepared to run in your truck.

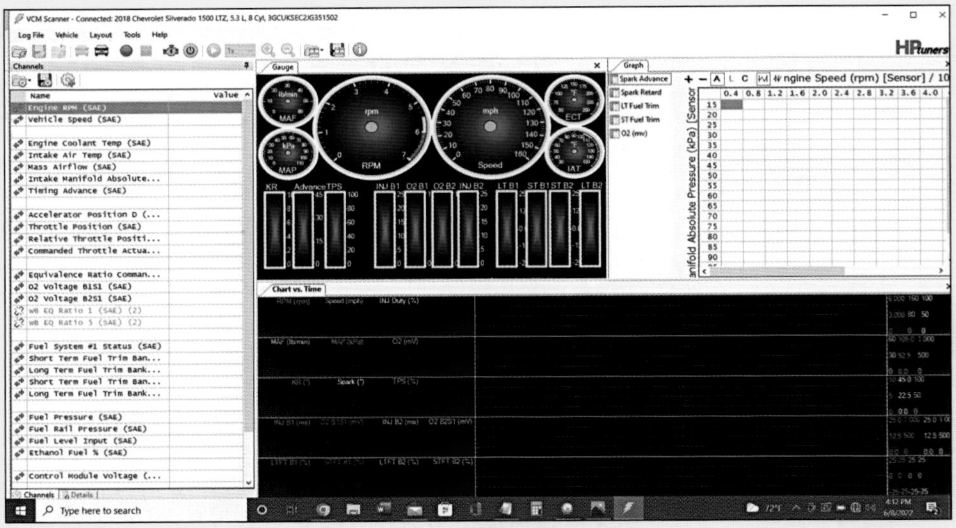

1 ***Stock ECMs must be unlocked in order to start your new swapped vehicle. Send it off or buy the software and do it yourself. This is the HP Tuners software to unlock the 2018 L83 in the 1991 1500.***

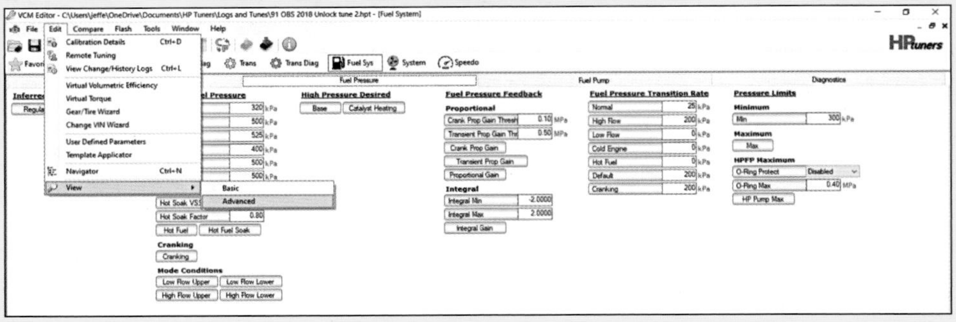

2 ***Switch the view from "Basic" to "Advanced" in the "Edit" tab. This will show all the parameters, whereas Basic mode won't let you get to the vehicle anti-theft system (VATS), which is what we have to disable.***

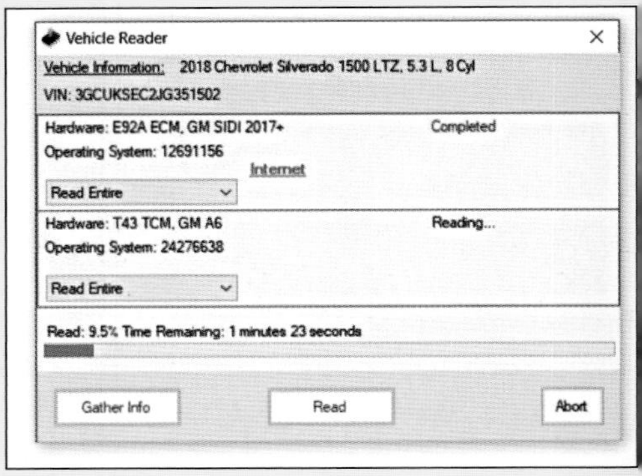

3 ***Read the ECM, which needs to be set to "Read Entire." Save the stock file as the vehicle stock file. Do not delete this because it can be used in the future if a mistake is made.***

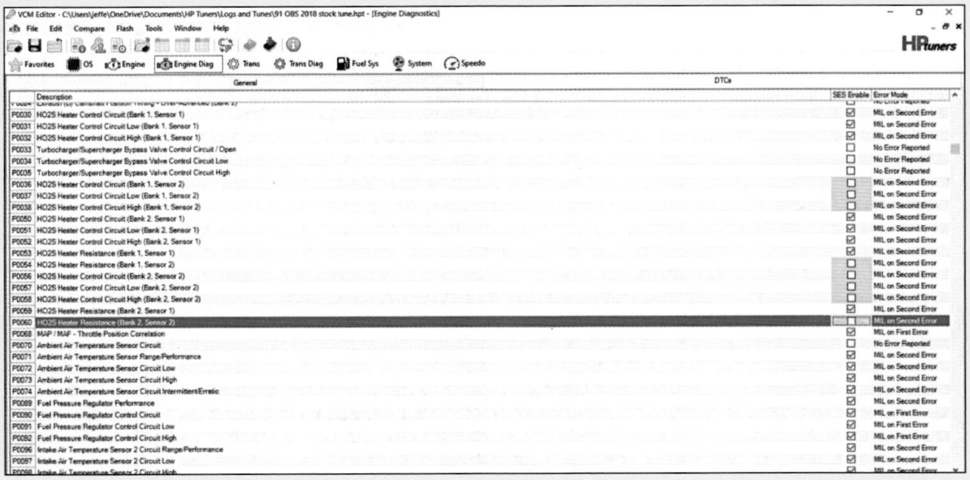

4 ***Next, go into the check engine light (CEL) code file and disable all of the rear oxygen sensors. If you do not do this, the CEL will light up.***

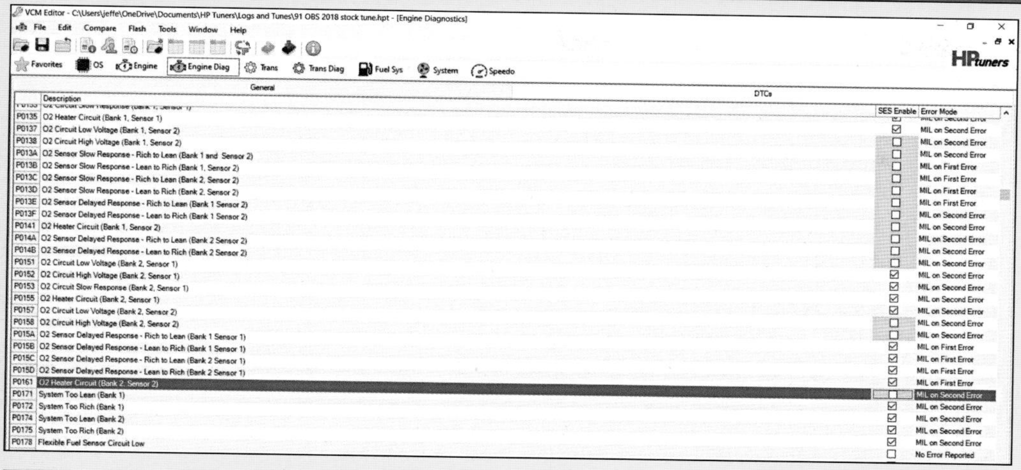

5 *The oxygen heater circuits, slow response, and low voltage must be turned off too.*

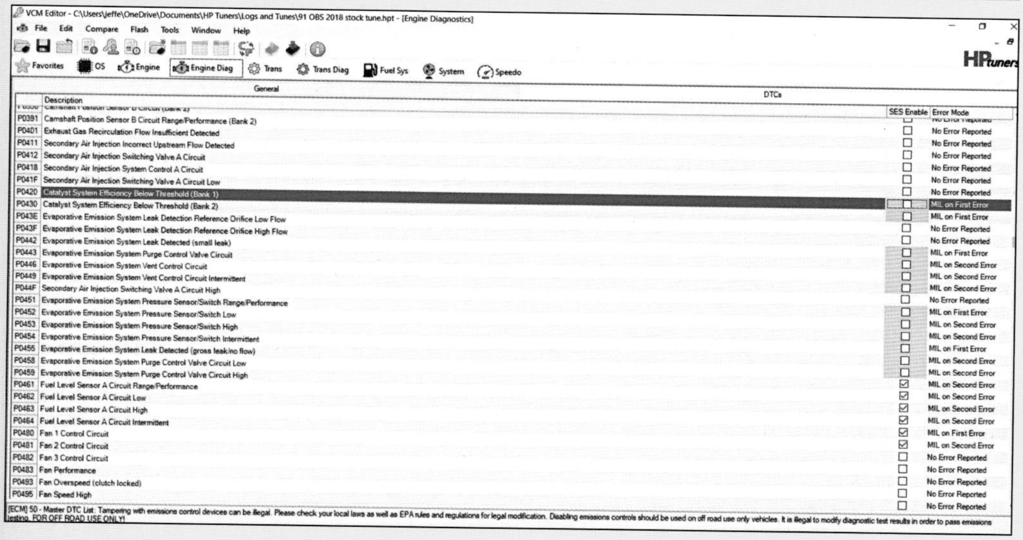

6 *Also, deactivate the evaporative emissions control (EVAP) system codes.*

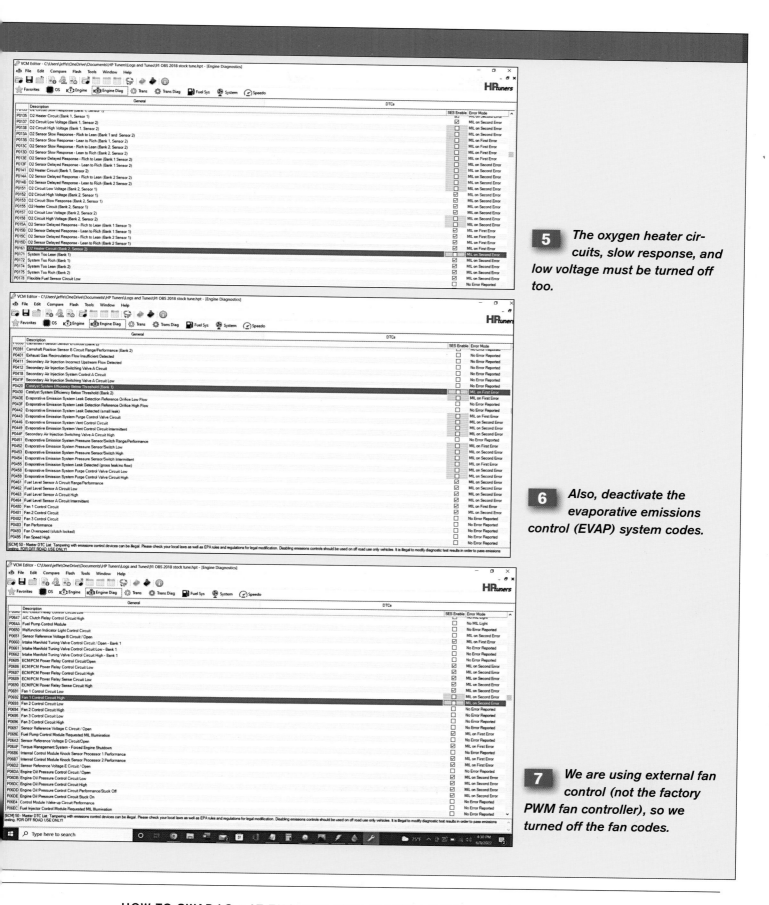

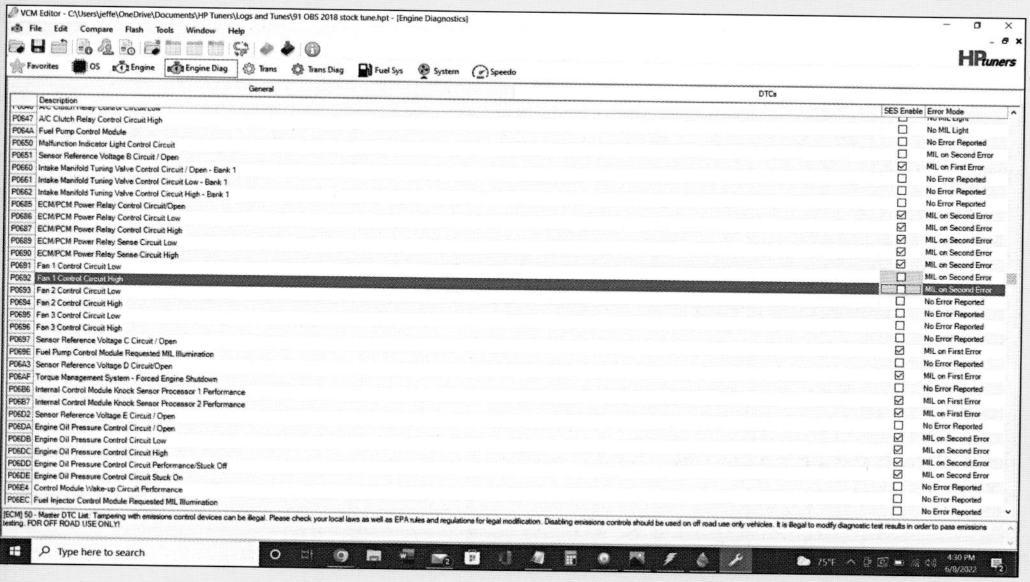

7 *We are using external fan control (not the factory PWM fan controller), so we turned off the fan codes.*

ECM Initial Startup *continued*

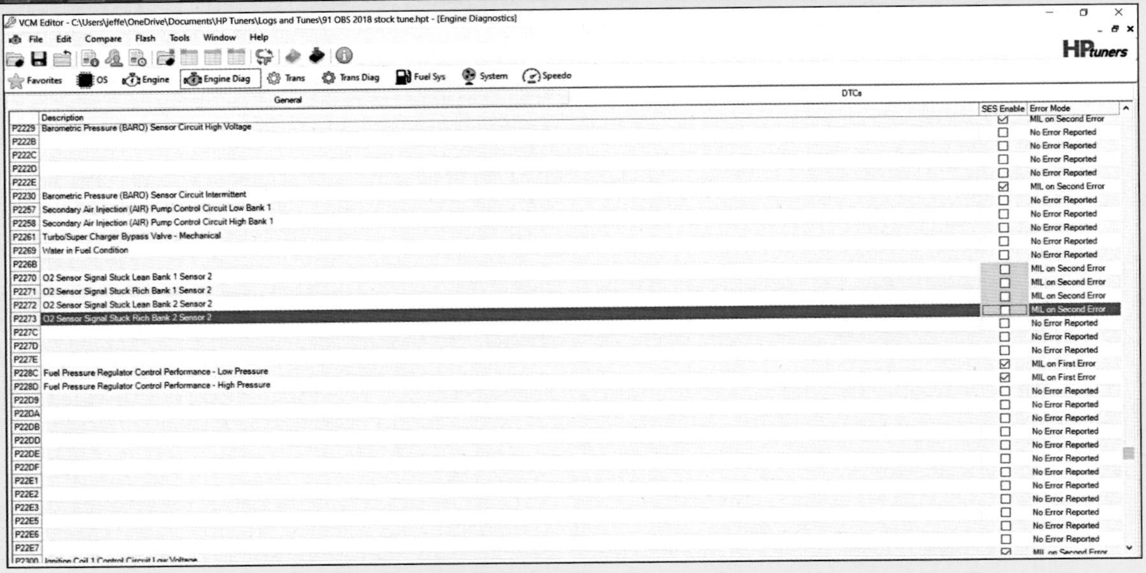

8 *Don't forget to turn off the oxygen signal stuck codes.*

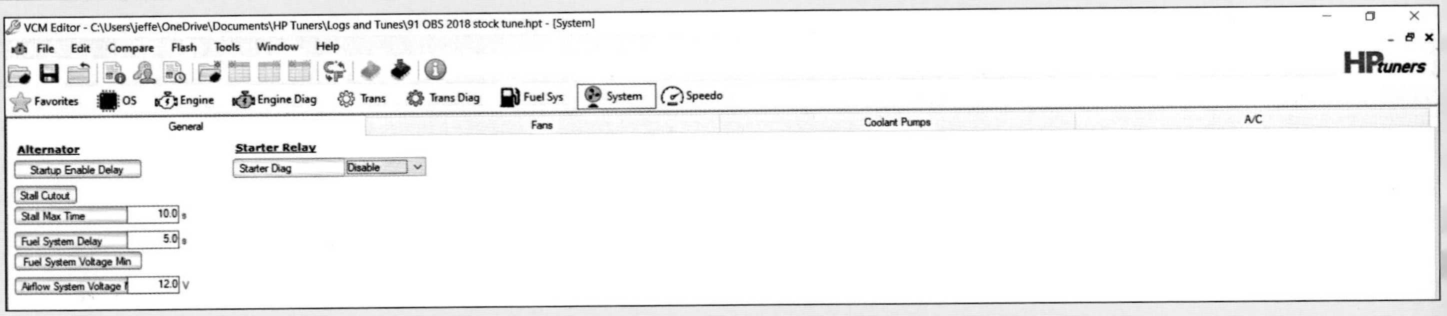

9 *Now, go to the "System" tab. Under "General" and "Starter Relay," disable "Starter Diag."*

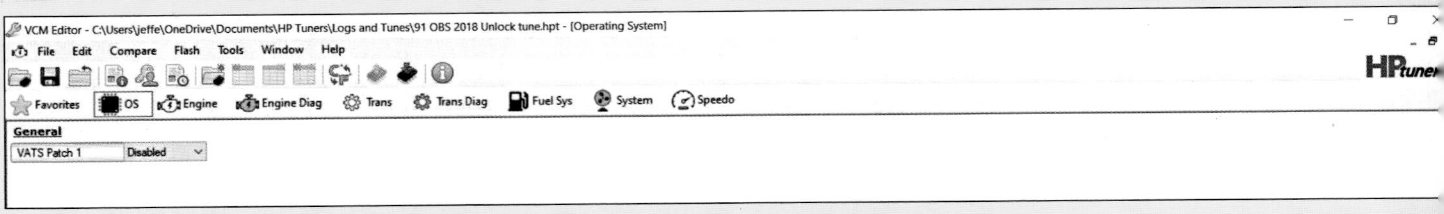

10 *Click on the "OS" tab. Under "General," Find "VATS Patch 1" and disable it.*

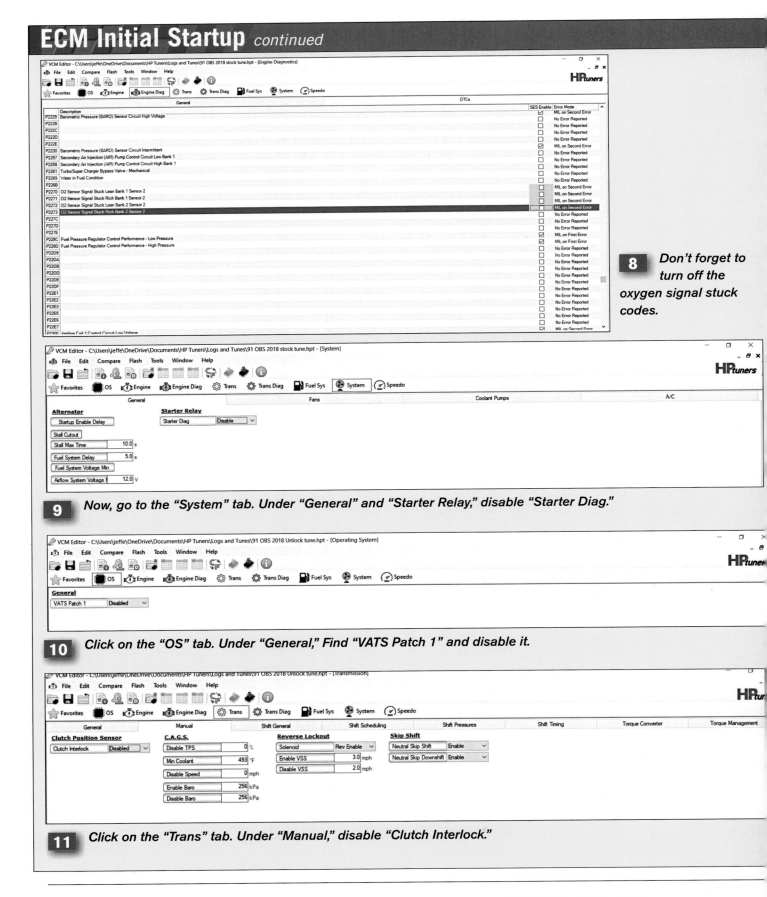

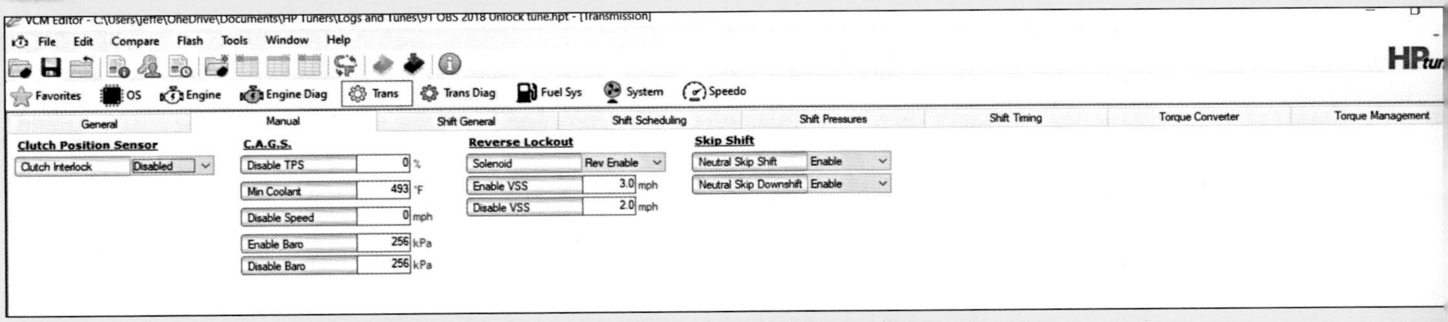

11 *Click on the "Trans" tab. Under "Manual," disable "Clutch Interlock."*

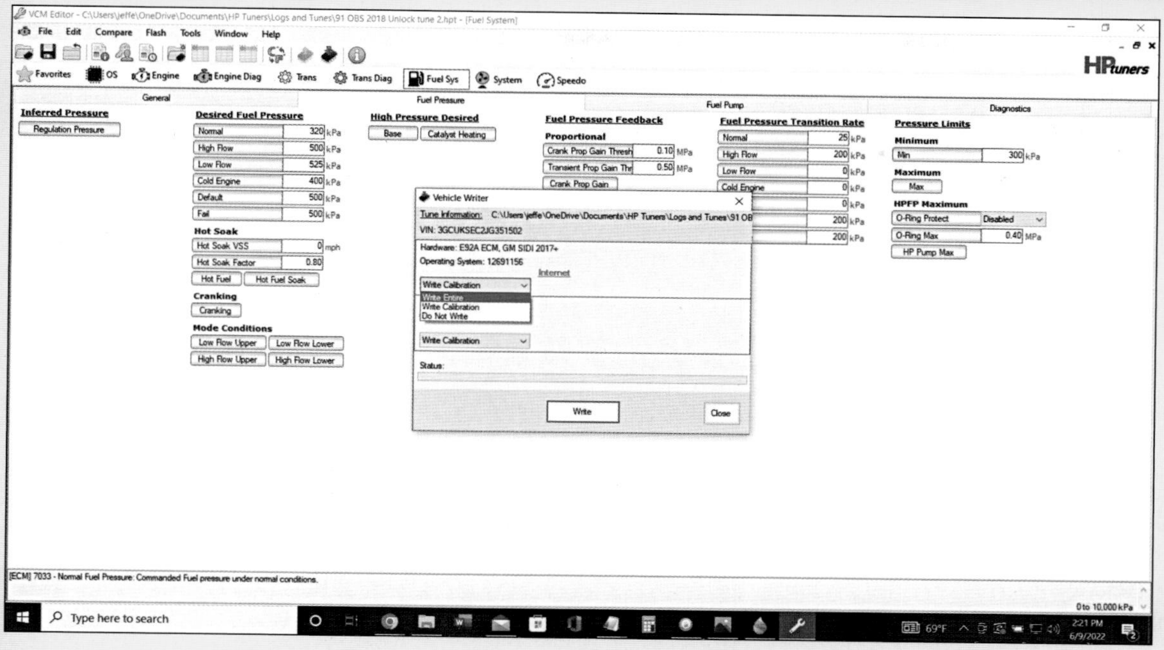

12 ***We saved this tune as "99 1500 L83 Unlocked," set the software to "Write Entire," and wrote the new tune to the ECM. The truck fired up minutes later without any of the factory security.***

To unlock an ECM, a full-blown tuning package, such as HP Tuners or EFI Live, is needed. Handheld tuners are great for basic upgrades and on-the-fly tuning, but they can't get deep enough into the ECM software to make the necessary changes for a swap.

Using the latest version of HP Tuners, we reprogrammed the E92A ECM that came with the 2018 L83 and 6L80 transmission featured in the 1991 C1500 LT swap in this book. The process is very similar for LS ECMs, the main difference being the location of the VATS table(s). A few things are needed to get started with this process: a laptop or desktop, the HP Tuners GM tuning package, enough credits for your application (typically two credits), and a completed engine swap that is ready to run.

The newest version of HP Tuners uses a Bluetooth OBD-II dongle. Once synced to a computer, this dongle gets attached to the OBD-II port and then the computer talks to the ECM via Bluetooth, eliminating the hardwire connections. It is imperative that the software is updated to the latest version before starting, as this can create problems. If tech support is needed, this is the first thing they ask.

Using the VCM scanner tool, first connect to the ECM with the key in the "Run" position (*do not start*). Once the computer has connected to the ECM, select "Read" and then make sure the box "Read Entire" is selected. At this point, read the ECM and save that stock file for future use. It is imperative that you save this file without any changes. Once a new tune is created, save all future tunes as a "Save as" file so that you do not lose the original stock tune for your vehicle. Once saved, you can go into the ECM and start changing things.

There are three main steps: removing the VATS, turning off the starter diagnostic disablers, and deleting some codes that will set the CEL on the dash. First, go into the table that says "Engine Diag," as this is the code list for the CEL. Simply uncheck the box to turn off a function. The main functions that we turn off are the rear cats, the fuel evaporative emissions control (EVAP) system, and fan control (we are not using the Gen V PWM fan).

Next, jump to the "System" box, and under the General tab, disable the "Starter Relay Diag." This is part of the VATS disable. Next, go to the "OS" tab under the "General" sub-tab, and "VATS Patch 1" should be set to disable. The last piece of the puzzle is in the "Trans" tab, under the "Manual" sub-tab. Make sure the "Clutch Interlock" is set to disable. The VATS system is now completely disabled. For some LS ECMs, the main VATS patch tabs are located in the "System" tab, and there are two "VATS Patches" that must be disabled.

After making these changes, the new tune is saved (remember to save it as a different name) and then loaded to the ECM. You must select "Write Entire" in both of the vehicle writer tabs, otherwise your engine will not start. This takes about 10 to 15 minutes. Once the tune is loaded to the ECM, simply cycle the key off and then back on. Then, start. ■

CHAPTER 8

FUEL SYSTEM

Gen III, Gen IV, and Gen V engines use high-pressure fuel systems to feed the engine at the proper level. This means that the entire fuel system needs to be redesigned for most GM C/K10 trucks but not all. Any fuel-injected truck or SUV already has the main components in the original fuel system to greatly simplify the upgrade to support an LS/LT engine swap.

Starting in 1987, GM trucks and SUVs went from a carbureted system to the first throttle-body fuel-injection system. Along with this came in-tank fuel pumps and return lines. For most swaps, this eliminates the need to add anything beyond an upgraded pump in the tank and a fuel-pressure regulator.

Gen III through Gen V engines require 60 psi of pressure and a minimum of 40 gph with a free-flowing return line. This is a very simple fuel system that is easily adapted to most C10 trucks with stock fuel tanks. Early-model trucks with fuel tanks behind the seat are a little trickier, but the stock vertical tank can remain in place.

The Gen V LT-series engines are direct injection, meaning the fuel is pressurized and injected directly into the combustion chamber, much like a diesel engine. The NA Gen V engines reach about 2,175 psi, while the supercharged versions run closer to 2,900 psi. Direct-injection engines have much greater fuel economy and more power potential because the ECM has far better control of how much is being burned. This is due to the three types of combustion modes in the ECM: ultra lean, stoichiometric, and full power.

Ultra-lean is used during cruising, when there is no acceleration and light loads. The engine may see air-to-fuel ratio (AFR) readings as high as 65:1. This is possible due to the swirl chamber design in the combustion chamber. The highly pressurized gasoline is injected directly at the spark plug, keeping the heat away from the cylinder walls. The fuel injection is also performed later in the compression cycle. This burn is much cooler than in a conventional engine, which is how they get away with such high AFR figures. This is the hyper-economy phase of the engine.

Stoichiometric burn is what we all know to be the typical burn mode.

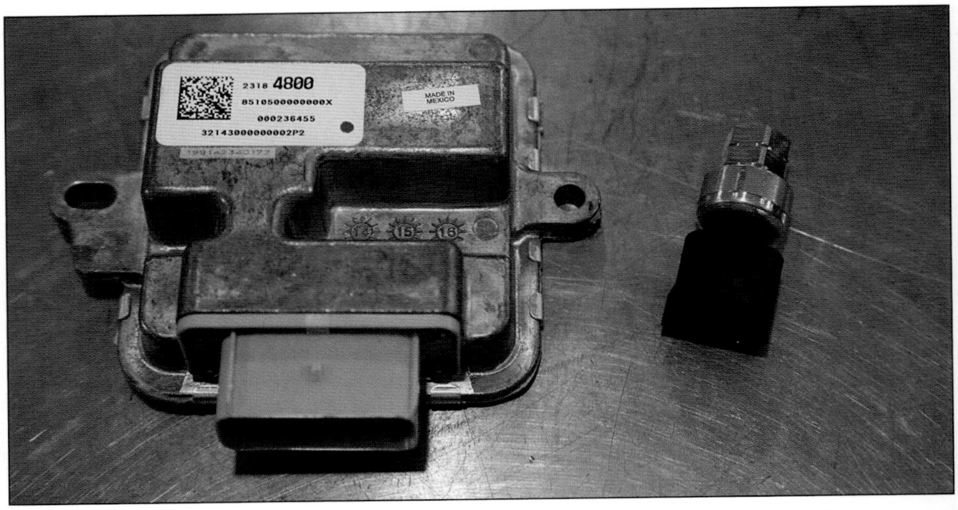

A fuel control module (FCM) helps your LT engine run well. This small computer controls the fuel pressure that the engine receives based on demand. You can run a static pressure system set at 60 psi, but the PWM system is much better.

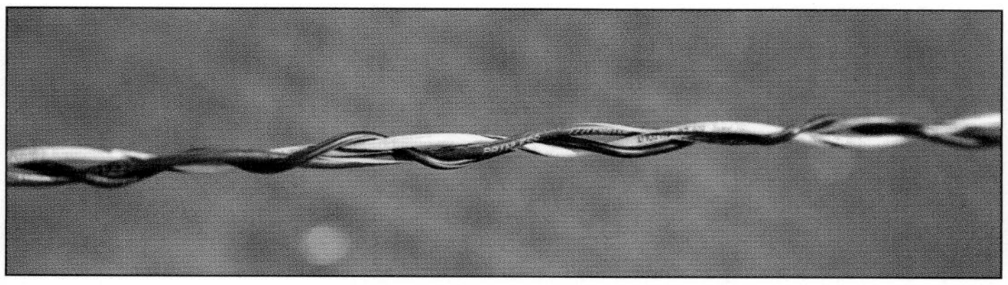

Three wires run from the FCM to the fuel pump, and they must be twisted with a shielded ground wire. We braided our wires, but the minimum is 27 twists per 8 feet. The cleaner and more consistent the twist, the better the signal wires are protected. A loose braid is best, as a really tight twist or braid can stress the wire itself.

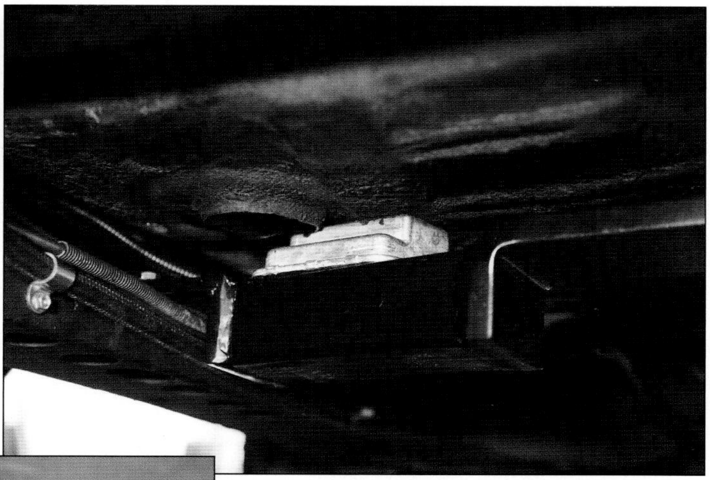

The FCM must be mounted between the engine and the fuel tank, and the Chevrolet Performance wiring harness has a very short pigtail for the FCM to fuel pump run, so you may need to extend it. This FCM was mounted under the car to the transmission crossmember.

Several versions of the fuel-pressure sensor can be used with LT-series engines. The Corvette and truck sensor is on the upper left, and the sensor used with Camaro LT engines is on the bottom right. Internally, they are the same, but the Camaro sensor has hose barbs, while the other requires a 10-mm male-threaded adapter.

Depending on the fuel-system plumbing, the Camaro sensor may work better, as the truck/Corvette sensor can become a bit clumsy without a direct-fitting adapter. If you use AN fittings, the truck/Corvette sensor works better.

An AFR of 14.7:1 is the target for the ECM, and the fuel is injected during the intake stroke, generating the type of air-fuel mix that is experienced in a conventional engine.

Full-power burn is just like the stoichiometric mode, only more fuel is added to keep detonation at bay. The LT1 has 11.5:1 compression, so this is a critical function for hard acceleration. In the LT4 supercharged version, compression is lower at 10:1 to reduce cylinder pressures with the 9.6 psi of boost.

To achieve these burn modes, the ECM has full control of the fueling system. There are two fuel pumps, an electric supply pump in the tank, and a mechanical-pressure pump underneath the intake. The mechanical-pressure pump runs off a tri-lobe wing on the camshaft. Aftermarket upgrades to the fuel-pump lobe can be made through the camshaft, such as Comp Cams offers, which can increase fuel flow as much as 74 percent. The electric supply pump in the gas tank is different from a standard electric pump as well.

Instead of a basic fuel pump and regulator, the factory supply pump is controlled by the ECM through a fuel pump module. This controls the base fuel pressure as it reaches the mechanical direct injection fuel pump. A special pressure sensor in the fuel line monitors the pressure of the fuel to maintain adequate pressure for the current engine demands. The primary spec that General Motors states for LT-series engines is 72 psi at 45 gph. This is slightly misleading, as this number is for high-demand peaks.

Under part throttle, the LT fuel system runs as low as 54 psi for cruising. Rather than use a regulator, the pressure is managed through pulse width modulation (PWM) control of the pump. Essentially, the ECM switches on and off the voltage and current sent to the pump at a very fast rate to control the speed of the pump, ensuring full pressure at all times with no delays. This complicates the fuel system for the LT-series engine swap. You can't use just any old fuel pump. Direct injection fuel pumps have to be PWM capable, and not all electric fuel pumps are.

Another factor is that the LT fuel system is returnless, which was done to keep the fuel temperature down. Because hot fuel does not cycle through the pump to the engine and back to the tank, the fuel temperature remains even. Returnless fuel pumps are rarely suitable for EFI use without PWM control, and the ones that are available cannot support the type of pressure and flow needed for an LT. The pump requirements are 72 psi at 45 gph and an 84-psi pressure relief to be compatible with the Chevrolet Performance control system, which is a pretty high burden for a street-driven electric fuel pump.

Installing the PWM controller is relatively simple, but the fuel-pressure sensor is a bit tricky. First, an inline adapter is needed with a pressure-sensor port positioned at 90 degrees or 5 to 85 degrees to the flow of fuel, according to the GM manual for the fuel controller. This is fairly easy, as there are plenty of these fuel-sensor adapters out there. The problem is that most of the adapters are for 1/8-inch NPT fittings and not the 10-mm threads required for the GM sensor.

Finding a 1/8-inch NPT male to 10-mm male adapter is difficult. It is easier to find a -6 AN male to 10-mm adapter. To use this, an aluminum fuel log or Y-block fuel splitter and a -6 to 10-mm male to male adapter is needed. This allows the sensor to connect into the fuel system. We made one with a leftover piece of fuel rail from another project.

Wiring the PWM pump controller is a plug-and-play affair, but the pump wiring itself is not. There are three wires coming off the pump module: yellow with a black stripe, gray, and a smaller-gauge black wire. The yellow/black wire is the ground, the gray wire is the power side, and the small black wire is the shield.

If using a GM pump with a shield-wire pin, connect the small black wire to that pin. If you are using a pump without a shield-wire

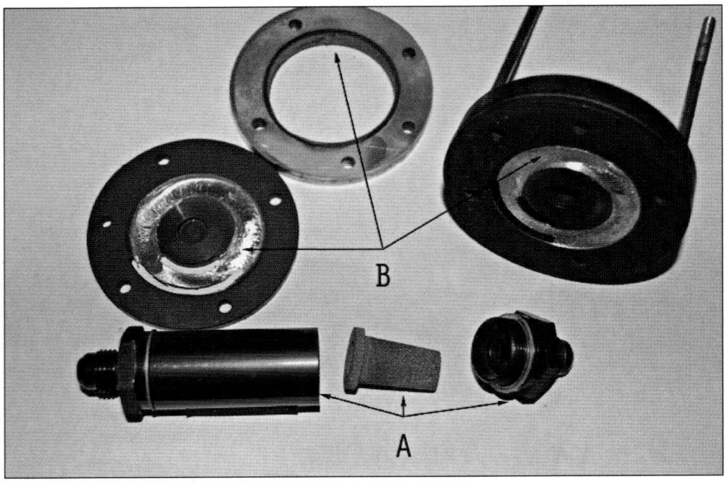

These parts show what happens when the pump cavitates. Part A shows a typical off-brand filter. The small, sintered metal filter restricts flow to the pump. Part B shows the actual damage inside the pump. The cavitation grooves out the aluminum, sending shavings into the system and ruining the pump. (Photo Courtesy Aeromotive)

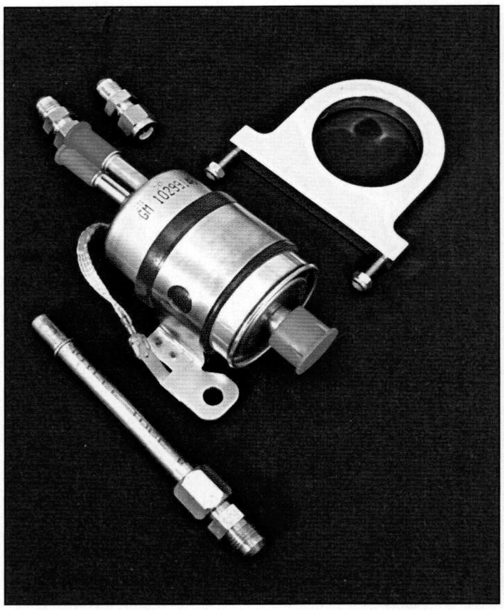

Installing a Corvette-style filter regulator is a simple option when running a static pressure system. This unit acts as the fuel filter and regulates the fuel pressure.

The Corvette filter regulator mounts under the car and near the tank, so the return line is very short. This design is simpler, but some prefer a dual-line system to keep the fuel cooler. However, the performance difference is negligible in a street-car application.

Holley offers in-tank pumps, such as this one, which use HydraMat technology to eliminate the need for a baffle, as the HydraMat soaks up fuel at any angle as long as it is touching it. (Photo Courtesy Holley)

pin, leave the wire unterminated and tape it to the other wires. Because of the nature of PWM control, there is a very real potential for electromagnetic interference (EMI) from other electronics in the vehicle. To eliminate this from interrupting the control signal, the two main power control wires are twisted with a third shielding wire. This wire is grounded to the chassis near the pump.

The Chevrolet Performance wiring harness only comes with a certain length; most C/K chassis absolutely require longer wires. To maintain the shielding, twist the wires at a minimum of 27 twists per 8 feet of wire. The best way to ensure that the wires are correctly twisted and won't unravel is to braid the three wires together. It does not need to be a tight braid, rather a consistent loose braid, wrapping the wires around every 3 inches or so. Do not use crimp connectors for these wires. Instead, make sure to solder them well and use shrink tubing.

It is possible to run an LT-series engine without the PWM control. This is done with a standard regulator and return line system set to 72 psi. This is the process that is used for engine dyno testing, which is often done at 60 psi. There are a couple of issues with this in a street car. First, 60 psi is not 72 psi, so the direct-injection pump will not be functioning at full capacity, meaning it will not be full of fuel under full load. While this works on the dyno, it could run into some drivability issues in real-world street applications, as has been reported by some LT swappers.

If the regulator is set to maintain 72 psi, the system should work as intended, but the return line can cause some issues with fuel temperature. Because a return line sends fuel back to the tank, the result is an incremental rise in fuel temperature. While vapor lock should not be an issue, hot fuel at 2,000 psi becomes more volatile, which can cause some issues. Many retrofit systems drop the hot returning fuel directly in the flow path of the fuel pickup, meaning that most of the returned fuel gets sent right back through the pump and to the engine, where it gets returned again, this time even hotter. If this route is chosen, the return line needs to be located as far from the pickup point of the fuel pump as possible.

Running a return-style fuel system with a Gen V has become more commonplace. In fact, most aftermarket wiring harnesses and even Holley's aftermarket engine management system revert to a return-style system set with static fuel pressure. The key is maintaining enough flow at the higher pressure to make sure the mechanical pump does not have even a split second of no fuel. This is very bad for the mechanical pump and will shorten its life.

Fuel Pumps

When it comes to fuel pumps, there are two categories: in-tank or external. The in-tank pumps last longer, hold higher pressure, are more efficient, and are quieter. In-tank pumps are generally more complicated to install, and retrofitting an in-tank pump can be costly. However, an in-tank pump does not come with the ground clearance issues that external pumps do.

Virtually any aftermarket EFI in-tank pump that can supply the 60-psi fuel-pressure requirement is suitable for an LS or static-pressure Gen V swap. Many builders suggest the Walbro 340 in-tank pump because these pumps hold higher pressures and are excellent for supplying LS engines. There are many in-tank pumps available. The key is to buy a pump that is suited for your application.

Replacing the fuel tank may be part of your plans already, as the older the truck, the more damage and rust may be lurking inside the tank itself. This is not a requirement, but it is easy to replace the entire tank and get an in-tank pump for not much more than just the tank itself. For most C/K10 trucks, a stock replacement tank can be sourced for less than $400.

Converting to an in-Tank Pump

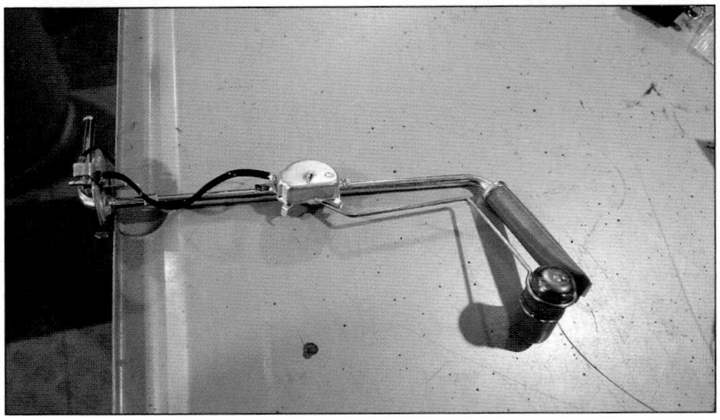

1 *For the 1966 Suburban, we converted the stock pickup tube to an in-tank pump unit. This pickup is for the new Brothers truck tank that we installed in the truck. We placed it on a bench and marked the length of each component.*

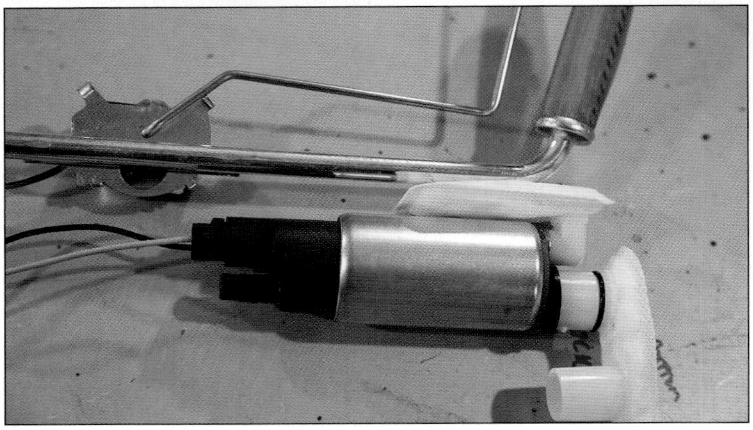

2 *The new pump is a stock GM in-tank unit for a 2000s-era 1500, and it will work perfectly for this upgrade. Mark the pickup tube to length so that the pump sock will just touch the floor of the tank.*

3 *Next, cut the tube and install the new pump at the end, making sure the sock would just touch the bottom of the tank.*

4 *After cutting the tube, make a hole for the wires. Make two holes so that the wires will be separate.*

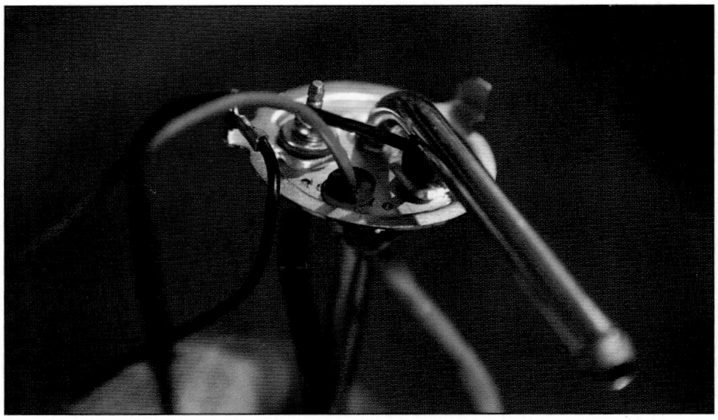

5 *Using a few fuel-safe grommets and some red RTV, seal the wires to the pickup assembly.*

6 *Finally, install the assembly into the tank.*

External or inline pumps offer a simpler installation and are usually cheaper. Inline pumps are much easier to change, making roadside swaps bearable. The main gripe over inline pumps is the noise. The relatively quiet and smooth-running Gen III–V engines do not drown out many external sounds, including these inline pumps. Therefore, drivers may hear the whir of the electric pump sound over the engine with a stock-style quiet exhaust. For most builders, the added noise isn't a problem. Rather, it is an inconvenience. For a show vehicle, a noisy pump might be considered a significant annoyance.

The real drawback for an inline pump is that the fuel line is only pressurized after the pump, so the tank to the pump is gravity fed. Anyone who has dealt with a modern high-performance external fuel pump can tell you that life is really difficult when the siphon is lost in the tank. Simply having the pump in the tank maintains a constant supply of fuel to prevent those hard-cornering and acceleration woes that come with a stock tank and an inline electric fuel pump.

Inline fuel pumps also require a more substantial return-line system because of the long distance the regulator will be from the fuel tank. Inline pumps are also subject to failure through heat. The only thing that cools the pump is the gas flowing through it.

Not all inline pumps are created equal. External pumps come in all different shapes and sizes with the majority of the market consisting of low-pressure units designed for carburetors. These pumps deliver 6 to 14 psi, which is not close to the 60 psi required to operate an LS engine. Any less than 60 psi, and it leans out and does not run well, if at all. There are plenty of inline EFI pumps to choose from. Many builders prefer the Walbro GSL 392 external pump. These pumps are well suited for Gen III and Gen IV engines and can supply the pressure needed.

A common cause of failure with an inline pump is installing a filter between the tank and the pump. If using an actual pre-filter with a 100-micron filter and large diameter, then it is fine, but using a 10-micron post-filter in front of the pump will certainly reduce the life of the pump, leaving you stranded.

Post-filters restrict the flow to the pump, causing cavitation, which is incredibly damaging to the pump. If there is a clean filter sock on the pickup tube in the tank, a pre-filter isn't really needed, but you can use one as long as it is 100 micron. The higher the micron number, the larger the pores are in the filter, reducing large contaminants without reducing flow.

Cavitation is a natural process that occurs when vapor bubbles are induced in liquid under pressure. All electric fuel pumps are susceptible to this force. Its most common cause is installer error where an inadequate fuel supply increases the suction on the inlet side. Cavitation is literally boiling the fuel through pressure. Vapor bubbles form and then split, imploding and causing a micro explosion. This is extremely damaging, even a few minutes of cavitation can ruin a fuel pump.

Another cause is overheated fuel. Not running a return line (deadhead style) or attempting to plumb the return line into the feed line (not into the tank) will cause hot fuel to cycle back through the pump, heating it up more. The hotter the fuel, the easier it is to cavitate or even vapor lock. Yes, EFI systems can vapor lock too. This is why a proper return system is so important for EFI.

Aftermarket Pumps

There are multiple ways to achieve this task, but it really depends on the type of tank in the truck. The aftermarket has really come a long way in recent years when it comes to fuel pump upgrades and engine swaps. For some trucks, a drop-in module that fits into the stock fuel-sender location can be purchased. It needs a feed line, a return line, and a new fuel level sender. It cannot be any easier than that. There are multiple companies offering these drop-ins, including Holley Performance and Aeromotive. Both are featured in this book. For older trucks, the situation requires a little more effort.

1960–1972

These model-year trucks almost all came with gas tanks behind the seat. There is currently no retrofit EFI pump for these tanks, and they are too tall (deep) to use an off-the-shelf universal retrofit in-tank pump. The only option is to cut and weld, which can be done safely on a used tank with the proper precautions. This means removal from the vehicle, rinsing at least three times with water and soap, and thorough forced-air drying between rinses. If you smell a hint of gas, do it again. Only then can you proceed with welding.

Welding a thin gas tank is not easy, and it usually ends up with leaks and rust on the inside, where it is very difficult to apply sealer for the fresh welds. It just isn't worth the hassle unless you are a really good welder and your tank isn't rusty at all.

Installing an Aeromotive Pump Module

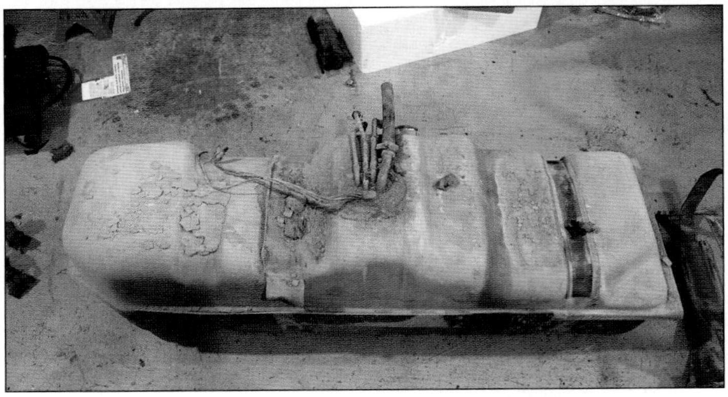

1 *We pulled the tank from the 1991 1500 to upgrade the pump with a new drop-in module from Aeromotive, but we didn't expect what we found. Remember, this truck has been sitting in a field for the previous 10 to 15 years.*

2 *Using a screwdriver and a mallet, tap the locking ring loose to pull out the sending unit.*

3 *When the pump came out, we saw that it was rotten. The inside of the tank is just as bad; this tank is junk.*

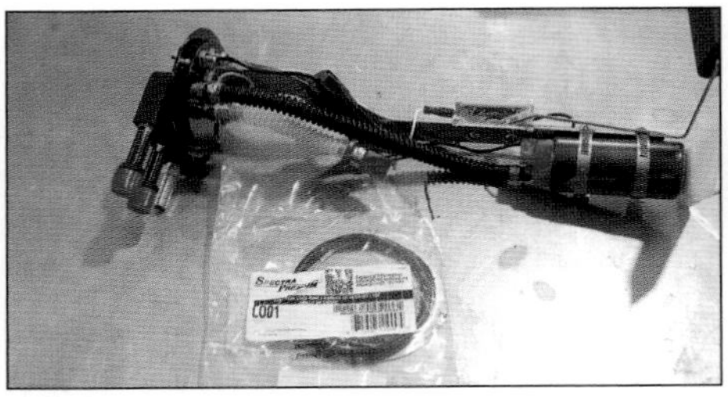

4 *The new pump module came from Aeromotive, and it is capable of supporting far more power than this truck will ever have. This is a direct replacement for the factory pump in this 1991 Chevy.*

5 *Slip the new O-ring onto the pump assembly. Always use a new O-ring.*

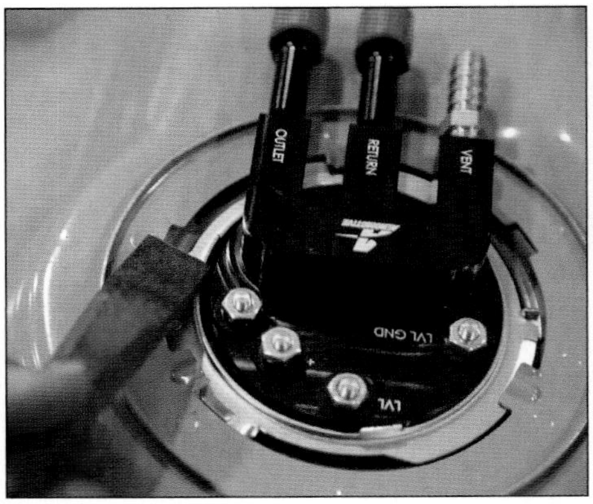

6 *Then, the pump unit drops right into the new tank just like the factory assembly.*

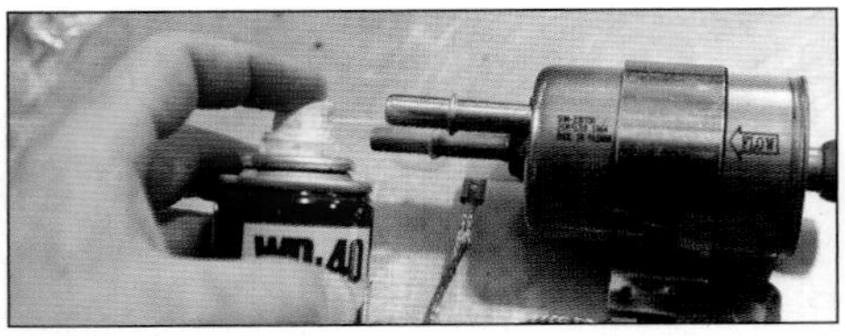

7 *We selected a Corvette-style regulator filter for the 1991 1500, as we are running the L83 with a static fuel-pressure system. The nipples of the regulator were lubed up with WD-40 to ensure that the O-rings on the fittings don't grab and roll out. These are notorious for leaks, and it is usually because the O-rings were pushed out of place.*

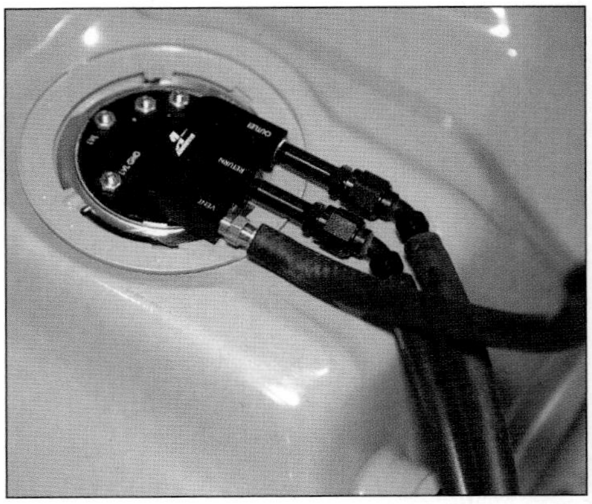

8 *Pre-wire and plumb the pump with hose before installing it, as there is very little gap to reach the terminals once the tank is in place.*

For these models, the best solution is an external pump or retrofit underframe tank. Because the tank is in the cab, getting an external pump below the bottom of the tank is easy; the underside of the cab floor will do that. Adding a return line to the tank is as simple as drilling a hole next to the sender opening and using an O-ring or nylon washer fitting to ensure a good seal. Many early C/K10 owners want to get rid of the in-cab tank, as it takes up all the room behind the seat, so underframe tanks are used.

For the 1966 GMC Suburban featured in this book, we went this route. Granted, the suburban already had an underfloor tank, but it was rotten. We sourced a tank from Brothers Truck and installed it under the frame of the Suburban. While we were at it, we retrofitted the tank with an in-tank fuel pump.

1973–1987

The aftermarket for these years has grown substantially, and there are now multiple options for fuel pumps. Holley now offers a replacement drop-in sending unit with everything ready to go. Just pull out the original and drop in the new one, wire and plumb the lines, and reinstall the tank. There really isn't any good reason not to use one of these drop-ins, as they are just as affordable as a new fuel pump. The 1987 trucks already have an in-tank pump. For more details on this year, see the OBS truck section that follows this.

Holley Muscle Truck 255-LPH Module (Part Number 12-308)

Built for 1973–1986 trucks, this module comes with a new fuel-level sensor, 255-liter-per-hour (lph) pump, and a HydraMat filter sock. The HydraMat filter socks act as reservoir for fuel, so in situations where there is sloshing or low fuel, the sock holds onto the fuel that touches it, so it always has a supply. The fuel level sender is pre-calibrated to match the factory gauge (0–90 ohm), and the pump itself can supply up to a 550-hp engine. For engines making up to 750 hp, the larger 350-lph module (part number 12-378) is recommended.

What makes this module different is that it is internally regulated at 58 psi. This is enough to support any Gen III or Gen IV engine, and there is no need to plumb in a return line. It even connects to the factory fuel line. Although 58 psi is a little low for a Gen V engine, Holley says that it has used it successfully on Gen V LT swaps with its Holley Terminator engine management system.

1988–1998 GMT400 OBS

These trucks already have in-tank fuel pumps, so there are a few options. The factory pump is not capable of producing enough pressure to feed an LS/LT engine because the pump only generates 12 to 20 psi. The pump

We reused the main engine-feed hardline on the frame, which is a time-saving measure.

With the tank in place, it is clear how little room there is. It is possible to access the terminals, but there is no way to read what they are.

Grounds are critical for fuel pumps and fuel-level sensors, so we cleaned a section of the frame, drilled a hole, and bolted the grounds in place.

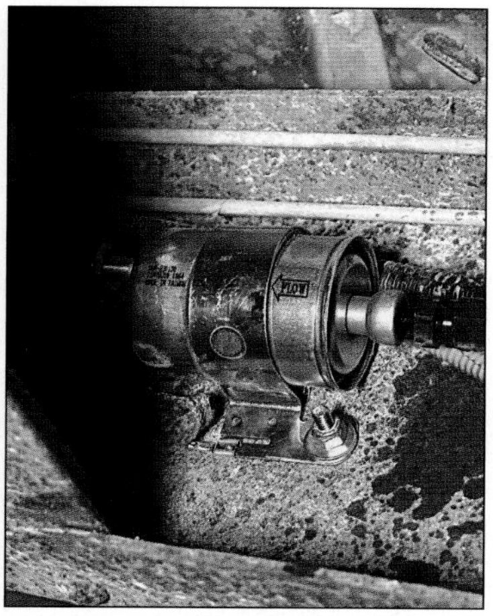

We mounted the filter to the frame as well. Note that the flow arrow is backward. This is a manufacturer issue; the flow of the fuel is the opposite direction that this arrow shows.

Underfloor Tank Install

One of the most common upgrades for 1960–1972 C/K10 trucks is swapping out the in-cab fuel tank. Relocating the tank from behind the seat has been happening for decades, with truck owners using any tank they could manage to fit between the rear frame rails. With the Camaro tank, GM A-Body tank, Blazer tank, and Suburban tank, or even fuel cells in the bed (this author had one in a 1965 C10 almost 30 years ago), there are many options to make it happen. To simplify the process, Brothers Truck has a kit that makes the process easy. Using a brand-new 1969–1972 Blazer tank makes it easy to relocate an in-cab tank to under the bed and gain some room.

1 ***Because this 1966 C10 is actually a Suburban, the fuel tank is a little tricky. We had to notch the top of the frame rail to provide access for the new filler neck.***

2 ***The tank comes with straps for trucks, but we discovered that the front-most bolt hole in the tank matched up with an existing hole in the frame. This greatly simplified the process.***

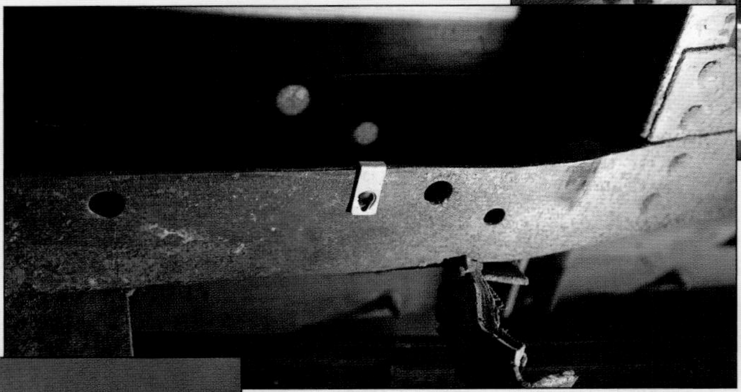

3 ***Insert speed nuts onto the holes, and drill the rear holes.***

4 ***A little tab on the top of the tank rail is a locating feature, but it interfered with the speed nuts, so we cut it off.***

5 ***To cut down on any rattles and provide a little tension, lay some closed-cell foam on the outer flanges of the tank.***

6 *You have to be able to fill the tank, so pick up a fuel cap kit and make a new filler neck. This cap has a pass-through hole that is spring loaded, so the cap doesn't have to be removed to fill the tank.*

7 *Using fuel-safe silicone elbows and a section of aluminum tubing, make the filler neck. This drops in through the filler door and lines up with the tank neck. Note that most silicone hoses are not fuel safe; only use fuel-safe hoses for fuel. This hose has a rubber fuel-safe liner.*

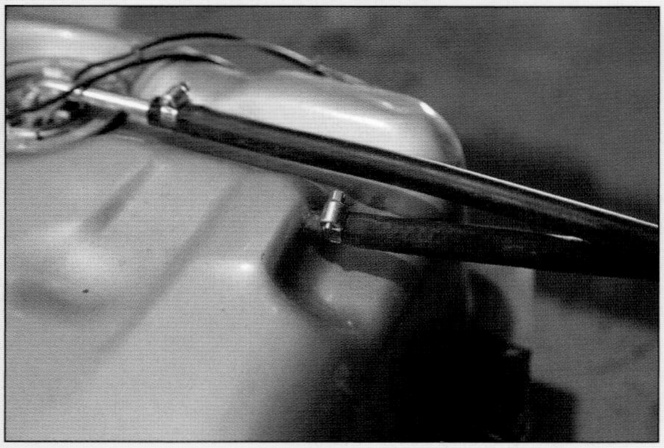

8 *Before installing the tank, we pre-plumbed the hoses and wiring. The tank vent is now the return-line port.*

9 *You can cut a piece of exhaust tubing to serve as the filler-neck angle mount for the hose. Weld the cap bung to the pipe along with an angle bracket to secure the neck to the filler recess in the side of the Suburban.*

10 *The angle bracket was secured with a sheet-metal screw to the inner wall. This does not pierce the interior of the cab; we checked multiple times before mounting the neck.*

11 *Under the truck, we secured the filler neck with a clamp to ensure that it didn't rattle or move around. There is just enough downward angle for the tank that the fuel doesn't pool in the filler neck.*

Underfloor Tank Install *continued*

We decided to go this route on our 1966 GMC Suburban. While the Suburban already had a tank under the floor, it was not original to the truck and was seriously damaged, so it was pulled before we started the engine swap. With a phone call, we had a new Brothers Truck Blazer tank on the way.

There are two options for these tanks: top or side fill. We opted for the side-fill tank, as we already have a side-fill door. If you are working with a truck, you can install a side-fill door or, as most owners do, go for the top-fill tank and add a filler flap in the bed itself.

Because we are LS swapping this Suburban with an LM7 5.3L, we need a fuel pump. Instead of using a universal module, which would fit under the bed floor, we chose a low-buck method: retrofit the new sending unit to accept an electric fuel pump. This works, and the truck runs and drives. However, there is very little room to install the pump with the filter sock. It was difficult, but it can be done.

First, we removed the sending unit from the tank, placed it against the edge of our workspace, and marked the location of the filter sock. This is the depth of the pickup, and where we need to position the new sock of the electric pump. The important thing here is to make sure the pump is mounted about 1/4 inch off the floor of the tank with a filter sock resting on the bottom of the tank. This keeps the impurities out of the pump while getting the most fuel out of the tank. The pump was secured to the sending unit using a short piece of fuel-injection hose and hose clamps.

On our sending unit, the pivot mechanism was just above the point where the pump needed to go. We removed the lower tab from the pickup tube and secured the pivot mechanism with a hose clamp. The assembly is quite rigid and did not need any additional support.

The tricky part is the wiring. The wires have to get from the pump to the outside world. If the sender had a second line, as some do, we would have used that. However, this one does not, so we drilled two holes in the mounting plate. To keep the wires safe from chaffing, we installed a fuel-safe Viton grommet in each hole with a dab of silicone just to help keep them in place. We chose to go with two holes, one for each wire so that we could easily seal the wires in the grommets with silicone. This protects the wires and keeps them separate and sealed.

The wires that connect to the pump require crimp connectors, which we installed. We then wrapped both wires together with self-vulcanizing fuel-safe tape. This tape fuses mechanically and chemically to itself for a tight seal around the wires, and it is fuel safe.

With the pump installed, the tank could be installed in the truck. Because this tank has the side fill, the driver-side frame rail required a small notch on the top to clear the filler hose. This was cut with a small reciprocating saw, and the edges were cleaned up.

The Brothers Truck tank can be mounted two ways: bolts or straps. Brothers Truck supplies a pair of straps that bolt to the existing bolt holes on one side, but installing the tank requires drilling the other hole. We found that on the 1966 Suburban, two of the factory holes lined up perfectly, so we installed a set of 3/8-inch body clips (also known as speed nuts) to the lower frame holes and bolted the tank to the fame.

With the tank supported and in place, we marked and then drilled two more holes and installed another set of body clips. This allows the tank to be bolted in easily and securely without dealing with the straps. Before installing the tank, we lined the edges that touch the frame with some closed-cell foam to ensure that there are no rattles.

Because the original neck is gone, we had to fabricate a new neck. This works for top- or side-fill tanks that need a filler neck. Using a Williams Hot Rods quick-fill cap and bung, along with some 1.5-inch steel tubing and 1.5-inch silicon elbows, we built a new neck that runs from the filler door to the tank inlet. For this specific vehicle, we used one 90-degree and one 45-degree elbow.

The filler neck assembly was secured to the bed floor with U-straps and screws. The key to a fuel filler neck is to make sure the line runs downhill to the tank, if there are any low spots between the cap and the tank inlet, fuel will get trapped in the hose, and that is generally not a good idea. Sometimes it is unavoidable, but it is critical that there are now sections lower than a quarter of the filler-neck diameter. Any deeper than that, and you will have a hard time filling the tank, as the fuel will back up in the hose. ■

has to be replaced with a different unit that can handle the job. This is easy, though, as all you have to do is pull the sending unit, disconnect the pump, install the larger pump, and reinstall the module. This is not the only way, though, as Aeromotive has a drop-in replacement module that can handle just about anything you need.

Aeromotive Drop-In (Part Number 18474)

If you want a simple solution, this is it. Yank the tank, pull the factory sender, drop in one of these modules, and reinstall the tank. It really is that simple. The Aeromotive fuel modules come with a new fuel-level sensor, machined aluminum head, and two pump options.

The 200-lph pump supports EFI engines at power levels up to 600 hp naturally aspirated and 450 hp boosted, and it supports carbureted engines up to 750 hp naturally aspirated and 600 with forced induction. The 200-lph unit is not E85 compatible.

The 340-lph pump is E85 compatible and can handle even more power. EFI systems on gas can handle 850 hp NA and 700 hp with boost. Running E85, the system supports up to 595 hp NA and 490 hp on boost. In carbureted applications, the power goes up to 1,000 hp NA on gas and 850 hp with forced induction, while E85 carburated engine supports 700 hp NA and 595 hp with forced induction. The Aeromotive system uses a return-line system and requires a separate fuel-pressure regulator.

Universal Modules

If you are using a non-standard tank or there isn't a drop-in module that fits your needs, a universal drop-in module from Aeromotive or Holley Performance is an option. Just like the model-specific modules, these allow installation of a truly high-performance fuel pump into a stock fuel tank without welding. Aeromotive offers two retrofit in-tank pump kits: the Phantom and the A1000 Stealth systems. For basic street performance use, the Phantom 340 kit is suitable. This kit allows a hole to be cut in the top of the tank, the pump dropped in and bolted down, the lines hooked up, and you are done. The kit comes with the seals, hardware, and a drill jig to ensure that the holes are in the right place.

The 340 supports up to 700-hp supercharged EFI engines or 1,000-hp supercharged carbureted systems. That means there is plenty of room to power a stock 430-hp LS3. The Phantom system can fit in just about any tank, so this is a really good option that takes out the guesswork.

For more serious performance engines, the Stealth A1000 system feeds up to 1,300-hp EFI systems and 1,500 for carbureted engines. Installing these systems takes slightly more effort than the Phantom kit but not much. The Phantom pumps are PWM compatible, so if you are swapping a Gen V engine and want to use the factory PWM fuel control, these will work.

Holley's universal modules are available in multiple options—from 255-lph pumps to the massive dual 450-lph module that can support 1,700 hp for EFI and 2,200 hp in carbureted applications. There are return and returnless modules as well. These are not PWM compatible, only standard 12-volt power.

The most important aspect of any electric fuel pump is the wiring. In addition, it is most difficult to get solid grounds because paint, rust, and scale inhibit the ground. Always be sure to remove the paint and anything else from the ground location so that there is clean metal. Electricity requires equal grounding and positive current flow. A bad ground is just as bad as a faulty positive feed.

Electric fuel pumps require a lot of current, so running a relay circuit from the pump trigger lead, along with 12-gauge positive and negative wires to the fuel pump provides ample capacity. This ensures that the pump gets the required amperage without overheating the wires. Do not run a 16- to 24-gauge primary wire to a fuel pump because it will cause a fire. All fuel pumps require at least 12-gauge power wire, with the larger pumps needing 10-gauge wire. This includes both power and ground wires.

Most EFI engines (except for 2014-and-newer Gen V LT-series engines) require return lines. This can sometimes be confusing because Gen III and Gen IV motors use a single-line fuel rail. The 1997–1998 Corvettes and 1998–2002 F-Body LS1s used a dual-line fuel rail. In 1999, the Corvette LS1 went to a single-line rail, using a filter regulator near the fuel tank and running a short return line back to the tank. This configuration is much simpler and requires only a single line run the length of the vehicle.

There are many builders who prefer to run two lines the distance of the vehicle with the dual-line fuel rails. The benefit of running a full-length return system is cooler fuel. The fuel does not sit in the lines, heating up from the pressure. Instead, a constant flow of fuel is running through the lines, ensuring cooler fuel and, therefore, more power. This of course, requires two sets of fuel lines—a 3/8-inch line for the feed and 5/16-inch line for the return.

When choosing the simple one-line route, the 1999-and-newer Corvette filter regulator is needed. This unit has two lines (an input and an output) on one side for the fuel tank, and one output on the other, which goes to the engine. This preset regulator provides the correct 60 psi to the engine, which pressurizes the entire fuel line while pumping

LS/LT fuel rails use these little push-on connectors. They are easy to use and wrench-free. On the 1966 Suburban, we used the stock fuel rails, which have a built-in regulator, but we used a Corvette filter regulator at the pump so that we didn't have to run the return line to the engine. This fitting will be a cap for the return line.

The fuel rail has the cap on the lower exit port. Another push-on fitting is at the top for the fuel feed line.

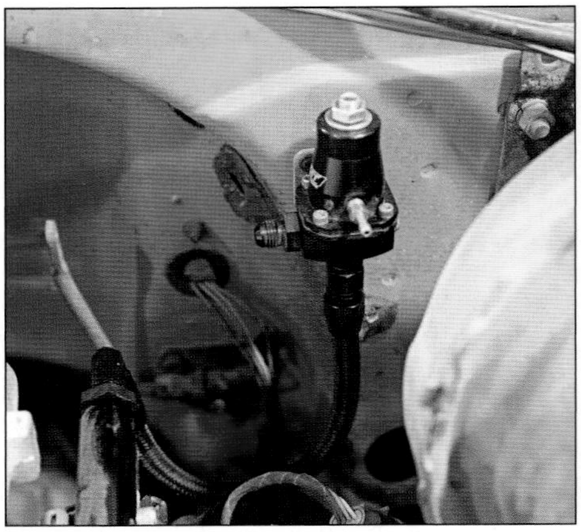

On this 1967 C10 with a 6.0L engine that has a supercharger, we opted for a separate regulator that has boost referencing to add extra pressure under boost.

The LT fuel rails use the same fittings. This is a -6 AN adapter, which makes plumbing very easy. The LTs are dead-head systems, as there is no return line.

the excess fuel back to the tank. This is typically mounted as close to the tank as possible to minimize the length of feed and return lines to the tank.

For a dual-line system with the pump in the tank, a filter is needed between the pump and the fuel rails. It is best to filter the fuel as soon as possible, keeping the fuel lines as clean as possible. Beware of cheap import filter regulators, as many of these leak at the fittings and cannot be fixed. You are much better off buying brand-name filter regulators with tighter tolerances that won't leak.

Installing new lines is a fairly simple process, but it can be nerve-racking at the same time. There are three ways to accomplish this task: run braided hose, bend new hard lines, or install pre-bent hard lines. Using pre-bent hard lines is the simplest method if the vehicle has the fuel tank in the stock location. Pre-bent lines, such as those from Classic Tube and Tube Tech, are patterned after the original lines in the vehicle and should fit just like the originals. That is not to say that there are not compromises and tweaks that must be made along the way.

Bending and installing custom lines most effectively transports fuel the length of the vehicle, but it is much easier said than done. This is a challenging task that requires some metalworking skills, and therefore the task will be frustrating at best for the novice. There are tubing makers, such as Classic Tube, that offer custom bending services. Using coat hangers or other wire, a pattern is bent by hand and sent to the maker. They, in turn, will bend a set of hard lines to your specifications and ship them to you. This ensures quality bends with proper flares where you want them (without kinks) and without the aggravation of doing it yourself.

The other option is to use flexible hose for the long runs. This works, but braided hose should be used rather than plain rubber hose to protect from road debris damage. The chance of road debris snagging a long braided fuel line is much higher than with a hard line. Rubber lines are not the best option, either. Rubber lines dry out and crack much faster than hard lines corrode, so the rubber lines will have to be replaced eventually.

Steel-Braided Fittings and Hoses

While regular rubber hoses are adequate for factory installations, braided lines and hoses provide the best look, performance, and fit for a custom install. For decades, steel-braided lines have long been the standard for custom vehicles, and they have been cutting fingers and being the bane of existence for many street rodders. There are a few tips and tricks that can take the strain out of plumbing your ride and getting the best look possible.

Earl's Performance Plumbing, a division of Holley Performance, offers a few products that bring the braided look under the hood while reducing the strain of stainless steel. The Pro-Lite 350 hose is a high-quality rubber hose with a black nylon braid that protects the rubber from chaffing, flying debris, and cuts. The nylon is easy to cut, saves your fingertips, and adds a serious look to your plumbing. The dark braid look is all business, but it really cleans up the engine bay. The Pro-Lite 350 can be used with all the AN fittings and simple hose clamps, adding to its versatility.

Working with AN fittings requires some extra knowledge and planning of each system. Typically, the local parts store

1 *Running AN lines means assembling the fittings to the lines through a specific process. Here is a set of -8 fittings, -8 hose from Earl's, some Royal Purple assembly lube, and some AN wrenches.*

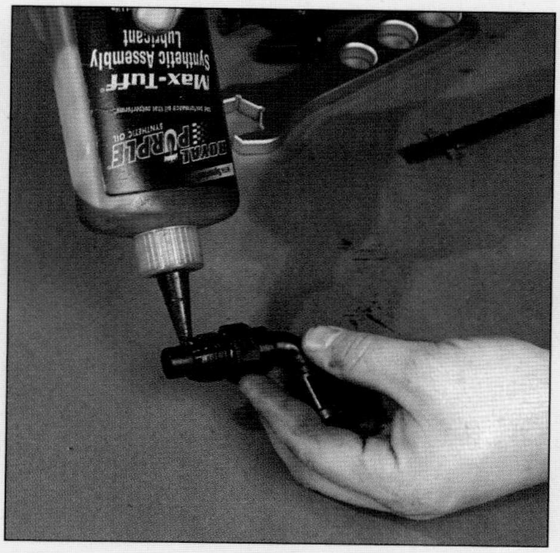

2 *Lube up the main fitting to accommodate the hose and the threads on the collar.*

3 *Next, install the collar on the hose. The hose should be 1/16 inch from the threads on the inside of the collar. Wrap tape around the hose flush with the base of the collar.*

4 *Clamp the main fitting into a vise. We are using a set of Earl's aluminum jaws to protect the finish of the fitting.*

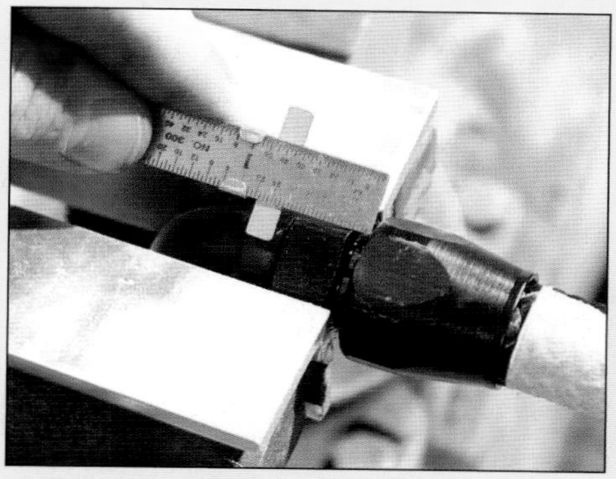

5 *Installing the hose to the fitting takes a little effort. Push the hose into the fitting and then spin the entire hose/collar assembly until you can't thread it by hand anymore. Then, use the AN wrenches to seat the collar 1/8 inch from the end of the fitting.*

6 *The hose should not have pushed out from the collar more than 1/16 inch. If it did, it must be reinstalled.*

Steel-Braided Fittings and Hoses *continued*

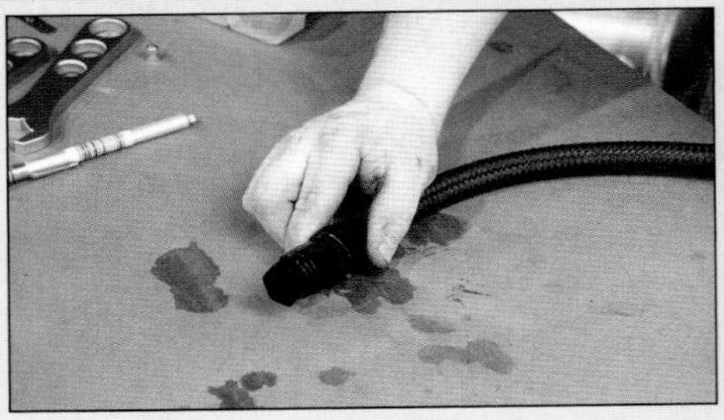

7 ***Most people just stop here, but the fitting needs to be pressure tested. Using a kit from Summit Racing, cap the ends. One end has a Schrader valve for adding air.***

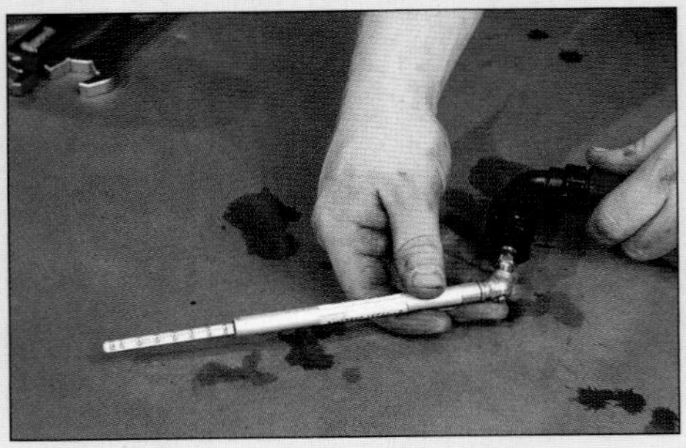

8 ***Pressurize the line to the capacity of the system. In this case, about 65 psi. Check the hose at or above the pressure of the system.***

9 ***While holding pressure, place the assembly in a jar of water. Test both fittings. Let the hose sit for 5, 10, and 20 minutes, checking to see if the hose loses pressure over time.***

doesn't carry AN fittings, so unless you have quick access to a speed shop, ordering fittings is the only option. Have the system planned out beforehand so that you don't waste time with parts you don't need or end up waiting for the ones you don't have.

Each AN size directly correlates with a specific outer diameter (OD) of metal tubing. Each size is listed as "-X", each number after the hyphen indicates a 1/16-inch increase in size, and therefore a -3 fitting would be 3/16 inch, -4 would be 1/4 inch, and so on.

If the vehicle sees a lot of street time, running hard fuel lines is recommended. Even braided lines can collapse over time, and a properly routed steel line will last almost forever. Depending on the stock system, it might be possible to reuse the stock hard lines. A 3/8-inch feed line and 1/4-inch return line (if using a return-style system) are the minimum requirements for a high-performance fuel system. These sizes are good to about 500 hp. If your LS engine produces more than 500 hp, you need 1/2-inch lines.

There are two ways to convert from hard lines to braided lines with AN fittings: install a hose clamp on bare hose or do it the proper way using a tube sleeve, tube nut, and an AN fitting. There is a trick to it, though, and if it is not done properly, the fitting will leak.

The automotive industry's standard flare is 45 degrees. This is the angle of the inside lip of the flare, which is what seals against the fitting. All commonly available flaring tools come as 45-degree kits. However, AN fittings require 37-degree flares. Those 8 little degrees can mean the difference between a proper seal and a nasty leak. Finding a 37-degree flare tool might prove to be a little difficult, as the local parts store won't carry them. We sourced ours from the Matco truck, and it had to be ordered. A basic double flare is all that is needed once you have the right tool for the job.

Planning out the system requires a little work and can be a tedious task. Careful measuring is important, as you don't want to order 25 feet of hose only to end up needing 26. Using a simple drawing of a vehicle and marking out the route for the lines and hoses can greatly simplify the task. Determining the placement of the fuel pump is key for fuel systems.

For the transmission cooling lines, route the hoses through the frame whenever possible to reduce the amount of exposed line. To make a sharp turn, figure in an angled fitting, such as a 45 or 90 degree instead of trying to bend the hose. A 3-inch radius is the maximum bend for rubber hose.

Choosing which components to use depends on your budget and level of performance. Earl's Performance Plumbing offers several different types of fittings and hoses to suit each system's needs. Black Ano-Tuff hard-anodized fittings resist corrosion and wear better than the more common red and blue anodized type, and these fittings are perfect for Earl's Pro-lite nylon braided hose.

Pro-Lite 350 hose is best suited for the fuel, heater, and transmission hoses because of its light weight and flexibility. Stainless-steel Teflon lines or nylon-braided high-pressure hose are needed for power-steering lines. Swivel Seal hose ends add flexibility to the lines because these ends keep the hose from twisting when assembling the lines in the vehicle. Otherwise, they can collapse.

Often, there will be things that don't fit or additional fittings will be needed. If you are ordering parts online or from a catalog, you will have to wait for them to arrive before planning your system. Discuss your plans with the tech advisors because they will be able to help you get exactly what you need. Once all of your lines are fit and installed, test each system for leaks before setting out on a road trip. ■

AIR INTAKE AND EXHAUST

Swapping an LS/LT engine into your truck is a big project, and it effects almost every single aspect of the overall project. By the time the engine and transmission are installed, wired, plumbed, and running, there is a sense of relief at almost being finished. The last steps are at hand: getting the air in and out of the engine. Most builders save these two sections for last because it is difficult to prefabricate the exhaust and air intake until the engine is physically in the vehicle. It is also important to make sure that everything else is done before trying to tackle these projects.

The air intake and exhaust systems should be thought-out and planned like the rest of the build. An air filter can be slapped on an engine to get it running, but it won't yield optimal performance. Maintaining the coolest, least turbulent pathway for the intake air charge gives an engine the best opportunity to make power.

All engines are in essence air pumps. Air comes in, gets squeezed, and is ejected under pressure to generate power. Optimizing the airflow in and out maximizes the engine's performance.

All EFI systems require oxygen sensors to read the oxygen gas levels in the exhaust, and these vital sensors tell the computer if the engine is running rich, lean, or just right. However, that is not all. LS/LT engines all come with catalytic converters, four of them, which are used to burn up the exhaust gases to reduce emissions. This is a very important factor to consider that requires a bit of homework.

Most states have a classic-car provision that exempts older vehicles from emission standards and/or safety inspections, but it is imperative to research the current laws in your state before completing your swap. Some states require the vehicle emissions to match the standards for the year of the engine, not the vehicle, which would require the engine to retain all of the original smog equipment (including the EGR, AIR, and catalytic converters) in working order. Every state is different, and the laws are constantly being revised and changed, so it is up to you to make sure that your LS/LT swap is legal in your state.

Building Custom Intake Tubing

1 ***Every engine needs filtered air, and LS/LT engines are no different. They do need some intake tubing, though. If a filter is put on the end of the throttle body, you won't get as good of airflow as you will with a properly designed intake tube. Plus, there needs to be a place for the mass airflow (MAF) sensor. We used a Holley universal air intake kit on the 1966 Suburban LS swap.***

Building Custom Intake Tubing *continued*

2 *We cut off the sections we needed from the large piece of pipe. This kit is pretty slick; it has many segments and coupler sleeves to simplify the process. For this vehicle, we need this section of tubing, the adapter sleeve for the throttle body, a coupler, and the filter adapter.*

3 *Secure the filter adapter to the pipe with hose clamps.*

4 *On the other end is the throttle body adapter coupler, which also uses hose clamps.*

5 *Place the MAF sensor just ahead of the first bend to give it as much straight piping in front of it as possible.*

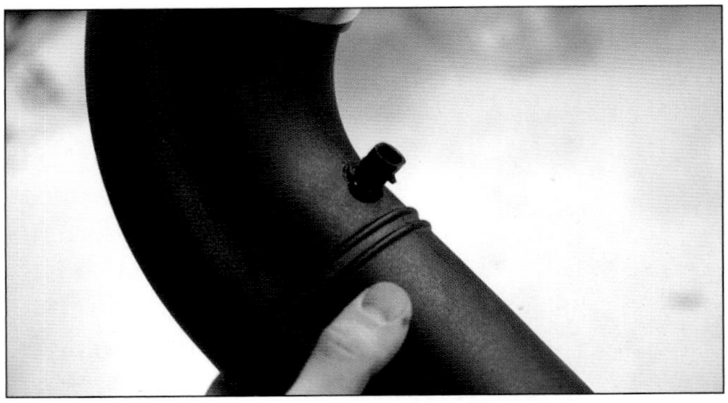

6 *Carefully add some silicone to secure the sensor to the tubing.*

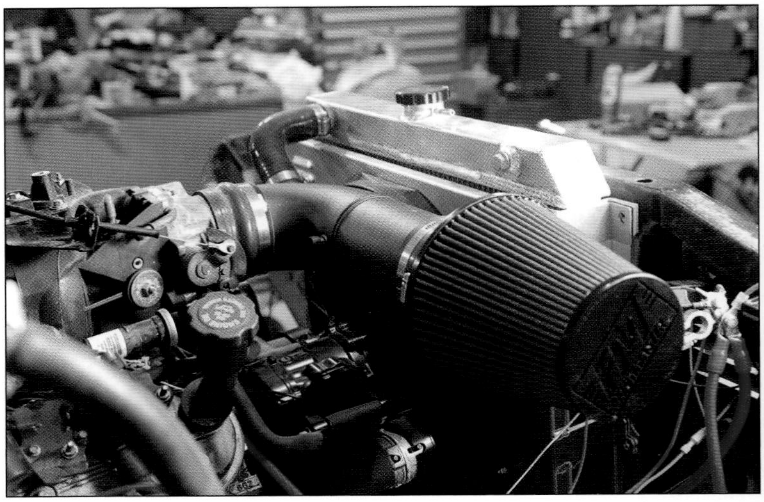

7 *The finished intake tube pulls air from the passenger's side of the engine bay. The kit comes with a nice mount that secures the filter, which we bolted to the radiator shroud.*

Air Intake

While the exhaust gases are managed by the mufflers and exhaust system, the incoming air charge requires some attention as well. Unlike the exhaust, the intake system is very simple: an air cleaner element, some tubing, and the mass airflow (MAF) sensor are all that is required for the EFI LS/LT engine.

It is possible on some swaps to simply install a cone-style air cleaner onto the throttle body with a built-in MAF sensor between the two, but more often than not, some sort of ductwork is needed. For LT engines, the recommended spec for the MAF location is at least 10 inches before the throttle body in a straight section of tubing at least 6 inches long. This is not always possible, but this is the minimum recommended length.

The air inlet for LT engines needs to be 4 inches in diameter as well, which could cause some issues in tight engine bays. Even with the cavernous engine bays of C10 trucks, it is surprising just how fast a 4-inch pipe fills the space between the throttle body and radiator, especially with electric fans.

The key to a good intake system is large, smooth bends in the piping. Air does not like to make abrupt turns, which creates a vortex effect inside the tube, drastically slowing down the air. Slow air means less air in the engine. Short air filter elements require the air to make fast direction changes, and that pulls away potential horsepower. The best bet is to make the intake tube as straight as possible, preferably grabbing the cooler air outside of the engine bay.

Building an intake system usually involves some tubing, silicone elbows and couplers, along with some band clamps. A hard-pipe intake can also be fabricated with steel, aluminum, or stainless-steel tubing, if you have the ability to cut and weld sections of thin pipe together. The hardest part of fabricating a hard-pipe intake tube is getting the cuts just right. The 1966 Suburban and 1991 C1500 swaps featured in this book used a kit from Flowmaster.

The 615400 Delta Force Universal Performance Air Intake system comes with a 4-inch XPLE polyethylene segmented intake tube with multiple angles and turns, silicone couplers, a throttle-body adapter, and an eight-layer cotton gauze reusable air filter. What is really cool about this kit is that it includes a blade-style MAF sensor bung that just happens to be the style most commonly used with LS/LT engines.

Building an Air Intake

Creating an air intake with smooth curves is simple when you have a Flowmaster universal intake kit. The kit has everything needed to build one complete air intake, and in most cases, enough left over to build a second one for something else (with another filter, of course).

For the 1991 C1500 L83 swap, we ran into some clearance issues for the intake piping. The battery is on the passenger's side, congesting the space where we wanted to put the filter itself. We could have moved the filter over the passenger-side wheel well, but we didn't like the amount of heat it would see there.

On the driver's side, the upper and lower coolant hoses were in the way of getting the tubing to the area behind the headlights, so we settled for a shorter intake with the filter behind the radiator. This will, of course, mean that the intake charge will be slightly heated by the radiator. However, when driving, the air will be much cooler than stagnant air hovering around the headers on the sides of the engine.

We selected a section of the tubing with a 45-degree bend and trimmed it to fit up against the throttle body with the supplied throttle body–to–pipe adapter sleeve. This put the remaining section into the radiator, so we cut away the next section at the segmented ribs. The ribs provide a really nice demarcation line for cuts and the rib makes for a nice stop for positive retention of the clamp and silicone sleeve. You can't always use the segments as provided, so it is critical to use the segments in this manner.

We slipped a coupler on the intake pipe and found another section of the supplied pipe that had a short 45-degree bend. After trimming this from the main pipe, it was attached to the main intake section and rotated until we had good clearance for the filter between the radiator, accessory drive, and the upper radiator hose. This position allows us to install the MAF sensor far enough away from the throttle body in a long straight section of the intake and have a good mounting point for the air filter and enough airflow to feed the engine. In this install, the supplied mounting bracket for the air filter was not suitable, so we made a simple bracket that slips under the band clamp on the filter to the inlet tube junction.

Building a Vacuum Source

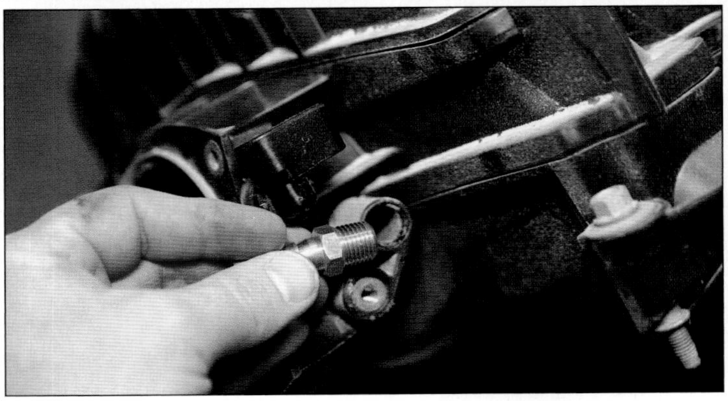

1 *If you have power brakes or anything else that needs vacuum, you can pull vacuum from the idle air control (IAC) valve port, which we do not need, as this engine is drive-by-wire. This is a 1/4-inch NPT nipple, which fits perfectly.*

2 *Tap the intake with an NPT tap to create threads so that the fitting will seal and be removable for service.*

3 *Once the port has been tapped, it is ready for use.*

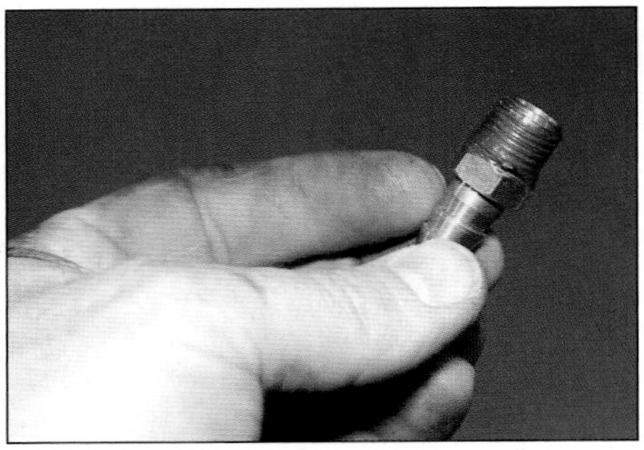

4 *Apply thread sealant to the nipple to seal it from any possible leaks.*

5 *The vacuum port is in place and can be plumbed for the power brake booster or other vacuum accessories.*

6 *The factory LT positive crankcase ventilation (PCV) system is convoluted and doesn't work very well, but the fittings that push-lock onto the valve covers can be reused. Plumbing the draw side of the PCV into the intake tube needs to be done in front of the throttle body. Otherwise, the air going into the engine is not metered and will be a giant vacuum leak.*

Once the fabrication was done, we picked a location for the MAF sensor. We opted for a position that was 10 inches away from the throttle body but not in the center of the 6-inch straight section. It is in the 45-degree elbow at the end of the inlet tube. This is the best position we could find that provided clearance for the MAF sensor wires and the recommended distance from the throttle body. We used the supplied boss, marked the pipe, and then cut the pipe to accept the sensor.

If you are building piping, use an aluminum mounting boss from ICT Billet (part number 551545) to secure the sensor to the air inlet tube. This is a weldable piece, but it is aluminum, so either the tube needs to be aluminum and TIG welded or you can use epoxy to bond it to plastic or steel tubing.

The MAF sensor is directional; it must be installed with the narrow side in the path of airflow and in the right orientation. The easy way to identify the flow on the LT sensor is to look for the wire terminal to flow toward the throttle body. If it is installed backward, the engine will not run right. The same process works for LS engines.

Vacuum and PCV Issues with LT Engines

Truck versions of the Gen V engines have a vacuum pump mounted down low on the driver's side of the block. This pump is for the PCV system and the vacuum brake booster. It helps draw the crankcase fumes out and recirculates them through the intake, as it provides more vacuum than manifold vacuum. This pump has caused a lot of problems on 2014–2018 trucks, to the point of a large recall.

Locating the MAF Sensor

1 ***LT engines and some late-model LS engines use cartridge-style MAF sensors. This is the bung that comes with the Holley air intake kit. These can be installed in the wrong direction, so we marked the top with a flow arrow to make sure we did it right.***

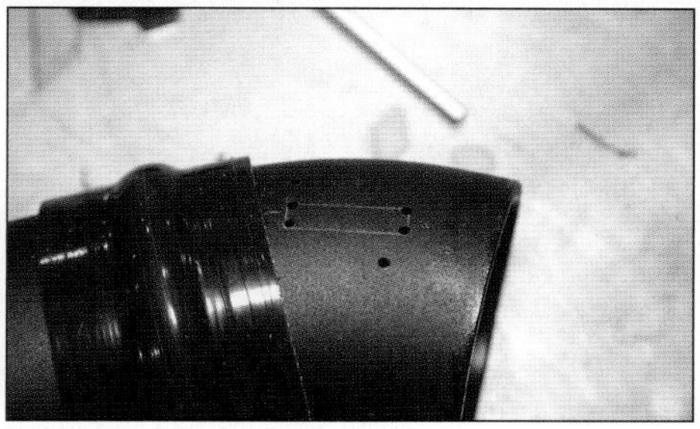

2 ***This is a little close to the air filter, but it was the only suitable location for the sensor. After marking the mounting holes and opening, drill the corners and cut out the center.***

3 ***We installed a pair of stud bolts from the inside of the tube. Do not put the nuts on the inside, as they could vibrate loose and damage the engine. The bolts were epoxied in place to prevent this.***

4 ***Insert the MAF sensor into the fitting and secure it with nuts. Note the flow direction arrows on the small tab on the front of the sensor.***

5 ***We used one kit to make intake tubes for both the 1991 1500 truck and the 1966 Suburban. We just had to supply our own filter and fabricate a mount for the 1991 1500 truck.***

One issue with direct-injection engines is that there is no fuel that flows over the intake valves. Over time, within 20,000 miles in fact, the intake valve will be covered in carbon deposits. Eventually, valves start sticking, which requires a very expensive repair job. This issue can be eliminated by running a can of intake cleaner through your engine every other oil change.

The feeder tube slips into the inlet just before the throttle body.

Start the engine and run it at 1,500 to 2,500 rpm (varying the speed up and down consistently) until the can is empty. The can has a locking top, so once you start, it stays spraying.

The problem is that the pump has a filter screen that over time clogs up with trash and slowly reduces the vacuum required to operate the brake booster. This has caused a few wrecks and has spawned a new market for vacuum-pump deletes. In most swaps, the vacuum pump doesn't clear the frame (it will clear in some trucks), but the reality is that deleting it is required for most aftermarket accessory drives and power-steering add-ons.

Once the pump is gone, a solution is still needed for the power brakes. This is easily rectified by plumbing the brake booster into the manifold. Additionally, there must be vacuum for the crankcase pressure. The GM recommendation for all of the Gen V crate engines is to plumb the crankcase vents on the valve covers to the air intake tube between the MAF sensor and the throttle body. Unfortunately, this leads to an entirely different issue: carbon buildup on the intake valves.

Because the Gen V is direct injected, there is no fuel washing over the tops of the intake valves. Over time, the oil vapor from the crankcase ventilation burns onto the valves and creates a sticky mess. If left unattended, this buildup can require a complete head rebuild. There are a couple solutions to this: an intake-valve cleaner and an oil catch can.

The intake valve cleaner should be run through the engine at least every other oil change. For less than $20, this can be done at home in the driveway. Even on a completely stock Gen V, this is necessary. Intake-valve cleaner washes the intake valves and removes the carbon buildup. Even one treatment can increase fuel economy and performance. This should be done to every single used Gen V engine immediately after a swap, as it is unlikely it has been done prior.

The second solution will reduce the amount of carbon buildup on the intake valves so that there isn't as much oil consumption. This is another issue with the Gen V engines: they can burn as much as 2 quarts of oil between oil changes. This is because the PCV system has a bad habit of just dumping oil into the intake.

The catch can is typically installed on the vents coming out of the valve covers, which then filters the oil vapor out of the crankcase gases. Then, gases are drawn back into the engine through the air-inlet tube between the throttle body and the MAF sensor.

The port on the intake valley

just below the throttle body is then ported to fresh air or to the catch can, depending on what catch-can system is used. Some systems made specifically for Gen V engines only service the valley cover port to the PCV valve on the intake behind the throttle body. These systems require using the original air-intake system, which is not practical or even feasible in C10 trucks. A universal catch-can kit works just as well while treating the entire crankcase system.

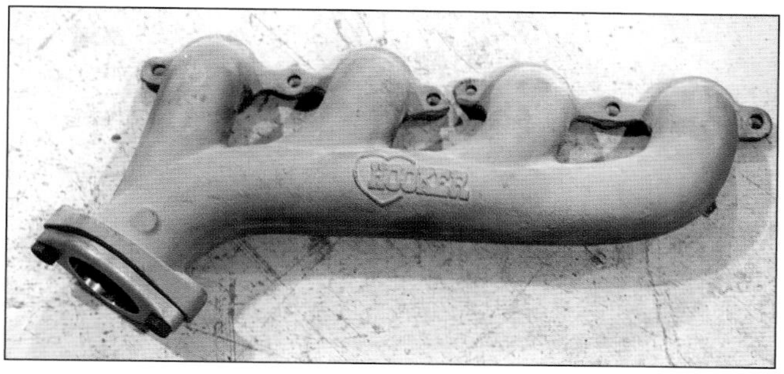

These LS cast-iron manifolds from Hooker are perfect for C10 swaps. They fit most trucks, flow as well as or better than the stock manifolds, and come with flanges to weld the exhaust pipes to.

Exhaust

The factory components of the LS engines are decent, and the LT-series stock manifolds are actually pretty good. To squeeze out every available drop of fuel economy to meet the strict modern standards, the factory exhaust has to perform well while being quiet and efficient for emissions too. This means that the stock manifolds are acceptable for swaps, and in many cases actually work better than any aftermarket offerings. There are a few reasons for this, but the bottom line is that getting good flow out of an LS/LT engine is not too hard.

The ECM has to monitor the exhaust system. This is critical to any EFI system, and even more so in an LT-series direct-injection engine. Inside the combustion chamber, the fuel is injected at high pressures; any restriction of flow is a bad day for your engine.

In stock trim, there are four oxygen sensors: two just behind the exhaust manifolds and two more just after the catalytic convertor pipe, which is actually an assembly of two or three catalytic convertors. If you are planning on using catalytic convertors for legal reasons (varies by state), then you will likely want to retain the rear oxygen sensors. If you are not using cats, then you need to delete the rear oxygen sensors in the ECM programming. Most preprogrammed ECMs from harness companies already do this.

It is highly advised that you check with local and state laws regarding engine swaps and emissions equipment. These laws vary by state, and when you get a vehicle inspection, it would not be good to be missing emissions equipment that is required. Most states have classic-car exemptions, so it depends on the age of the vehicle.

Stock LS Manifolds

Stock Gen III and Gen IV exhaust manifolds are fairly efficient and help make 400-plus hp for most engines. The trick is finding a pair that fit your truck. The motor mounts and engine installation typically determine exhaust manifold compatibility. One set of manifolds may fit one install and not fit another, as your engine adapter mounts may or may not clear, or they may shift the engine to where these manifolds might not clear the chassis or steering box. Test-fitting is the only way to verify fitment. The Trailblazer/Envoy stock manifolds fit most C10 series trucks, as do the 2010-and-newer Camaro manifolds.

Stock exhaust manifolds also need a compatible flange that can be welded to the rest of the exhaust system.

Coat all exhaust bolts with copper anti-seize to prevent the threads from galling to the heads and breaking off.

We used new gaskets on the LS, but LT engines use MLS sheet-metal gaskets that are reusable many times.

The cast-iron manifolds look great in the 1966 Suburban. They clear the chassis without issue because we are using the Hooker Blackheart swap kit.

Several different flanges are used on the stock exhaust manifolds, but not all of them are reproduced. The trick here is to make sure that you get a little bit of the stock exhaust, the section just below the flange, so that you will have the right flanges for the exhaust manifolds you are using. If the flange your engine has is not available, fabrication is the only other option.

Speedway Motors is reproducing the exhaust flanges for the LS1 and Vortec manifolds. Another source for flanges would be used catalytic converters. While you can't buy a used converter, you can buy the flanges. Most salvage yards will gladly cut them off and sell them to you.

Stock LT Exhaust Manifolds

There are several factory manifolds for Gen V LT-series engines, including one for trucks, one for Corvettes, and one for the other passenger car models. The following list has the GM part numbers for the factory exhaust manifolds. Because LTs don't currently have many options for headers, factory manifolds get used more often.

Corvette

The Corvette manifolds are center dump, which does not clear any aftermarket motor-mount adapters. For the non-supercharged 6.2L (LT1), the left part number is 1269724, and the right part number is 1262975.

LT4 Supercharged Engines

For LT4 supercharged engines the left part number is 12629726, and the right part number is 12629727.

Camaro

The Camaro manifolds are center dump, which does not clear any aftermarket motor-mount adapters. The left part number is 12629728, and the right part number is 12629729.

Trucks

Manifolds are the same for 5.3L and 6.2L engines. These manifolds are swept back, so they dump to the rear of the engine. They clear most aftermarket motor-mount adapters and are suitable for C10 LT swaps. The reality is that there is just not much available in the aftermarket for LT-swap headers, so most swaps will use a version of the truck manifolds or headers. The left part number is 12629337, and the right part number is 12629338.

If you are using factory headers in a Gen V LT swap, some flanges are going to be needed. The factory flanges are not readily available in the aftermarket, so you have to build your own. They could be cut off of a factory Y-pipe, which is also the catalytic convertor for 2014-and-newer GM trucks. This might be a fairly costly option, as the catalytic convertors cost about $1,400 brand new, so the used ones will not be cheap.

Building flanges is not that complicated, but it does require attention to detail and some heavy steel plate. If you do not have the ability to fabricate them, any local machine shop or steel fabrication shop could make them quickly, and it should not cost much more than a few hundred dollars.

To make a set of flanges you need the following:

- 1/4-inch plate steel
- Torch or plasma cutter
- Carbide drill bit set
- Drill
- Cardboard (for template)
- Pencil
- Grinder
- Center punch

The flanges begin as a piece of flat plate steel. The minimum thickness for the flanges is 1/4 inch, but 3/8 inch would be even better. You want a thick flange to avoid warping. We had an original flange; it happened to come attached to one of the manifolds from the salvage yard, but we only had one, and the yard that we bought our engine from did not have any others available, so we used the one we had as a pattern.

Use the factory manifold, which in this case is a 2015 Chevy truck manifold, to trace the shape of the flange onto a piece of cardboard to create a template. We traced our flange several times to make extras, as we are doing several swaps at the moment. If you make several, you can cherry pick the best ones to use for your project.

We used a plasma cutter to cut out each flange and then used the grinder to clean them up. Using a large metal-cutting band saw could provide cleaner results. The center hole for the exhaust itself can be cut with the plasma cutter or with a hole saw. We used the plasma cutter for this example.

Making Clearance for the Headers

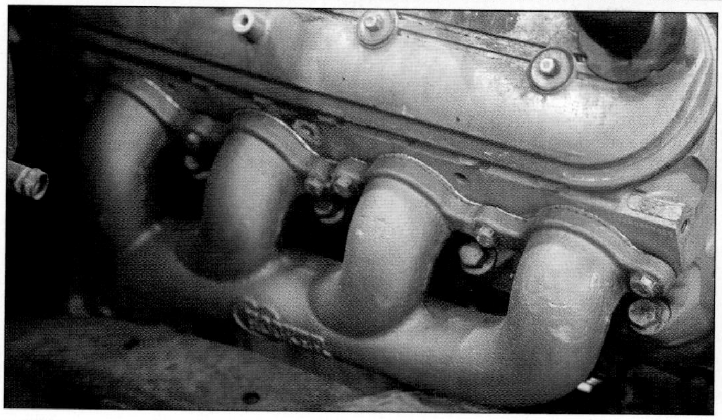

1 *The stock frame stands on the 1967 C10 hit the manifolds on both sides.*

2 *The driver's side was just as bad. It doesn't look like much, but if the engine was started, the interference would have damaged the manifolds.*

3 *Mark the offending areas so they can be fixed.*

4 *Heat up each frame stand with a torch until it glows red.*

5 *Use a small sledgehammer to bend the metal. It didn't need much of an adjustment, so it was a quick fix.*

6 *Now, the manifolds clear with ample room for engine flex.*

The critical area for this project is the three bolt holes. If it is off even a little, it will not get a good seal. Using the center punch, we marked the center and drilled a small 1/8-inch pilot hole in each flange bolt hole and then used a series of increasingly larger drill bits to open up the hole. Do not do this in one step, as 1/4-inch plate is hard enough to drill as it is and breaking a bit is no fun.

The flanges are pretty simple to make, and they work really well, but there is now another issue. Making flanges means that the factory donut gasket cannot be used. To rectify this problem, get some steel-lined exhaust gasket material from Fel-Pro, specifically Fel-Pro part number 2449 Pro-Ramic Gasket Material. This stuff is made from a

Corvette manifolds are not suitable for any truck swap, as they are "center dump," and there is not space available for them. These are LT1 manifolds. The LS Corvette manifolds are basically the same design.

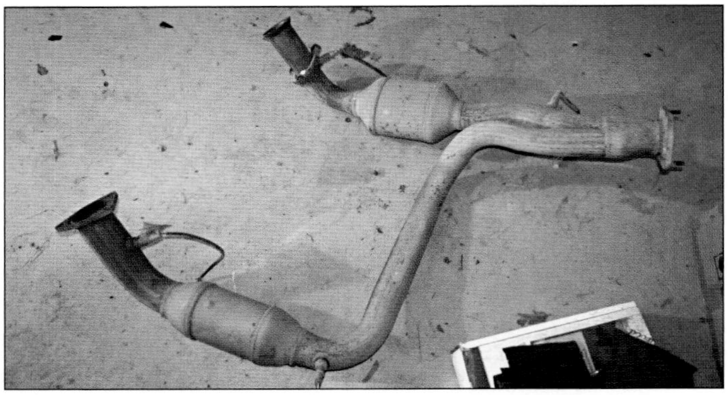

If the front catalytic convertors came from the donor truck, then you can just modify the flanges (or use stock manifolds) and have a clean-emissions truck. This is especially important for swappers who have to meet Environmental Protection Agency (EPA) restrictions based on the year of the engine in the vehicle.

sheet of perforated steel coated on both sides with ceramic gasket material. Cut it with tin snips, and it will hold up to the heat of engine exhaust. If the flanges are flat, they won't have any issues with leaks.

Making a gasket is not difficult, and this process works on standard gasket materials as well. Non-steel-lined material is much easier to work with because you don't have to cut through the steel core, but we made the gaskets shown here with relative ease. Three tools are needed: tin snips, a hammer, and a set of hole punches. Our punches came in a set of six, and while they won't be used often, you will be glad you spent the $10 on them when they are needed.

We used the new flanges as a pattern and traced the shape of the gasket with a pencil. This needs to be as accurate as possible. Next, we used a punch that was the closest to the required hole size and made the holes. A couple of blows with a hammer cut right through the gaskets without any tearing or jagged edges. Then, we used a pair of tin snips to carefully cut out the outside shape. Cut slow and carefully. The metal core can cut you pretty badly, so be careful and wear gloves.

The center hole is the toughest, as it needs to be cut clean. We used the hole punch to get the center hole started and then used the snips to finish the job. Work slowly and have lots of patience. The Pro-Ramic material is not expensive, but it isn't exactly cheap, either. It is a really good idea to make several sets of gaskets at once. That way, replacements are on hand should one need to be changed out.

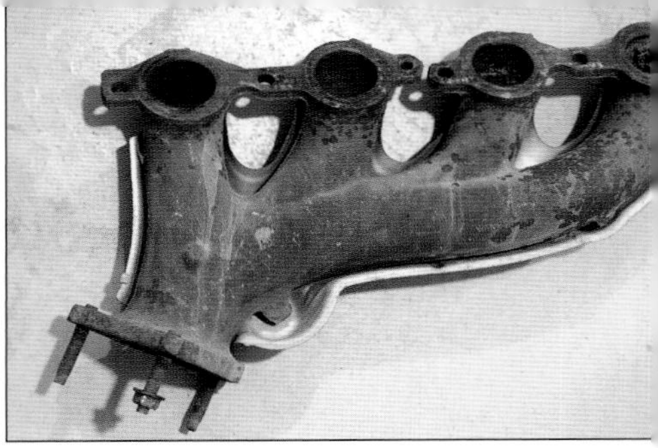

These truck LS manifolds show how good they really are, as they are not your typical SBC-style cast manifolds. These fit most trucks, but the triangular flanges are hard to find and can cause some interference on tight-fit chassis, depending on the engine setback.

These will last a while, but they are not going to last nearly as long as the factory-style donuts.

Aftermarket Headers

When it comes to aftermarket exhaust, the LS-series engines are covered, just about every header manufacturer has an LS swap header that will fit a C/K10 truck. Most are universal, but some are specifically designed to work with that manufacturer's engine swap components. BRP Hot Rods and Hooker both offer LS swap headers and manifolds that work with their specific swap systems. They will work with other components as well, but they are specifically made to fit their swap components.

LT engine swaps are a different story, as there are very few options on aftermarket headers designed for engine swaps at the current time. A few are available from Hooker and BRP Hot Rods, but that is all there is at the moment. The issue is that General Motors not only changed the exhaust flange for the Gen V LT-series engines but also the angle of the exhaust flange itself is about 3 degrees sharper. Hooker offers several options that work with C10 trucks and SUVs, including manifolds and long-tube and mid-length headers.

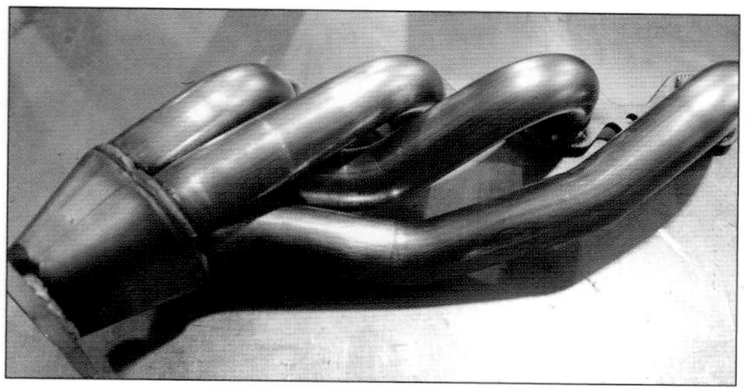

The shorty headers from Hooker are designed for 2014-and-newer trucks, and they work quite well in swaps. The flange can be cut off and a V-band type of flange can be welded in to get away from gaskets and interference issues.

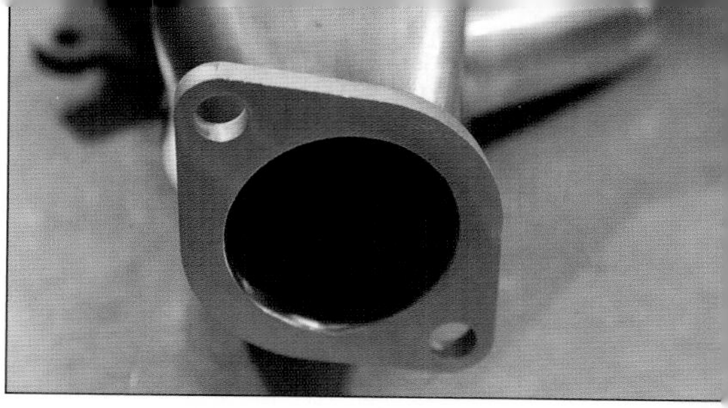

Hooker has switched to a two-bolt flange, which works pretty well in most applications.

All LS/LT engines require oxygen sensors, which should be mounted about 18 inches from the manifold or header collector. This is a weld-in bung for an oxygen sensor. Some are hex, some are round.

We drilled out the pipe with a step-bit to get the right-sized hole. Some bungs have a nice step on the flange to lock it into the pipe.

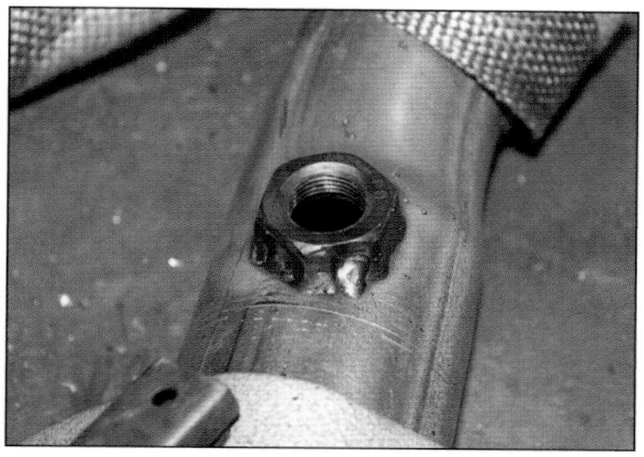

The bung was placed onto the pipe and welded to the pipe. A good weld to seal the perimeter is required.

Hooker's cast-iron Gen V manifolds clear the chassis on all C10 trucks, and they flow really well. These are an excellent solution to the budget swap. Mid-length headers work on C10 trucks but need a two-bolt flange over the stock LT three-bolt flange, which can have some fitment issues between the frame rails.

BRP Hot Rods has several swap kits available: a 1964–1972 Chevy truck kit, a 1973–1987 Chevy truck kit, and a 1988–1998 GM truck kit. This represents a huge segment of the LT swap market, but the headers for these applications appear to be designed specifically for the rest of the BRP LT-swap platform. It is unclear whether or not the headers will fit with other swap adapters. In addition, they are quite expensive at $1,149, although they are very nice quality. Built from stainless steel, they are worth the price, but that might be out of reach for the average low-budget swap project.

Until the aftermarket catches up with the increasingly popular LT swap, there are options beyond the factory manifolds. Most aftermarket LT-powered truck headers are a mid-length style of header, where the collector dumps at the bellhousing about midway between the oil pan flange and the head deck. This makes 2014-and-newer GM truck headers the best bet for most applications. That doesn't work on every chassis, but it will get you pretty close. Mid-length headers work on C10 trucks, but you want a two-bolt flange over the stock LT 3-bolt flange, which can have some fitment issues between the frame rails.

Catalytic Convertors

For those who live in emissions-controlled states, chances are high that some sort of catalytic convertor must be installed with your LS/LT swap. Most of the mystery lies in the construction of a catalytic converter. The most important part is the ceramic matrix.

Shaped like a honeycomb, the matrix is made predominantly of a ceramic material called cordierite. The honeycomb is created through an extrusion process in which lengths of the honeycomb shape are squeezed through a die and supported by computer-controlled jets of air that keep the honeycomb straight as it leaves the machine.

Once the ceramic honeycomb is fired and set, it receives a washcoat of various oxides combined with the precious metals that function as the actual catalyst. The washcoat is used because it evenly disperses the metals throughout all the pores of the matrix. The metals are generally mixed to best use their individual properties. Most cats in the United States use some combination of platinum, palladium, and rhodium.

Outside of the United States, copper has been tried but will form dioxin, which is a toxic substance with carcinogenic properties. In other places in the world, materials such as nickel, cerium in washcoat, and manganese in cordierite are used, but each has its disadvantages.

If you need (or just want) catalytic converters, Magnaflow builds high-flow cats for performance applications. This is a good way to go for adding them to your exhaust.

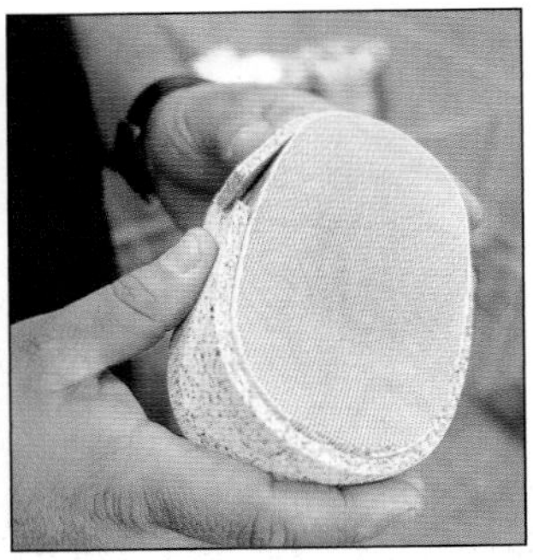

Inside the catalytic convertor is a honeycomb of palladium, platinum, or rhodium. This is why cats are expensive: all of these are considered precious metals.

Although it's not part of the exhaust, EGR-equipped engines may not be required by law in your state to have the EGR system. It can be removed by using one of these EGR plugs.

Originally developed throughout the 1930s and 1940s for industrial smokestacks, catalytic-converter inventor Eugene Houdry began to develop a cat for automobiles in the 1950s. The first cats were mandated in 1975. These catalytic converters were of a two-way type, which combined oxygen with the carbon monoxide and unburned hydrocarbons to form carbon dioxide and water. As the science progressed, more strict environmental regulations brought about a change to three-way converters in 1981. These more advanced cats also reduce nitrogen oxide.

Cats work by using what is called a redox reaction. This means that once the catalyst is up to operating temperature (anywhere from 500 to 1,200 degrees Fahrenheit) both an oxidation reaction and reduction reaction are occurring simultaneously. That sounds a little complicated but what it means is that molecules are simultaneously losing and gaining electrons. These types of reactions are extremely common. Photosynthesis and rust are both good examples of redox reactions.

In the first stage of the catalytic converter, the reduction stage, the goal is to remove the nitrous oxide and especially the nitric oxide. When introduced to air, this quickly changes into nitrogen dioxide, which is very poisonous. The reduction stage works because the nitrogen molecules in the nitrogen oxides wants to bond much more strongly with the metals of the catalyst than it does with its oxygen molecules, and the oxygen molecules would rather bond with each other, forming O_2, which is the type of oxygen that we breathe.

Once the oxygen molecules break off from their nitrogen molecules, the nitrogen molecules move along the surface of the catalyst, looking to make friends with another nitrogen molecule. Once it finds one, it bonds and becomes the stable, harmless nitrogen that we find in our atmosphere. Once it becomes atmospheric nitrogen, its bond with the walls of the catalyst is weakened and the gas moves along to the second phase of the catalytic converter: oxidation.

Once the gases have finished in the reduction stage of the catalytic converter and we've eliminated all the nitrogen oxides, we are left with atmospheric nitrogen, atmospheric oxygen, carbon dioxide, carbon monoxide, water, and unburned fuel. The oxidation stage of the catalytic converter uses platinum and palladium, which want to bond with the various oxides. The oxygen molecules bond with the surface of the catalyst and break up and eventually find carbon monoxide molecules to bond with, creating carbon dioxide. The carbon dioxide bond is again stronger than the bond with the catalyst and moves through the matrix, allowing the process to begin again. At the same time that this is happening, some of the freed-up oxygen molecules begin to bond with the unburned fuel (hydrocarbons) and are changed into water and more carbon dioxide.

This brief history of the design of catalytic converters is important because it goes to show the advancements in cat technology. The original cats were very inefficient and clogged up quickly, causing serious performance issues. Modern performance catalytic converters are designed for free flow while doing their job of cleaning the exhaust gases. Magnaflow makes high-flow California Air Resources Board (CARB)–legal and New York–Legal cats that ensure the emissions of your LS/LT swap will match the necessary specifications for your area.

Some silicone was applied to the plug. The O-ring seals the hole, but the silicone keeps it from popping out.

How to Properly Dimple Headers

Headers help the engine breathe, but there are often interference issues that make fitting a set of headers in a vehicle difficult. Most aftermarket designs are tested, but different components don't always gel, so it may be necessary to take matters into your own hands.

Contrary to popular belief, dimpling headers makes no discernable difference in power. In fact, in some tests, dimpling even increased power by a few ponies. One dyno test in particular showed that even severe bashing of all eight primary tubes in multiple places had zero effect in performance. So now that you know that it is okay and won't hurt your engine's performance, what is the best way to do it?

There are several methods to dimple a header tube. Most folks just go bananas with a hammer, but this leaves an ugly mess that, while effective, is not very scientific. Others suggest filling the tube with sand to add some resistance; supposedly this makes a more uniform dent. The other method, the one we will demonstrate here, uses heat to soften the steel and a hammer to make the magic happen.

The first step is finding the location of the problem. On this Buick GS, we have a set of custom headers that were built to test the clearance of an LT1 in the A-Body. These are LS-swap headers with LT1 flanges. Unfortunately, the angle at the flange is not quite right, and the primary tubes hit the starter flange and the knock sensor on the passenger's side. Eventually, we will get a proper set of headers, but for now, a dimpling we shall go.

With the headers marked, they were removed and loaded into a sturdy bench-mounted vise. Then we applied some heat with an oxyacetylene torch in just the area we needed to dimple. This is important, as we want to make just enough of a dent to clear the area, and we don't want to distort the surrounding pipe. Be careful not to melt through the tubing.

Once the pipe is glowing red, we hit it with the hammer in the center, working out. For smaller dimples, the round ball side is best, but for larger areas, we used the flat side of the hammer. Then, we let the headers cool naturally. Placing them in front of a fan will cool them off in just a few minutes.

The fitment was checked and any additional dimpling was performed until the headers fit. While it is not something swappers want to do, it is often necessary to get the headers to clear the chassis or other engine components. Just be careful not to close the tube or cut a hole in it, but if you do put a hole in it, you can always weld it up. ■

1 ***Sometimes, parts don't fit as they should, especially headers. A 1-degree variance at the top of the head can result in a few inches at the bottom of the header. These headers were modified LS-swap headers with LT1 flanges. That didn't quite work as planned, as the passenger's side hits the bellhousing.***

2 ***Mark the offending area with a marker. Two pipes are at issue, so they need to be dimpled.***

3 ***Using a torch, heat the pipe until it is cherry red. Be careful not to melt the metal.***

4 ***Then, hit the pipe with a hammer to dimple it. This is a trial-and-error process, it usually only takes a few tries to get it right.***

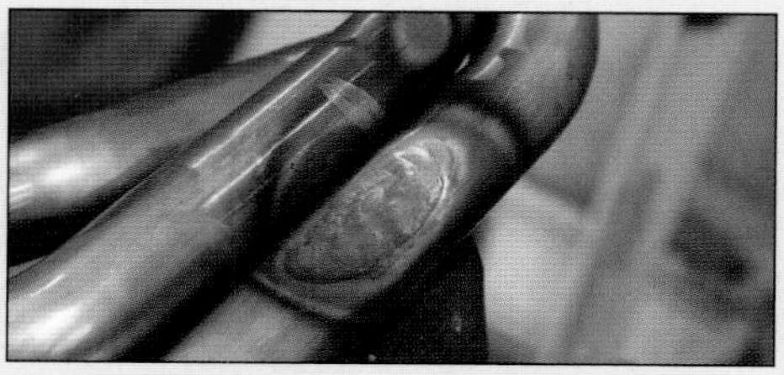

5 ***This pipe has been dimpled.***

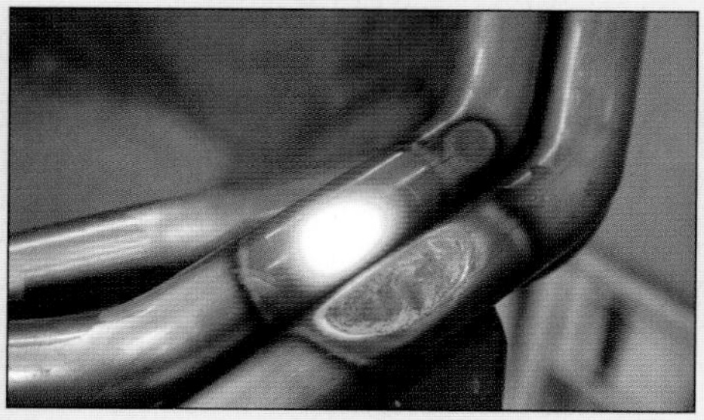

6 ***Heating the pipe to a cherry red color is the ticket to a smooth dimple. This allows for a more precise dent, as opposed to crushing the surrounding metal too.***

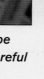

7 ***The ball-side of the hammer is good for working the corners of the dimple. The dimple should be as smooth of a transition as possible.***

Advanced Clutch Technology
206 East Ave. K-4
Lancaster, CA 93535
661-940-7555
advancedclutch.com

Aeromotive Inc.
7805 Barton St.
Lenexa, KS 66214
913-647-7300
aeromotiveinc.com

American Powertrain
2199 Summerfield Rd.
Cookeville, TN 38501
931-646-4836
americanpowertrain.com

Automotive Racing Products
1863 Eastman Ave.
Ventura, CA 93003
800-826-3045
arpfasteners.com

AutoMeter
413 West Elm St.
Sycamore, IL 60178
866-248-6356
autometer.com

B&M Racing & Performance
9142 Independence Ave.
Chatsworth, CA 91311
818-882-6422
bmracing.com

BRP Muscle Rods
5849 Rogers Rd.
Cumming, GA 30040
770-751-0687
brphotrods.com

Comp Cams
3406 Democrat Rd.
Memphis, TN 38118
800-999-0853
compcams.com

Chevrolet Performance
chevroletperformance.com

Current Performance
6330 Pine Hill Rd. #16
Port Richey, FL 34668
727-844-7570
currentperformance.com

Dakota Digital
4510 W. 61st St. N.
Sioux Falls, SD 57107
800-593-4160
dakotadigital.com

Deatschwerks
415 E. Hill St.
Oklahoma City, OK 73105
800-419-6023
deatschwerks.com

Detroit Speed and Engineering
185 McKenzie Rd.
Mooresville, NC 28115
704-662-3272
detroitspeed.com

Dirty Dingo Motorsports
506 E. Juanita Ave. Suite 3
Mesa, AZ 85204
480-824-1968
dirtydingo.com

DynoTech Engineering
1731 Thorncroft
Troy, MI 48084-5302
800-633-5559
dynotechengineering.com

Earl's Performance Plumbing
19302 S. Laurel Park Rd.
Rancho Dominguez, CA 90220
310-609-1602
holley.com

Edelbrock
2700 California St.
Torrance, CA 90503
310-781-2222
edelbrock.com

EFI Live
efilive.com

F.A.S.T.
3400 Democrat Rd.
Memphis, TN 38118
877-334-8355
fuelairspark.com

Flex-a-Lite
7213 45th St. Ct. E
Fife, WA 98424
800-851-1510
Flex-a-Lite.com

Griffin Radiators
100 Hurricane Creek Rd.
Piedmont, SC 29673
800-722-3723
griffinrad.com

Holley
1801 Russellville Rd. 42101
P.O. Box 10360 42102
Bowling Green, KY
270-782-2900
holley.com

Hooker
1801 Russellville Rd. 42101
Bowling Green, KY
270-782-2900
holley.com

HP Tuners
725 Hastings Ln.
Buffalo Grove, IL 60089
hptuners.com

ICT Billet
1107 S. West St.
Wichita, KS 67213
316-300-0833
ICTBillet.com

Jet Performance
17491 Apex Circle
Huntington Beach, CA 92647
800-535-1161
jetchip.com

Lingenfelter Performance Engineering
1557 Winchester Rd.
Decatur, IN 46733
260-724-2552
lingenfelter.com

Lokar Performance Products
Throttle Pedals and Cables
865-966-2269
lokar.com

Koul Tools
928-854-6706
koultools.com

Magnaflow
22961 Arroyo Vista
Rancho Santa Margarita, CA 92688
800-824-8664
magnaflow.com

Miller Electric Manufacturing Co.
1635 W. Spencer St.
P.O. Box 1079
Appleton, WI 54912-1079
920-734-9821
millerwelds.com

Moroso
80 Carter Dr.
Guilford, CT 06437-2116
203-453-6571
moroso.com

MSD
Autotronic Controls Corporation
1350 Pullman Dr., Dock #14
El Paso, TX 79936
915-857-5200
msdignition.com

OPTIMA Batteries, Inc.
X-33 Optima Batteries
5757 N. Green Bay Ave.
Milwaukee, WI 53209
888-8OPTIMA
optimabatteries.com

Painless Wiring
2501 Ludelle St.
Fort Worth, TX 76105
817-244-6212
painlessperformance.com

PerTronix Performance Products
440 East Arrow Hwy.
San Dimas, CA 91773
909-599-5955
pertronix.com

PRW Industries, Inc.
1722 Illinois Ave.
Perris, CA 92571
888-377-9779
prw-usa.com

Red Dirt Rodz
4518 Braxton Ln.
Stillwater, OK 74074
405-880-5343
RedDirtRodz.com

Rock Valley
800-344-1934
rockvalleyantiqueautoparts.com

Royal Purple, Inc.
One Royal Purple Ln.
Porter, TX 77365
888-382-6300
royalpurple.com

Speartech
3574 E. State Rd. 236
Anderson, IN 46017
765-378-4908
Speartech.com

Summit Racing
P.O. Box 909
Akron, OH 44398-6177
800-230-3030
summitracing.com

Tanks Inc
P.O. Box 400
Clearwater, MN 55320
320-558-6882
tanksinc.com

TCI
151 Industrial Dr.
Ashland, MS 38603
888-776-9824
tciauto.com

Trans-Dapt
12438 Putnam St.
Whittier, CA 90602
562-921-0404
hedman.com

VaporWorx
Newbury Park, CA 91320
805-390-6423
vaporworx.com